ANIMAL HEROES

Anthony Hill is a multi-award-winning, bestselling author. His most recent book for adults, *For Love of Country*, was published in 2016.

His novel *Soldier Boy*, about Australia's youngest-known Anzac, won the 2002 NSW Premier's Literary Award for Books for Young Adults. His most recent children's book, *Captain Cook's Apprentice*, won the 2009 NSW Premier's Young People's History Prize. It follows *Soldier Boy*, *Young Digger* and *Animal Heroes* as further testimony to his remarkable ability to extensively research historical material and, from wide-ranging sources, piece together a moving and exciting story.

He is also the author of two novellas, the beautiful *Shadow Dog*, and the award-winning *The Burnt Stick*, illustrated by Mark Sofilas, as well as the picture book, *Lucy's Cat and the Rainbow Birds*, illustrated by Jane Tanner.

Anthony lives in Canberra with his wife, Gillian. Their daughter, son-in-law and granddaughter, Emily, live in Melbourne.

anthonyhillbooks.com

Also Available from Penguin Books

Young Digger

The Story of Billy Young

Soldier Boy

The Burnt Stick

For Love of Country

ANIMAL HEROES

ANTHONY HILL

MICHAEL JOSEPH
an imprint of
PENGUIN BOOKS

MICHAEL JOSEPH

UK | USA | Canada | Ireland | Australia
India | New Zealand | South Africa | China

Penguin Books is part of the Penguin Random House group of companies
whose addresses can be found at global.penguinrandomhouse.com.

Penguin
Random House
Australia

First published by Penguin Group (Australia), 2005
This revised edition published by Penguin Random House Australia Pty Ltd, 2017

1 3 5 7 9 10 8 6 4 2

Text copyright © Anthony Hill, 2005, 2017

Cover design by Louisa Maggio © Penguin Random House Australia Pty Ltd
Text design by Samantha Jayaweera © Penguin Random House Australia Pty Ltd
Cover photographs: soldier and dog in Vietnam courtesy Australian War Memorial
(COL/67/0552/VN); soldier and dog in Afghanistan © Commonwealth of Australia 2015;
stack of photos and paper texture © Shutterstock
Typeset in Sabon by Samantha Jayaweera, Penguin Random House Australia Pty Ltd
Colour separation by Splitting Image Colour Studio, Clayton, Victoria
Printed and bound in Australia by Griffin Press, an accredited ISO AS/NZS
14001 Environmental Management Systems printer.

The author thanks the ACT Cultural Council and the ACT Government for the
generous assistance that enabled this book to be researched and written.

Supported by

ACT
Government

National Library of Australia
Cataloguing-in-Publication data:

Hill, Anthony, 1942– author
Animal heroes / Anthony Hill
9780143784609 (paperback)

Animals – War use – Australia.
Animal heroes – Australia.

355.424

penguin.com.au

For Michael McKernan, who suggested this book

IMPERIAL TO METRIC CONVERSIONS
To keep to the spirit of the times, we have retained the imperial system
of measurement in the early parts. For readers interested in converting
distances and weights into metric units, 1 mile is approximately
1.6 kilometres, and 1 pound is approximately 0.45 kilograms.

CONTENTS

FOREWORD

Animal Heroes

Visitors leaving the galleries of the Australian War Memorial pass through a long corridor. On one wall hangs a series of large photographs of Australian servicemen and women of different eras, snapshots of lives given in the service of our nation and its values.

Visitors have taken to placing poppies on the photographs. One is more heavily laden with this symbol of love and memory than any other. It is a photograph of two young soldiers and a dog.

Photographed the day that all three were killed by a bomb blast in Afghanistan, Sappers Darren Smith and Jacob Moerland are leaning back in their gear smiling at one another, relaxing before going back in search of improvised explosive devices. Between them, looking attentively to camera, is Herbie, Sapper Smith's beloved explosive detection dog. Darren and Herbie died together. They are buried together. Darren and Jacob are among forty-one Australians who died in Afghanistan named on the Australian War Memorial's Roll of Honour, which commemorates lives given for us and our freedoms. The list would be longer but for the service, devotion and skill of these remarkable dogs.

The most popular sculpture in the Memorial's grounds since its installation has been Peter Corlett's depiction of Simpson and his donkey. Competing closely with it now is Ewen Coates' magnificent explosive detection dog and handler. It depicts the bond between man and dog and the dangers faced by both. Inscribed into it are the names of dogs killed or missing in Afghanistan. Darren Smith's name is alongside Herbie's. The EDD sculpture is so loved by four-legged visitors we have designed and installed a bronze drinking bowl next to it.

Visitors to the First World War galleries can choose from a menu of six interpretive narratives to complement their tour. The most popular is 'animals in war'.

Whether in our exhibits, statues, artefacts, relics or commemorative days, animals are increasingly regarded as a powerful way of telling the stories of the men and women whose lives and service stand behind the Memorial. Animals, so loyal and trusting, stimulate the imaginative capacity within us to see the world and its conflicts through the eyes of others.

The paradox of the Australian War Memorial is that it is, in the end, not about war. It is about love and friendship. Love for friends and between friends. Love of family and love of country. It is about men and women who devote their lives not to themselves but to us, and their last moments to one another. And then – whether horses, dogs, pigeons or camels – the bond between animal and man, the devotion to one another and the resources invested in them speaks to the innate good in all of us, even in the worst of all possible times.

Animal heroes – for that is what they are.

Hon Dr Brendan Nelson AO
Director of the Australian War Memorial

INTRODUCTION

When my book *Young Digger* was launched at the Australian War Memorial, a friend, Norma Allen, suggested I should tell the story of 'Horrie the Wog Dog' – another wartime waif who was adopted as a mascot by his soldiers and smuggled back to Australia.

'But that book has already been written,' I said. 'Horrie was destroyed by quarantine officials during the Second World War.'

'I mean,' Norma replied, 'that you should tell what *really* happened.' And for the first time in nearly sixty years, she broke her silence and whispered Horrie's secret. The true end to his tale as told to her by Horrie's late master, Jim Moody. Even then, Norma said a silent sorry to those still in the know: for it was a deep secret, and the past can throw long shadows.

In the months that followed, I was able to confirm the main details of Moody's story with some members of his family and close friends. I saw the little dog's khaki jacket, with his corporal's stripes, and the smuggling pack displayed at the Australian War Memorial in Canberra. I visited the AWM website, looked at the photographs, and read the files. And in doing so, I not only discovered Horrie's story, but also came across many other stories of animals that have served beside Australia's fighting forces in war and peace for more than a century.

There were the messenger dogs of the First World War, the tracker dogs who went to Vietnam (and didn't come back), the patrol dogs and sniffer dogs of more recent conflicts. The gallant steeds of the Australian Light Horse carried their soldiers into many battles in South Africa and Palestine, yet only one ever returned home. The carrier pigeons saved countless lives during the Second World War by carrying messages through storm and gunshot. Two pigeons received medals for their valour, though in truth every animal who goes to war is a hero. White mice and canaries taken in cages to test for poison gas have been no less brave in their way than the mules that hauled the big guns through bursting shellfire in France, or the dolphins hunting for underwater mines in Iraq.

All acted as their training and instinct told them to. They had no choice about going to war. And all found their own levels of courage and loyalty in the face of death, even if faithfulness was too often in the past repaid by official indifference. Some, like Jack Simpson and his donkey, Murphy, who carried the wounded at Gallipoli, became famous. Most are now almost forgotten, surviving only in old photographs, fading letters and newspaper columns.

Then there are the many animal mascots adopted by the armed forces – from pygmy gliding possums, cats and dogs, to kangaroos, crocodiles, merino rams, eagles, ponies and tigers.

Some have been official mascots, symbolising those military virtues of strength, pride and endurance. They've been cared for by their units – paraded, promoted, demoted, reported upon – to represent the continuing aspirations, traditions and life of the group. The esprit de corps in fact. And often, through unselfconscious humour and parody, the animals can make the strictures of military life more bearable for their humans.

But by far the greater number of mascots have been stray

creatures, found on the road to war and taken in by soldiers for what these animals have to give. Companionship. Unconditional and uncomplaining affection. Hope. Laughter. Relief from the daily horrors and stresses of conflict. The knowledge that, however far from home, servicemen and women have *someone* close to share their gentler feelings.

For very often there are powerful bonds between the forces and their animals. Of suffering, survival, and salvation. Time and again I came across stories of human lives saved by the warnings of pet dogs and even monkeys. Stoic packhorses pulling drowning men from the Flanders mud. Injured sparrows that gave new hope to the prisoners of war who rescued them, that another life did exist beyond the jail walls.

Given all this, it's no wonder that so many soldiers risked much to bring their pets home. A few succeeded. The man who smuggled home Horrie the Wog Dog was one of them. Yet most animals were left behind or caught by Australian quarantine officials.

To those who knew them, however, the memories are as vivid and painful as ever. Not all the animals were heroes in a conventional military sense, winning medals for valiant deeds. But they all faced the dangers of a battlefield – or were ready, and tried to do so. And to those who love them, every soldier is a hero.

In the twelve years since this book was first published, a new generation of animal heroes has grown up and entered the lives and consciousness of the Australian armed services and the public at large. In particular, the explosive detection dogs working with the forces fighting Taliban insurgents in Afghanistan have become justly famous: none more so than the black Labrador-cross Sarbi, who was taken captive and recovered after more than a year, received the RSPCA Purple Cross on behalf of all the Australian dogs serving in that conflict, and who is now mounted and on permanent display at the AWM.

It may not be widely known, but the RSPCA generally does not make the dogs it shelters available to the defence forces. It certainly draws attention to the wonderful service these dogs render – but at the same time it has a long-standing policy opposing the use of animals for work 'where injury, pain, suffering or distress is likely to be caused.' As warfare, by its very nature, usually leads to such things, the Society doesn't make its animals available to the military. To what extent this may be at odds with the public recognition it gives to their service is a matter of opinion – though one can be opposed to conscription yet still acknowledge the bravery shown by conscripts on a battlefield.

Still, it does raise the broader ethical question of the use of animals in war, for none of them ask to go. They're all sent by humans. The RSPCA's position, a spokesperson says, is to encourage other methods that don't place animals – or people – in harm's way, and to reduce the number of animals used in conflict and seek alternatives to them. But in a violent world, there remains the dilemma of competing practical and ethical priorities any commander may face: is it better in an emergency to have a dead animal or a dead human as the victim of an attack? And where a dog has traits that can be of use to the protective services, is it not better to let it have a useful working life with a high standard of care, than have it put down – as sometimes happens – when it cannot find a suitable domestic home?

Whatever view one takes on this, the fact is that many new memorials have been erected in public places recently for the six explosive detection dogs and four combat assault dogs that were killed in Afghanistan, and to commemorate military working and service dogs generally. Their value in detecting hidden explosives and other illegal substances, as well as their ability to track enemies, find people who are lost, guard military facilities, and assist as faithful friends those who are suffering the wounds of war, have become even more recognised by the authorities. The dog sections are now highly regarded units within the army and air force. The animals themselves are now recognised with service medals. A number of organisations have been introducing assistance dog programs for veterans facing post-traumatic stress disorder and other problems. The very successful travelling exhibition A is for Animals, mounted by the AWM, the animal open days that have been held, Ewen Coates' sculpture *Elevation of the senses* dedicated to the Afghanistan dogs, and Steven Holland's memorial to all animals in war, attest to the intense public interest in – and compassion for – the subject.

There are many more photographs of the animals and people featured in this book than could fit in the picture insert. As well as visiting the monuments, museums and collections mentioned in the stories, interested readers can find these additional photographs using the references and search terms collated in the chapter notes.

The very welcome decision by Penguin Random House to publish this revised edition of *Animal Heroes* has allowed me to add the Afghanistan dogs to this collection of stories, where they may take their place among their fellows from earlier wars. I've updated information on those who are still living – both Snappa the crocodile and Courage the wedge-tailed eagle are warrant officers now – as well as explored new material that's come to light concerning the eventual fate of Horrie the Wog Dog.

I've also taken the opportunity to add some new stories: a couple from the colonial wars of the nineteenth century; a few great mascot stories including, from General Peter Leahy, the pig Willy; the late George Gray's tale of his tracker dog Pedro; and an acknowledgement of the very small creatures – the flies, fleas, lice, spiders, ticks and mozzies – that are part of every soldier's life in the field . . . companions-in-arms as it were (and under-the-arms, and in many other places as well).

So let me thank everyone mentioned in the acknowledgements and chapter notes who has helped with this project over the years. As I remarked in the introduction to the first edition of this book, while the memories are still there, and the old photographs and letters can still be found, may these stories of just a few of Australia's animal heroes stand for them all. Lest We Forget.

Anthony Hill
Canberra, 2017

Colonial Wars

For Aboriginal people, Australia's foreign wars doubtless started in April 1770 at Botany Bay, when two Gweagal warriors threw their spears and Captain Cook's landing party returned fire . . . and they properly got under way when Arthur Phillip came ashore with the First Fleet soldiers and convicts eighteen years later.

The 'Black Wars' continued through most of the nineteenth century as European settlement spread across the continent. Indeed, some armed raiding parties continued in remote areas until the first decades of the twentieth century.

For Europeans, of course, the concept of Australia's foreign wars is a matter of 'us' going out to fight 'them' overseas, in some other corner of the world.

Even before the last British colonial troops departed in 1870 and the six colonies took responsibility for their own defence, some 2500 individual colonists had joined the British forces that left for New Zealand to campaign in the Maori Wars of the 1840s to 1860s.

The first truly Australian colonial force raised for an overseas war was the New South Wales contingent that went to the Sudan in 1885 to avenge the death of General Gordon at Khartoum. It saw very little action and returned with only a donkey as a war trophy.

The outbreak of the Second Boer War in October 1899 was a more serious test of Australia's youthful defence capability. Eight or nine contingents went. The first light horse regiments were formed. With the colonies coming together at Federation in the middle of the war, the infant Commonwealth of Australia raised three contingents, but most arrived in South Africa after the war ended in May 1902.

Overall the Australians acquitted themselves well, although generally the quality of the horses was not high and they suffered heavy losses. Among the 16 000 Australian soldiers the casualty rate was 8.5 per cent . . . nothing compared to the two world wars of the twentieth century that followed, in which our forces came of age.

THE SUDAN DONKEY

Sydney, 1885

A small white donkey, with a short tail, a thin summer coat, and very big ears, was feeling angry and insubordinate. With good reason.

He'd been enjoying a handful of hay in the shelter of a troop-ship just berthed at the Quay, looking forward to a little peace and quiet after weeks of seasickness, when one of the soldiers on board grabbed his halter and tried to lead him off to join their welcome home parade through the streets of Sydney.

The donkey didn't want to go. It was cold outside. And wet. The rain was coming down in slabs and everyone was drenched. There was no cover. Nothing to eat. And the donkey was far from *his* home: half a world away from his native village in east Africa.

He tried to dig his heels into the wooden deck of the troopship SS *Arab*. He raised his head, curled his lip, and began to protest.

Hee-haw! he brayed, as if to say, *Bugger off. Hee-haw! And leave me alone!*

But the soldier was having none of that. He'd been an officer's cook during their short and not terribly glorious campaign in the Sudan, from which the colonial troops were now returning. In fact, after the donkey's capture the cook had commandeered it to carry his provisions, and had since become wise to its ways.

'Don't you *Hee-haw* me!' he exclaimed, jerking the halter.

'If *we're* going to be soaked and miserable, so will *you*!'

He smacked the animal on the back of the legs with a stick. It didn't hurt especially, and the donkey had suffered much worse from his former masters in the Sudan. But as the *Arab* was already awash with rain and seawater, the donkey lost its footing and his hooves skidded along the slippery deck.

Hee-haw! Hee-haw!

Too late. Trying to regain his balance, the donkey's legs were already in motion, and the soldier-cook was dragging him from his tarpaulin shelter to the gangplank and the waiting crowd.

A ripple of laughter greeted the Sudan donkey's appearance at the ship's rail. There were even a few brave cheers from the people huddled beneath umbrellas on Circular Quay, or sheltering from the weather in the lee of the wharf buildings. Their applause was quickly dampened, however. Everything was sodden and dripping and half-drowned – not least the soldiers, lined up in waterlogged ranks on the dockside.

A brass band tried to liven things up with some military quicksteps and the sentimental air 'Home Sweet Home'. But the notes were washed away by the rain. A welcoming troop of volunteer infantrymen in scarlet coats, and the naval brigade in blue, stood up to their ankles in mud as their officers shouted orders.

Most miserable of all were the 750 men of the New South Wales Contingent, coming home after three months away fighting for Queen and Empire in the heat and desert country of the Sudan. To be sure, they hadn't seen much action and only three of their number had died – of disease. But it was the first time Australian soldiers had crossed the world to fight in the Imperial cause and prove themselves 'worthy of a place beside the flower of the British army', as the *Sydney Mail* described it. And if the contingent's drill was rough and their officers inexperienced, at least they'd shown the mother country what Australian fighting men were made of. Shown they were willing.

Now, having disembarked from the *Arab* and paraded on the wharf, they were showing every sign of catching their deaths of cold.

Rain cascaded off their tropical helmets, as if from verandah awnings. It spilled onto their khaki jackets, soaked their breeches, ran down their leggings, and overflowed into their boots.

Nor was this all. The men were upset they'd been forced to wait days in quarantine before landing in Sydney to greet their families and friends. They were tired, for reveille had sounded long before dawn, and they'd been given no breakfast. And here, on this wet June morning of 1885, they had to stand for an hour in the rain before setting off on a march through streets running like rivers.

How different from the sunshine, jubilation and excitement of their departure only sixteen weeks ago! Now they'd all rather go straight home to a hot meal, dry clothes, a kind wife and a warm bed.

The soldiers' mood was in this despondent state, when the white Sudan donkey appeared at the top of the ship's gangplank. Here was something to cheer them up! Their little mascot. The spoils of war. The only trophy they'd brought home with them in triumph from the campaign.

'Three cheers, boys!' And everybody laughed.

For the donkey took one look at the soggy mass of people on the wharf. He surveyed the steep and perilous gangway, rocking with the motion of the ship, down which he was supposed to walk.

No thanks!

He turned and tried to go back to his canvas shelter and the handful of hay. As the cook wrestled with his head at one end, the donkey kicked out his hind legs at the other and shouted defiance.

Hee-haw! Not on your bloody life!

Yet the cook was as strong-minded as the donkey. With liberal assistance from the stick and a couple of soldiers pushing from the rear, the little animal was persuaded to mount the gangway.

He braced his feet. He brayed. He tried to bite and buck. It was no good. However unwillingly, the donkey was dragged protesting down the gangplank; and probably for the first time in Australia's own military history (apart from those volunteer colonists who had returned from the Maori Wars twenty years before) a mascot acquired during an overseas campaign was landed on home soil.

Men cheered. Ladies waved handkerchiefs from beneath their umbrellas. It was worth going to war and getting wet, just to see the skill with which the soldiers manoeuvred the trophy ashore.

Once on terra firma, the Sudan donkey gave up all resistance. He shook the rain from his flanks. He lifted his head and cried *Hee-haw!* once more, as if to echo the crowd's laughter. And then he permitted the grinning cook to lead him on an inspection of the serried, sodden ranks, just like Commanding Officer Colonel Richardson himself.

People loved it. The dark clouds seemed to part briefly, and a bright ray of light and good humour shone on the rainy parade.

For the fighting men the sight of the donkey plodding among them once more brought back memories of the late campaign . . .

It began when the much-loved General Gordon was killed at Khartoum by forces loyal to a charismatic Muslim leader known as the Mahdi. Several Australian colonies volunteered to contribute troops to the army that Britain was sending to the Sudan to avenge

Gordon, but only the New South Wales offer was accepted.

The contingent left Sydney with much patriotic fervour in early March, gorgeously dressed in scarlet coats and blue trousers. Once arrived at the Red Sea port of Suakin, however, they had to change into khaki – the first time that Australian soldiers had put on the drab (if more serviceable) battledress of modern warfare.

Despite a few brief skirmishes, the infantry spent most of its time guarding the construction of a railway from Suakin to Berber on the river Nile. And it was then that the white donkey came into their possession.

One morning, a patrol of British mounted infantry heard someone groaning in agony. They crept through thick mimosa bush, to find a tribesman lying with his hand cut off and the donkey standing over him. They were near a well and it appeared the man had come down for water, been attacked by hostile locals, and left to suffer. The tribesman was taken to hospital and the donkey led back to camp – where it was conscripted by the officers' cook to carry his baggage for the duration of the campaign, and to return as a souvenir of war when the contingent left for home a month or so later.

The donkey wasn't their only captive. During one fruitless pursuit of their enemy, a party of Australians heard a sheep bleating high in a ravine. Drawing on their bushmen's skills, they mimicked the cry – and a lost black and white lamb came down in search of its mother. It, too, was taken back to camp and became something of a mascot: though somehow, in the telling, the young sheep at some point turned into a goat – and, unlike the donkey, it didn't come home. Probably it ended up in the cook's pot!

———

With such thoughts of hot food and dry woollen coats, the men of the contingent stood in the drenching rain at Circular Quay and waited for their victory march to begin. Who could say why the parade hadn't been postponed to a finer day? Or what, on this washed-out morning, was the reason for the delay?

In all likelihood they were waiting for the politicians to arrive: those gallant souls who always send soldiers off to war and, of necessity, must share their triumph when they come home.

Yes! Here indeed were the covered carriages of the Governor, members of the ministry and parliament, the mayor and aldermen, sloshing through the downpour to join the parade – though the occupants themselves, of course, remained snug and dry.

At last! The band struck up a lively tune. Officers barked their orders. Troops shouldered arms. And with as much bravado as they could muster, they set off to march through the saturated streets to Paddington and the Victoria Barracks. Where they had to stand in more rain, listening to speeches by the Governor and other dignitaries, before they were finally given three cheers, a tot of rum, and allowed to go home.

All except for the donkey, who was spared the march. As the soldiers departed, he was led back aboard the *Arab* and allowed to finish his breakfast. Eventually he was taken to the Sydney zoo, where it was expected he would end his days in retirement.

Yet long after the volunteers of the Sudan contingent had returned to civilian life, their donkey continued to maintain his presence in the public imagination.

For months, the cartoonist Livingston Hopkins ('Hop') kept up a campaign in *The Bulletin* magazine ridiculing what he saw as the contingent's folly, using the donkey as a principal figure of fun. Hop portrayed the donkey under the punning title 'An Asset, or what we got for our £400 000'. He drew the donkey emblazoned on a mock Sudan medal. When the supposed 'Sudan goat' turned out to be a furphy, he had the donkey kicking it to death at the zoo and hanged for 'murder'.

Eleven years later, when a British politician criticised the Sudan expedition, Hop had the donkey shedding tears, 'And *this* after all I have done for the Mother Country.' And in 1898, amid reports that the donkey had died at the zoo, he showed the patchwork animal being mourned by another comic figure of misplaced patriotism, 'A Little Boy at Manly'.

News that the donkey had died, however, seemed premature. In 1910, when veterans of the contingent met at a reunion in Sydney, *The Bulletin* reported that the famous Sudan donkey was still alive and living at Duntroon, a pastoral property near what was to become the new national capital of Canberra. Photographs and traditions from the period suggest this is probably correct, although nobody knows quite how it got there. But when Duntroon became the Royal Military College of Australia (RMC) in 1911, the first officer cadet, Walter Urquhart, took a picture of the white donkey in a paddock: looking rather sad and lonely, as if still missing his native Sudan.

It lived on until 1913 – the year before the Great War broke out and the Australian fighting forces really showed the world their qualities. Yet curiously, memory of the donkey survived in fragments through RMC traditions. In 1923 two cadets, Fred Scherger and Reg Pollard, found the skeletal jawbone of a horse or a sheep. Recalling the donkey, and the biblical story of Samson who killed a thousand men with 'the jawbone of an ass', they fashioned the bone into a trophy, later supported by two boomerangs, as in the RMC badge, and called it 'Enobesra'.

Enobesra survived for many years, being held aloft as a mascot at football matches and housed in the cadets' mess, where it was treated with much honour. For some time the RMC handbook even adopted Enobesra as a worthy, respectable title.

Then a few years ago, Enobesra disappeared. Which was a pity. Every institution – like every war – needs its trophies, and for RMC this one had its own links of memory to the Sudan donkey: one of the first mascots brought back to Australia from an overseas military campaign, and which went to its maker from the college campus.

Happily, others thought so too. Around 2008 a replacement trophy was made – a plaster cast from the pelvic bone of a sheep apparently, mounted on a plinth, and now kept with the battalion sports sergeant. It's still carried in triumph to RMC sporting events, still not allowed to touch the ground in case it brings bad luck, and still declaimed with the emphasis on the third syllable: 'En-o-*bes*-ra!'

As to what 'Enobesra' means? Try reading it backwards.

BUSHIE

Australia's first official war dog

The donkey that returned from the Sudan may have been turned into an object of ridicule and contempt by *The Bulletin* cartoonists. But a handsome black and white sheepdog called Bushie, who in 1900 went to the Boer War as a mascot with a Bushmen's Contingent, was celebrated by the public as never before.

Bushie was declared Australia's first official war dog with the regimental number 159. His portrait was painted standing in front of the contingent's colours. He was 'christened' by a lieutenant-governor and handed to Lord Roberts (affectionately known as 'Bobs'), the Commander-in-Chief in South Africa, for safekeeping. Lord Roberts in turn presented him as a gift from the Bushmen to Queen Victoria at the close of her reign in 1901. Indeed, from a working family's cottage in rural New South Wales, Bushie seems to have finished his days in the royal kennels at Osborne House on the Isle of Wight.

When the Second Boer War broke out in late 1899, the Australian colonies raised several contingents, mainly from their local militias, to support the Empire's cause. But there seemed a reluctance to get too involved. There may even have been a certain sympathy for the Dutch Boers, who'd attacked British forces and besieged towns in Natal. After all, they were seeking to forestall a feared British takeover of their own territories, following the discovery of vast gold and diamond deposits in the Transvaal and Orange Free State.

At that stage there was a good deal more enthusiasm for the war among the Australian people. In New South Wales subscriptions were called in December to pay for a Citizen's Bushmen's Contingent – and in fact it raised over £30000, two-thirds of that donated in the first week alone. Bushmen hurried to enlist: their renowned horsemanship, resourcefulness in living off the land, hardihood and independence were just the thing for a highly mobile war being fought over great distances on the South African veldt, especially in the later phase of the conflict. The country seemed not unlike Australia.

The corps began assembling in Sydney under the command of Lieutenant-Colonel Henry Airey, who'd also been with the Sudan contingent. Aware of the mutual dependence that exists between a bushman and his dog, the local Animals' Protection Society decided that the contingent should also have a dog: a 'pet' it was called by the press, although today we would properly call it a mascot, for it was to be an official dog.

On the advice of the president of the Kennel Club, a black and white collie was selected. It was owned by a Mr Chiplin who lived at Wentworth Falls in the Blue Mountains, west of Sydney. 'A useful and companionable canine' the *Sydney Mail* called him, the dog appeared from the accompanying photograph to be mainly English border collie, perhaps with a bit of kelpie or some other working breed in him. A very fine specimen nonetheless, a white blaze down his nose and muzzle, and a large snowy patch on his chest.

He was brought to Sydney in February 1900 to join his soldiers at the Paddington barracks, where he was put in the care of Lieutenant Arthur Battye from Forbes, second-in-command of

C Squadron. At thirty-one, Battye was the son of a station overseer: and as it happened, his father – also called Arthur – was serving as a trooper in the same squadron.

A remarkable amount of official fuss was made over the mascot dog. What he was called when he lived with Mr Chiplin is not recorded. But in late February, not long before the contingent left for the war, the *Mail* tells us that he was taken to the chambers of Sir Frederick Darley, the NSW chief justice and lieutenant-governor. Here, at a short ceremony, Sir Frederick 'christened' the dog 'Bushie'. And in a little speech added, 'He is a beautiful dog, and I wish him a hearty return from South Africa.'

In his new capacity Bushie sat (or rather stood) to be painted by the artist Wollaston J Thomas: the dog posing in front of a draped flag against a rolling landscape, with a military bugle beside him.

The presence of the bugle was a happy coincidence. For when the Bushmen's Contingent marched through the streets of Sydney from the barracks to the wharf on the afternoon of 28 February, Bushie was out in front of the band, led by a young trumpeter, Rupert De Lacey Peek from Maitland. They were just behind Lieutenant-Colonel Airey on his charger.

The procession was about half a mile long, and was one of the most enthusiastic ever seen in the city. The *Telegraph* thought it would be hard to imagine a more formidable array of 'rough diamonds' than these bushmen, whose 'stalwart bearing as they rode past elicited innumerable expressions of admiration from the many thousands who lined the way'.

The pavements were crowded with cheering citizens offering huzzas, flowers, fruit and more welcome gifts in bottles to their bushmen; ladies waving and blowing kisses from the balconies; children running alongside the mounted soldiers. The *Telegraph* considered the sight 'most picturesque'. But after the military's former scarlet jackets, it lamented that 'the khaki uniform is not calculated to impart much splendour to a military pageant. It looks a downright fighting costume, distinctly more utilitarian than artistic.'

The times they were a'changing, even then.

Still, there was Bushie to add some colour to the proceedings. 'He is a pretty animal,' the newspaper observed, and 'cut rather a unique figure as he was led along by the bugler'. His collar was decorated with red, white and blue rosettes, and he trotted along quite docile, the *Telegraph* reported – at least until the parade turned into Macquarie Street, where the mighty roars from the spectators so frightened the dog that young Rupert Peek could scarcely restrain him.

Nor was Bushie the only animal mascot in the parade. There were quite a few unofficial ones as well. The *Telegraph* noted there was a possum, 'which was swung by the tail in the air during the march by one of the contingent', and a small terrier dog was also brandished aloft. Indeed, after the troops had lined up on the wharf at Woolloomooloo for speeches by Sir Frederick Darley and the politicians – when the men had marched aboard the two transport ships (Bushie voyaging on the *Atlantian* with Lieutenant Battye) – a wallaby and a dingo also appeared on the decks.

Some things like scarlet coats might change; but more important matters, like the bonds between a regiment of soldiers and their pets, endure across the generations.

The Bushmen sailed for South Africa next morning. After a month at sea they reached Cape Town on 2 April, where they collected some more troops. The contingent sailed on to the Portuguese port of Beira on the east coast, where they disembarked. From there, they and their dog Bushie went by train to Marandellas in the high country of what was then Rhodesia (now Zimbabwe), but there were no Boers to be found. There followed a dreadful journey 350 miles south-west to Bulawayo. Some went by train, others marched or rode their mounts: and the horses suffered dreadfully.

The animals (and men) had been given no time to acclimatise to conditions in South Africa – not to the terrain, extremes of temperature, lack of trees and grass or, in particular for the horses, to the radical change in their diets. These Australian Walers (so called because they'd first been bred in New South Wales, as remounts for the Indian Army) were used to grazing freely on grassland paddocks. In South Africa, they had to subsist almost entirely on dry food, and had no time to adjust. Unlike their brethren who were sent to Egypt with the light horse in 1914–15 and had a year to acclimatise before the Palestine campaign, the Boer War horses were put to work almost immediately, and they paid the price. Their condition deteriorated, they began to starve or suffered the onset of Bluetongue disease. By the end of May, only two months into their campaign, when the NSW Bushmen reached Bulawayo to rest and re-equip, several hundred of their horses had already died.

In this, their experience was typical of that endured by Australian and most other imported military horses in South Africa. A T Yarwood, in *Walers*, cites figures suggesting that about 37 000 Australian horses were sent – some 15 000 with the contingents and 22 000 remounts. Not one of them came home. And while individual statistics for the Walers are not given, the casualty rate among the horses used by the British armies overall was more than 67 per cent, including those who died in battle, from disease, wounds, malnutrition and even thirst. It's a shocking figure, and the

Australian statistics would have been no better – if anything, worse.

Lord Kitchener, who succeeded Lord Roberts as commander-in-chief of the British forces, was very critical of the quality of the Australian horses. It's true that many of them were not up to standard. But it's been pointed out that the Imperial horse buyers, in a competitive market, wouldn't offer the amounts the best stock was going for. And there's a truism in business: if you buy cheap, you get cheap. While the inspector of remounts at Cape Town acknowledged that many of the Australian animals were not good, he nevertheless told Lord Kitchener in a private letter, 'You will go down to history as the largest horse killer of your or any other age.'

From Bulawayo the NSW Bushmen travelled by train some 430 miles to Mafeking in north-west South Africa. They arrived not long after the town had been relieved by British forces on 17 May and the Boers, who had besieged it for nearly seven months, had withdrawn. The mascot dog Bushie undoubtedly went with them, but his movements for some months after that are fairly unclear, as the Bushmen squadrons were sometimes split from each other and sent to different locations.

The war had entered its second phase. After the British reverses resulting from the initial Boer attacks, the Imperial armies were intent firstly on regaining their lost ground: not only Mafeking but the towns of Ladysmith and Kimberley had also been relieved. Secondly, the British went on to capture the principal Boer towns and capitals. Bloemfontein, capital of the Orange Free State, fell at the end of March. On 31 May Pretoria, the capital of Transvaal, capitulated, and Lord Roberts entered the city. In fact most of the principal Boer settlements had been captured by late September, and

Roberts thought the war was almost over. But rather than surrender, the Boer forces began a guerrilla campaign, forcing the British to pursue them over great distances across the veldt, dragging the war on for another twenty months.

It also led the British to adopt a 'scorched earth' policy to deny the Boers supplies. Farmsteads were raided and set ablaze. And, far more horrible, Roberts' successor, Lord Kitchener, began building camps to intern Boer women and children. 'Concentration camps' they were called – the first time that term had been heard. Kitchener's camps were a precursor to the greater evil that would follow later in the twentieth century: many thousands of people in the Boer camps – the great majority of them children – died of disease and malnutrition. It's not surprising that public opinion at home had turned against the war by the time it ended.

At the end of May 1900 one squadron of the NSW Bushmen left Mafeking with Colonel Airey and captured the town of Zeerust fifty miles away. They established a base and mounted patrols. Other squadrons joined them to help capture a town called Rustenburg, on the route to Pretoria, and later to strengthen the defences of an isolated post known as Elands River.

The local Boers were becoming more aggressive, however. Both places were under threat. Rustenburg was even evacuated – until two squadrons of the NSW Bushmen with General Baden-Powell's column helped recapture it in early July. The engagement saw the Bushies charge the Boers and drag many of them off their horses, killing thirty-eight. They were even congratulated 'for their dash and gallantry'. Lieutenant Battye was there with C Squadron, but it's uncertain whether his mascot dog was with him.

Nor do we know if Bushie was present at a far bloodier event in August. Some 105 NSW Bushmen were part of the garrison of just over 500 men at Elands River, when they came under siege by more than 2000 Boers under General de la Rey. The Boers were equipped with six field guns and three automatic 'pom-pom' guns, whereas the defenders only had one old Maxim gun and a screw gun, plus their rifles.

They appeared hopelessly outmanned and outgunned. In the first two days of the siege 2500 shells rained into the post, killing most of the 1500 animals: horses, oxen and cattle. The heat was relentless and after a week the stench became almost unbearable. Water was so low that men had to creep from the post under cover of night to find it. The one saving grace was that the Boers wanted the camp's supplies and eased up on the shell bombardment – but the small-arms fire continued around the clock.

Yet the Bushmen and their comrades would not surrender. Out of respect for their gallantry, the Boers offered safe passage to the nearest British position, but it was rejected. For twelve days – from 4 to 16 August – they held out and the battle raged. Two attempts to relieve the outpost failed: the first was ambushed and the second, under General Baden-Powell (later to found the Boy Scout movement), turned back too soon, thinking the fight was over. Not until 10 000 troops under Lord Kitchener set out from Mafeking did the Boers withdraw. By then twelve of the garrison had been killed along with seven native porters, and fifty-eight men were wounded.

The historian Chris Coulthard-Clark says the action was perhaps the most notable involving Australians during the war, earning high praise from the Boers' senior commander, General Jan Smuts, later to become Prime Minister of the Union of South Africa, who said they stood their ground with 'magnificent courage'.

It seems unlikely that Bushie the dog was there, amid such carnage to the animals. It's more probable that he remained in relative safety at Mafeking or thereabouts. The only thing we know for certain is that some time in June the dog was photographed. Indeed, the *Sydney Mail* told its panting readers that not only had Bushie's portrait been taken, but that an enlargement had been sent to Queen Victoria. Moreover, Her Majesty was 'to be asked to accept Bushie, should he survive the perils of war, as a living memento of Australian loyalty'. The dog was then still under the care of Lieutenant Battye, and the paper remarked that 'probably he will be entrusted with the duty of taking Bushie to England'.

It was quite a remarkable elevation for an animal that had already risen from the working ranks of a rural sheepdog to the singular status of Australia's first official war dog, in the care of a regimental officer. Now it was proposed he should be presented to the Queen and take up residence in one of the royal palaces.

And that, it appears, is how things transpired.

Certainly Bushie next made a public appearance in October 1900, when Lord Roberts inspected the colonial troops camped at Daspoort, just outside Pretoria, some of the NSW Bushmen among them. Lieutenant-Colonel Airey was there, with Lieutenant Battye and of course the regimental pet. The *Sydney Morning Herald* reported that Lord Roberts inspected the numerous troops who were present, and thanked them for 'the devotion and bravery which they displayed during the campaign', and made particular mention of the events at Elands River.

Subsequently Lieutenant Battye came forward with Bushie and – having obtained Airey's permission to do so – handed the dog over to Lord Roberts to take back with him to England and present to the Queen. Believing the war was coming to a close, Roberts was preparing to transfer command to Lord Kitchener on 12 December 1900.

Roberts left South Africa soon afterwards aboard the SS *Canada*, accompanied by his aides and of course Bushie. They arrived in the Channel late on New Year's Day 1901: the first day of the new century – the day on which the six Australian colonies federated to create the Commonwealth of Australia, now responsible for the nation's defence.

The ship spent the night at Poole and next morning steamed to the Isle of Wight, anchoring off Cowes, where Queen Victoria was then at her residence, Osborne House. The *Canada* was surrounded by white sails and steamboats decked with colourful bunting, and cheering crowds come to see the Field Marshal's return. A pinnace arrived from the royal yacht to carry Earl Roberts – as he'd just been created – to Trinity pier, where he was greeted by members of the Royal Family, Princess Beatrice and the Duke of Connaught. He was then conveyed by carriage to a civic welcome as the warship HMS *Australia* fired a nineteen-gun salute.

Orders for Bushie must also have been sent ahead. For as Earl Roberts was being feted ashore Andrew Slater, the Queen's land steward for Osborne, arrived on board *Canada*. As *The Times* reported next day: 'One of the Queen's Scottish attendants had also gone off to fetch a collie dog which Lord Roberts had brought as a gift for the Queen.'

It was all rather reminiscent of the crowds and military ceremony that Bushie had known when he left Australia ten months before. Alas, he didn't have much time to enjoy the pomp when he came ashore at Cowes. Doubtless he was taken pretty quickly by the land steward to his new home in the royal kennels at Osborne.

Earl Roberts visited Queen Victoria for an audience later that afternoon, where she presented him with the insignia of the Order of the Garter, England's premier order of chivalry, and he was appointed Britain's Commander-in-Chief of the Forces, the last man to hold that title before the position was abolished.

Whether the Queen and the Field Marshal spoke about Bushie isn't known. But a fortnight later, on 14 January, Roberts came back to Osborne for an overnight visit. It would be remarkable if he didn't at some stage tell Her Majesty about the lovely collie dog he'd brought as a gift from her loyal Bushmen in South Africa. It was exactly the sort of gesture Victoria liked. Perhaps the old Queen even went to see the dog in his regal quarters. Who knows? But it would have been among the last things she did. The monarch was ailing, and a week later Queen Victoria died at Osborne House at the age of eighty-one, after a reign of over sixty-three years. She was succeeded by her eldest son, who became Edward VII.

How long Bushie survived at the royal kennels is not known. In Sydney, a considerable number of postcards were printed depicting Wollaston Thomas's painting of the dog, done before the Bushmen's Contingent departed. The cards still turn up from time to time. There is one dated 1908 at the Australian War Memorial with the printed inscription on the back saying: 'Bushie's first home was a cottage at Wentworth Falls NSW, his last a palace, for he has since died in the custody of the King's Land Steward, Andrew Slater.'

Not a bad fate for Australia's first official war dog.

World War I
1914–1918

The First World War, or the Great War, was triggered by the assassination of the Austrian Archduke Franz Ferdinand in June 1914. A chain of alliances led to the outbreak of conflict in August between the Central Powers of Austria, Germany and the Ottoman (Turkish) Empire, and the Allied Powers of Britain, France, Russia, Japan, and later the United States.

Australian and New Zealand forces, as part of the British Empire, went first to Egypt then Gallipoli, where they landed on 25 April 1915 (Anzac Day). They withdrew in December 1915.

In 1916, the Anzac infantry divisions went to France, where they fought until shortly before the Armistice ended the war on 11 November 1918. The light horsemen formed part of the Desert Mounted Corps, fighting the Turkish armies in Sinai, Palestine and Syria.

DRIVER

The puppy who went to war

A little Sydney silky terrier called Driver has a special place in the story of our animal heroes. He was one of the very few soldiers' mascots to leave Australia and be smuggled home again at the end of the First World War.

Driver was only ten weeks old when he left Sydney in November 1915, hidden in the pocket of his owner, Fred Roberts. Fred was a horse transport driver with a company of field engineers, and was afraid his wriggling grey puppy might not have been allowed on the troopship.

He needn't have worried. The men had carried many other pets aboard. There was a kangaroo, several wallabies, a possum, and another silky terrier called Sapper, who gave birth to a whole litter of pups during the voyage to Egypt.

We don't know what happened to all these animals. Perhaps Sapper went to another company of soldiers. The marsupials probably ended up in the Cairo zoo, joining their many cousins who'd come across with other Australian diggers.

What is certain is that Driver became the mascot of 7th Company Field Engineers. With them he went to France – to suffer the same cold and endless mud as the men, with all the despair of war on the Western Front. The only warm place Driver found was between his master's feet in the horse wagon, or back at camp.

Never mind which master. When Fred Roberts returned sick to Australia and Leslie Ross became Driver's new master, the dog's favourite spot was always curled up by Leslie's feet. But it wasn't safe. One night a bomb fell very close to the horses, and over forty animals were killed.

After that, Driver learned to listen for the sounds of approaching enemy aeroplanes. Whenever he heard a German bomber overhead he'd rush to the nearest trench, and shelter trembling until it had gone.

There were other terrors: deadly shellfire, shrapnel and bullets, and the seeping stench of poisonous gas across the battlefields.

To avoid the worst dangers, the transport drivers often carried their supplies to the front after dark, and Driver always went with them. But the guns pounded all night long, the sky alight with scarlet flashes. And the dog was once so frightened that he jumped from the wagon and fled. Driver was lost for two days until he limped back to his company.

It wasn't all dread, however. Somewhere in France, Driver became a father. Some said the mother was Sapper, the silky terrier who'd come with them from Sydney. Whoever it was, the pups certainly had long, silky grey hair and droopy moustaches like their father. In fact the engineers kept one of the female pups, who they called Minnie, to be a companion mascot with Driver. And together, father and daughter travelled northwards into Belgium with the armies as the Great War drew to an end.

When it was time to come home, Leslie Ross went to England to join the returning troopships. Driver went with him of course – but Minnie had to stay behind. Like so many mascots, she became lost, and Leslie was never able to find out what became of her.

As for Driver, Ross got him safely aboard the transport ship *Castalia*, which left for Australia in April 1919. But a problem arose when Driver was spotted by the ship's master, Captain Erskine.

By special proclamation that year, no dogs were allowed to enter Australia from Britain, for fear they might introduce diseases such as rabies. Driver would have to be destroyed. They wouldn't even allow him to be put in quarantine.

So Captain Erskine demanded that Leslie Ross hand Driver over to him. But the man refused. And when he persisted, the captain angrily threatened to throw the dog into the ship's furnace.

Still Leslie Ross held firm.

'Excuse me, sir, but I don't think you will.'

The soldiers, gathered around on the troopdeck, murmured their support.

'There are 700 men on this ship. Driver is our mascot. He's served through the war. Where he goes, we follow.'

Not even their commanding officer, Lieutenant-Colonel MacCartney, could make them give up the dog.

'Anyone who takes Driver's life,' the men warned, 'will suffer a similar fate.' Nobody dared find out if they were joking.

The issue simmered during the six week voyage to Australia, but the men knew it would reach a head at Sydney. The quarantine authorities would surely be told about the dog. Driver could be seized and destroyed as soon as he and Leslie Ross went ashore.

What could they do?

The answer was simple. A mate offered to smuggle Driver ashore at Melbourne. If he landed the dog safely, he promised to send Driver by train to Sydney, for collection at the railway station.

He even had an idea about the smuggling. He cut a canvas kitbag in half and sewed the bottom part inside his greatcoat. It made a snug pouch to hold a small silky terrier. As the ship steamed along the coast the men practised with Driver, getting him used to the bag and the need to lie very still inside the coat.

The *Castalia* berthed at Port Melbourne early one May morning. Just after breakfast, Leslie Ross popped Driver inside the pouch, and whispered encouragement.

'In you go, old chap. Not a sound or a wriggle to let them know you're there. I'll watch you ashore, and see you later in Sydney.'

With a wag of his silky tail, Driver disappeared inside.

The disembarking soldiers assembled on deck. Leslie's mate had a kitbag on his shoulder, and the khaki greatcoat with the dog slung over his arm. Slowly they moved down the gangway, past the quarantine men, waving to their families, who were crying, 'Welcome home!'

Orders were for the men to put their gear in front of them on the wharf, and line up while General Brand inspected them and made a speech. For fully twenty minutes the soldiers stood on parade – with Leslie Ross watching from the ship's rail, his heart in his mouth.

Surely Driver couldn't lie still and hidden in the greatcoat for all that time? Surely he'd get restless and start to whimper, and want to come out of the pouch? And then what? He'd be seized by the quarantine officers and never heard of again.

Not for one moment did Ross take his eyes off that coat.

'Good boy, Driver,' he murmured under his breath, willing the dog to remain silent. 'Not a murmur. Not a muscle twitching. The best you've ever been. Nothing to let them know where you are.'

And it worked.

'It was almost as if Driver knew,' Leslie remembered years later. 'He never moved an inch.'

At last, the parade was dismissed. The returning soldiers kissed and hugged their loved ones, and drove into town for a civic reception. But not before a certain greatcoat was handed over for safekeeping.

'Look after this for me, Dad.'

'It's a bit heavy for an overcoat, son.'

Quietly, Leslie's mate explained – and left instructions for a dog crate that would be needed for a railway journey.

Sure enough, when the *Castalia* berthed at Sydney a few days later, Leslie Ross and his parents went to Central Station. And there, waiting for them, was Driver.

How the dog barked when he saw them! How he threw himself into his master's arms, and joined in the celebrations when they got home! It took the silky terrier a long time to settle down that night – to curl up beside Leslie's feet and go to sleep.

What a day. What a dog.

'He deserves a medal,' they said.

But the family couldn't tell anybody else about Driver's war record. If the authorities heard, the dog could still be seized. So they kept the secret to themselves and the few comrades who knew, during all the years that followed.

Driver had just turned eleven when he died in October 1926. It was a good age for a silky terrier, especially one who'd been to the Great War. But the family took it hard, for they'd grown to love the dog. So Leslie took Driver's body to the taxidermist at the Australian Museum, to be mounted.

It was the sort of thing people did then with their animals, more than they do now. Still, it was a bit of a shock when Leslie's father found Driver standing on the dining table one day, his glass eyes catching the light and with a front paw raised, as in life.

A few months later, Driver was presented to the Australian War Memorial with his collar and tag. He is still in the repository, his silky grey coat well cared for. Thousands of people saw Driver in a glass case when he was on public display, and read the story of the little Sydney terrier who went to war as a puppy, and came safely home again an animal hero.

But only the family of Leslie Ross, and the men who served with him in Egypt and France, knew the living reality behind the mascot whose dog tag simply says:

DRIVER
7th Field Coy Engineers
AIF
Born 15/9/15

And they, too, have now passed on.

MURPHY

The donkey and his Simpson

Mid-morning on Wednesday 19 May 1915, a small grey donkey they called Murphy made his way down Shrapnel Gully, Gallipoli, towards an Australian ambulance dressing station.

He picked his steps carefully, for the path was stony and dangerous, and Murphy was carrying a badly injured soldier. The man had first been helped onto the donkey after being wounded in the leg. Since then, he'd been hit again – in a burst of machine-gun fire that also caught the donkey's master and sent him sprawling to the ground with a bullet through his heart.

But Murphy was unhurt. The donkey had escaped any injury at all during the three weeks since the landing, and he was faithful to his trade. So he continued to plod down Shrapnel Gully with his patient, who by now was almost fainting from loss of blood.

Down at the dressing station, a New Zealand padre heard the rattle of hooves on stone. Glancing outside, he saw the familiar shadow of Murphy approaching with his burden. And he called out to the donkey driver, 'Is that you, Jack?'

Padre Bush-King knew the tall, blunt Englishman, known as Jack Simpson, reasonably well. A few days ago he'd painted a red cross on a white brassard – an armband – to be tied between Murphy's ears, to show that he was a proper ambulance donkey.

'Is that you, Jack?' But no answer came, except a soft whinny.

Suddenly, the padre felt afraid. He went outside, and saw Murphy standing alone with the injured soldier slumped on his back. So many had been wounded that morning, for the Turks had launched a dawn attack, trying to drive the Anzacs from the heights above.

The padre quickly supported the suffering man, calling for the orderlies. They lifted the patient down and into the dugout, staunching the blood and trying to ease his pain, before the stretcher-bearers took him to the tent hospital at Anzac Cove.

But where was Jack Simpson? He must have been hurt somewhere up the track, caught in the hail of shrapnel that had given the gully its name. After twenty-four days making that journey up and down the path, escaping every danger, had Simpson's luck at last run out?

Padre Bush-King went to the donkey. Murphy's head was bent low, searching for something to eat in the scraggy soil. He'd barely found a nibble before the padre seized his halter rope and began leading him back up the path.

Closer they came to the sounds of battle on the ridges, shells exploding around them. Bravely they plodded upwards. And the clergyman knew the red cross he'd painted for Murphy wouldn't save them if their names were on a bullet. It would find them. As one had found Jack Simpson.

For turning a corner, close to the place men called Bloody Angle, Murphy and the padre saw him. Jack Simpson was dead. He'd been found by a group of his mates from the 3rd Field Ambulance, with whom he'd been joking on the way down just a little while before. They'd heard the machine-gun fire and rushed down. But there was nothing they could do, except lay Simpson's body beside the track, away from further harm.

Padre Bush-King prayed over Simpson a moment. Then he and Murphy went back to the living.

That night, however, the ambulance men returned and carried their mate down to the cemetery by the beach. They buried him and placed a simple white cross above his grave, with only his name on it. And the legend of Simpson and his donkey began to enter the very consciousness of Anzac and all that it meant.

They had both been at Gallipoli from the first landing on Sunday 25 April.

Murphy had entered army service only the day before. He was one of several hundred donkeys rounded up from their island homes on Imbros and Lemnos, and slung aboard the transport ships to join the mules brought from Egypt to haul guns and supplies.

Next morning, they steamed across the narrow sea: away from the peaceful life they'd known, to the thundering hell of war. And there, amid the roar of gunfire, the animals were loaded into barges and ferried ashore. Some even had to swim the last few hundred metres through blood-stained water to the beach, where Indian drivers were taking charge of the mules. But there were few to care for the donkeys. In all the confusion, some of them, being free spirits, wandered off to find a safe place to graze.

Now, Jack Simpson was a free spirit himself. Growing up in the north of England, he'd run away to sea as a young man and jumped ship in Australia. When the Great War broke out, he enlisted (though not under his full name, John Simpson Kirkpatrick) and went to the 3rd Field Ambulance.

Jack may have resented the discipline and drill of military life, but he didn't shirk danger. As Simpson landed on Gallipoli with his unit, he threw himself into the dreadful work. That Sunday, more than 2000 casualties were carried down to the medical staff on the beach.

By nightfall, Simpson was exhausted. Taking a quick breather in the darkness, he came across one of the donkeys who'd wandered off to graze. As a lad, Jack had often seen donkeys taking people for holiday rides on the beach. Now, on the shores of Anzac Cove, he thought they might also be good for carrying those injured in war.

'No time for supper, young Murphy. You're coming wi' me.'

Knotting strips of bandages together to make a leading rein, he tied it to the donkey's noseband and led him away.

Together they turned into one of the gullies, crowded with men and weapons travelling the rough path up to the ridges. A little way along, they heard a soldier groaning. He'd been hit in the leg by a bullet, and couldn't walk any further.

The ambulance man with the donkey stopped.

'Hello, dig. You look as if you could do wi' some help.'

Jack bathed the wound with iodine, applied a field dressing and bandaged the digger's leg. It hurt the soldier like hell. But hanging onto Simpson, he was able to hobble across to Murphy.

'Come on, chum. We're going for a donkey ride.'

With his good leg, the injured man straddled the little animal, his feet almost touching the ground. While Jack supported him, giving Murphy a 'gee up', they slowly trekked down to the medics working by the light of hurricane lamps.

'Smart idea, soldier, to use a donkey. Keep up the good work.'

Simpson and Murphy turned and went back up the gully to find more wounded and carry them to the beach. For hours they kept it up. Many times Jack passed his mates from the 3rd Field Ambulance and exchanged banter. But he was a loner who preferred working by himself – answerable to nobody except his own free will, and the good humour of his donkey.

At length, both man and beast needed rest. They didn't go back to the field ambulance, however, but dossed down with the Indian mule drivers. Simpson enjoyed their company, away from officers. The drivers had also brought plentiful feed for their mules – and good forage, as Murphy discovered, was hard to find at Gallipoli.

It set the pattern for the weeks to follow. They always camped with the muleteers. Jack's sergeant wanted to charge him for being absent. But the colonel said they were doing such good work it was best to leave them. After that, the man only reported to his unit when he wanted a haircut or a fresh pair of boots.

Every morning, Simpson and Murphy set off at first light. Jack usually had breakfast with the men who guarded the water tanks at the foot of Shrapnel Gully, leaving Murphy to browse, before heading further up the valley toward the first of the wounded.

All day and well into the night they worked, carrying the injured down to the ambulance stations. All through the firestorms that swept the gully they walked – the man upright and unflinching, the donkey plodding faithfully by his side.

Men never forgot it. None of the shrapnel that killed others ever touched them. Their names seemed written on no bullet. As an example of sustained courage under fire, it was extraordinary. And to those who warned him of the dangers, Simpson merely joked, 'Ee, they be *my* troubles.'

Always the same. Always a laugh and a cheery word. 'Hello, dig.' Though sometimes they also felt the rough side of his tongue. An officer, carried down to the dressing station, offered Simpson a pound note in gratitude. 'Keep your lousy quid! I'm not doing this for money.' And a man who once took Murphy and his patient down to the medics to give Jack a break met the full force of Simpson's anger when he rode the donkey back up the steep path.

'What are you doing, idiot? It's the only chance the poor beast has to rest.'

Jack was as concerned for his donkey's welfare as he was for the wounded. He made a saddlecloth from sacks to protect Murphy's back, and fashioned stirrups from rags to support the men.

Before long, Jack acquired a second donkey that he called Duffy – or Abdul – or any other nickname that came into his head. One night he was heard to murmur as the donkey stumbled, 'Come along there, Queen Elizabeth.' Calling his wee animal, not much more than a metre high, after the great British battleship.

For twenty-four days, Murphy and Duffy and John Simpson Kirkpatrick kept it up. Between them they carried perhaps two hundred wounded men to safety.

Then, on 19 May, Jack and Murphy went out early as usual, but breakfast by the water tanks wasn't ready. 'Never mind,' Simpson called. 'Get me a good dinner when I come back.' But he didn't come back. Not alive. A bullet *did* have his name on it.

They say the men at Anzac fell silent when they heard the news – even those who'd barely seen him. Such was the symbolic power of his deeds. The Indian muleteers picked wildflowers for his grave, and called him *Bahadur* – a title given only to those they respect greatly. And next day Colonel Monash, commanding 4th Division, wrote to headquarters bringing the man and his donkey to special notice.

Other ambulance bearers, inspired by Simpson and Murphy's example, had also acquired donkeys and faced the same dangers. But as the Simpson tale grew in the telling, one story merged with another, as if his valour stood for all of them. That is the nature of legends, when a man dies.

Jack's own commander tried to get an honour for him. But it was hard to find any one act to justify the Victoria Cross. 'The fact is, he did so many.' Ultimately, Jack Simpson was mentioned in dispatches, and his family received his service medals. Every other attempt to obtain higher recognition, however, met with failure.

Murphy was more fortunate. In 1997, the RSPCA awarded him a Purple Cross – not just for Murphy, but to all of Simpson's donkeys 'for the exceptional work they performed on behalf of humans while under continual fire at Gallipoli'.

Nobody knows what really happened to Murphy. There were many donkeys at Gallipoli, but everybody wanted a share of the most famous one. So, when the diggers came to write their *Anzac Book*, they said Murphy had sired a foal born at Gallipoli. They called her Jenny and, like Murphy, she seemed to lead a charmed life. Until, only six months old, Jenny was killed by shrapnel.

Scores of donkeys and mules were killed. Animal heroes pay the same price as the humans who take them into war. Even Murphy was wounded by a piece of shrapnel. But he recovered, cared for by the Indian mule drivers with whom he stayed while the Anzacs remained on Gallipoli. Then, after eight months of bitter fighting, Murphy was evacuated from the peninsula with the men.

An Indian Army ambulance officer, Dr Carey Evans, wondered if he'd have to shoot Murphy or leave him behind. But the muleteers begged him to save the gallant animal that had faced the same dangers as the *Bahadur*, Jack Simpson.

So Dr Carey Evans wrote on two large luggage labels, *MURPHY V.C. PLEASE LOOK AFTER HIM*, and tied them to the donkey's halter. On the night of 16 December, Murphy was led quietly down to the beach, loaded into a barge and ferried to the ships. Before dawn, he came ashore again – at Mudros Harbour on Lemnos.

The donkey was taken to the horse lines, given a feed, and tethered. But when the Indian drivers came to see him, Murphy had disappeared. The *Bahadur*'s favourite had gone.

The drivers searched the nearby villages and countryside, but no trace of Murphy was found. Dr Carey Evans suspected he'd been taken by some Australians who saw the luggage labels and claimed Murphy as their own. But nothing was ever proved.

A few months later official enquiries were made. The big brass thought about bringing Murphy back to Australia for a wartime recruiting campaign. There were several versions of what happened to him. One said he was taken to Egypt and landed at Alexandria. Another said Murphy ended up with the Australian ambulance near the French city of Abbeville. To be truthful, he could only be classified as 'whereabouts unknown'.

But it would be nice to think, that morning on Lemnos, the donkey had smelt the clear, peaceful island breeze once more, slipped his halter, and just gone home.

ZEP

Dog with a passport

It is a winter afternoon on the battlefields of France, near the river Marne. 1916. Cold oozes across the open landscape: but here, in a stone barn, a young dog has found somewhere warm for a nap.

A bundle of straw, tossed in a corner, makes a fine bed. The white and black spotted dog lies with his eyes closed, listening to the familiar sounds of the world around him: hens busy in the farmyard; the distant popping of artillery from the war front on the horizon; soldiers working in a battery just across the field.

Everything is much the same as usual. Stillness falls, and the dog settles down to sleep.

Suddenly, he's awake again. His ears have caught some strange mechanical noise, coming not from the road – but above him, in the sky. A whirling, whirring sound he's never heard before.

The dog springs up. Alarmed. Soldiers are shouting, 'Zeppelin! The airship has bombs. Make ready to fire.' The big guns from the battery boom and shatter the afternoon. But before anything else, the dog's own world is exploding in flame and terror.

A heavy bomb, dropped from the German zeppelin above, has missed the artillery and fallen into the farmyard. The far end of the barn is blown apart. Stones and timber and metal are hurled by the blast. The dog howls and falls, dazed by the shock. He can hear other animals screaming. The hens. A wounded calf.

And then, through the stinking smoke and rubble, the dog is running for his life.

It's amazing that he's not been injured. Perhaps the straw protected him. But the dog doesn't think about that as he runs, with ears flattened and tail down, as fast as he can. As far as he can, away from the noise and horror. Not stopping. Not looking back. Not knowing where he's running to, so long as it's somewhere safe.

At last, the dog begins to slow down. He's tiring, and he's many kilometres from home. His path has taken him over soggy country to a strange road. He's only young and hasn't been this way before.

His instincts are good, however. As his fear subsides, and silence and the cold settle over the world once more, the dog scrambles onto the muddy road. Perhaps he'll get a sense of his bearings there, or find somebody he knows.

Nothing.

The dog trots further down the road, stopping every so often to look behind him and to listen. Just in case. Still nothing, however. And as the feeling he is lost grows stronger, the dog begins to be afraid once more. Panic stirs again.

Then, faintly, he hears the familiar sound of a motor coming towards him. The dog pauses. Turns. And crouches by the roadside, in hope and fear, as the vehicle draws nearer.

It is an ambulance, bearing the distinctive red and black star of the Society of Friends, driven by an Australian, Frank Fryer. A dedicated pacifist, as are all Quakers, Frank has nevertheless come to France to help the Society in its mission of relief to those who suffer in war: the hurt, the homeless, the many orphans.

Frank and his emergency nurse, Ethel Ubsdell, had been out that afternoon, gathering victims of the zeppelin attack. Now, taking them in the ambulance back to the Quaker hospital at the village of Sermaize-les-Bains, he sees the dog by the roadside. He brakes. Gets out. And, squatting down in his grey uniform and peaked cap, Frank calls to the trembling animal.

'Are you lost, old chap? Come over here. See if we can help . . .'

He doesn't speak in French, such as the dog knows. But kindness is understood in any language, and carefully the dog comes to him. He slinks low in submission, though his eyes look up with a question. Friend? It seems so. The tip of his tail wags slightly, and he licks the outstretched hand.

'Were you frightened away in that zeppelin raid?' Frank strokes the dog, easing his tension. 'You've no tag to say what your name is or where you're from, and there's no time to find out. We've people who also need help. You'd better come with us.'

Little by little he reassures the dog, until he can pick up the animal and pass it to Sister Ubsdell, sitting beside him on the open passenger seat. The dog is nervous of the woman at first, and shakes in the afternoon chill. But held in Ethel's arms, her body warmth flowing into him, and hearing the soothing sound of her voice, the dog starts to relax. To feel a little safe again.

The ambulance moves off down the road towards the hospital at Sermaize.

It didn't take the dog long to recover his confidence. He was wary of strangers at first and kept close to Frank Fryer, who fed him, gave him somewhere to sleep and calmed him whenever the dog awoke whimpering from nightmares.

'What is it, old man? Still dreaming of that zeppelin? Eh, Zep?'

The name stuck. Zep. Everyone at the hospital called him that. For Zep was soon visiting patients with the nurses: the women, children, and the old men who'd lost everything in the war. It was good for him and it was good for them, to share the affection of a dog and to remember a life that had once been normal.

As time went by, Zep even went out with Frank and Sister Ubsdell in the ambulance. Afraid they might take him back to the bombing, he had to be coaxed aboard at first. But finding that they wanted to keep him as their own pet – part of the wider family of the hospital – he soon started jumping into the seat of his own accord. Though whenever they passed the ruined barn, Zep stared rigidly the other way, giving no sign he'd ever known the place.

There was one problem. Because the Society of Friends was a civilian organisation operating in a war zone, they needed a special permit from the French authorities to travel on military roads. Frank had a permit. So did the nurses. But Zep didn't. Perhaps he'd be arrested if the ambulance were stopped by the army.

So somebody at the hospital, with a sense of humour and knowledge of French, got to work. Perhaps it was Ethel, for she'd become very fond of the dog. She took a pen and paper, and made up a passport just for Zep.

At the top of the page she put the Mission stamp. And below, she listed the young dog's particulars (translated here into English) and stamped it with his pawprint.

NAME	Zep
NATIONALITY	French
BORN AT	On the front
AGE	9 months

OCCUPATION	Hunter on foot (say Light Infantry)
STATEMENT OF RESIDENCE	Sermaize-les-Bains
MADE AT	21 February 1916
RESIDENCE PERMIT	To live at Sermaize-les-Bains for the duration of the war with his family

PARTICULARS

AGE	9 months
TAIL	49 cm
EYES	Brown
FOREHEAD	White stripe
CHIN	Prominent
LENGTH from TIP of NOSE to TAIL	1m 11cm
HAIR	Black and white spots
NOSE	Long black
MOUTH	Big
SPECIAL CHARACTERISTICS	He often scratches himself.

For over two years, Zep travelled in the ambulance with Frank, taking the sick and lost to hospital. The frightened young dog had indeed found safe refuge. Eventually, Frank left Sermaize and went to a Friends' mission near Verdun in northern France. Ethel was already there. Six months after the Armistice they married, and returned to Frank's home in South Australia.

We don't know what became of Zep. It's to be hoped Frank found a new home for him. But one thing is sure. With the fighting over, dogs no longer needed permits to travel the broad highways of France. So Mr and Mrs Fryer brought Zep's passport back to Australia with them. They kept it among their precious souvenirs, until the family gave it to the Australian War Memorial.

Today anyone can see Zep's amusing little passport – and share the simple pleasure this one dog gave to those dedicated Quakers who offered him succour, even as they brought relief to other lives devastated by war.

LAST RACE

Tripoli, 1919

An Australian light horseman, Trooper Billjim, stood by his bay mare, Missy, in the mounting yard of the Tripoli racecourse, giving last-minute instructions. The place was crowded with men and animals, and noisome with dust, sweat and chatter. But it seemed to Billjim that he and Missy were alone in the world.

'This is the last race of the day, old girl,' he said softly, rubbing the hollow in her neck. 'The last time we'll ride out together, you and me.'

The mare turned her head and nudged him.

'You run your finest race ever, eh? For both of us. Show 'em what we can do. Save our best for last.'

Trooper Billjim gave her a piece of apple pinched from an Arab hawker. And then, hearing the stewards calling the riders onto the track, he sprang into the saddle.

Thronging spectators cheered as they entered the sandy course. Up the track they moved towards the starting line, the horses flexing their muscles, coats brushed till they gleamed.

For Trooper Billjim this could have been any one of those days during the two and a half years since they'd left Egypt with the squadron. They'd ridden so far, and fought so many battles.

But now, with the Turks defeated and the war over, they were

getting ready to come home. The men riding today weren't wearing khaki uniforms, but racing silks (Billjim in blue and green). And
the only extra gear their Waler horses carried was a number on their
saddlecloths.

For here in Tripoli, the Australian Mounted Division was holding its final race meeting. Sappers had blasted rocks out of the
flat land near the sea, and mule teams had levelled it into a track.
A sandstone cliff had been terraced like a grandstand, crowded
today with uniforms and Arab robes. A totalisator was doing good
business, with men laying bets as if it were the Melbourne Cup. And
grog flowed in the marquee, just like at Flemington too.

There were six races on the program. In the late February afternoon, the riders broke into a trot heading to the starter for the last
event: down the straight and once around the course to the winning
post.

Billjim felt Missy tense beneath him. She was like that going into
action, sensing the excitement. Some of the crankier horses began
to prance about a bit. He remembered one called Bill the Bastard
who almost always bucked to begin with. Missy never did that. She
merely arched her neck, and snorted, and swished her tail.

Her tail! The riders wheeled about and formed into line, holding their horses in check as they advanced towards the starter. The
watching mob grew quiet. Any moment, and they'd be off. But
Trooper Billjim wasn't thinking of that. He'd just noticed that the
horse to the right of him had no tail and no mane. They'd been cut
off by the vets only yesterday. And tomorrow . . .

*Steady, old girl. Hold yourself ready to spring as soon as the
starter fires his gun.*

Away! Down the straight, hooves thundering and dust clouds
rising. Billjim leaned forward in the saddle, gripping with his knees,

holding Missy back a little, saving her best. The chestnut gelding with no mane or tail was beside him, his rider in red and white jockeying, like Billjim, for position. The crowds on the terraces urged their horses on.

The horses. Those wonderful, tough little Walers. They had come from all over Australia, not just New South Wales where they'd first been bred: shipped in their tens of thousands to fight for King and Empire. Such courage. There was scarcely a trooper who hadn't wanted to buy his nag and bring it home when the fighting was over. Even Bill the Bastard once carried five stranded men for half a mile, without once bucking.

The racing crowd cheered as the horses pounded down the straight towards the first turn.

Doing nicely, Missy. Keep it easy. Long way to go yet.

The mare's tail streaming and her long mane flying.

The bloke in red and white on the gelding with no tail or mane looked over to Billjim. Sizing him up. And the two men laughed.

Such wild men, all of them. No respecters of persons. Never saluted officers, unless they deserved it. Remember that feller in the Holy Land who blew out a sanctuary lamp that had been burning for 500 years? Reckoned it needed a rest. And when they got blind drunk in Jerusalem, someone rode a donkey pell-mell into the officers' restaurant.

They weren't always louts. After the battle at Romani in 1916, a colonel and his men gave up their horses to carry seventy Turkish prisoners, almost dead of thirst, five miles across the sand dunes. But you touch their Walers without asking . . .

Pell-mell down the far side of the track. Missy and the chestnut gelding going hell for leather.

Hold it, old girl. Not just yet.

Of course, they'd known since November the horses wouldn't be returning with them. They were told it was cost and quarantine. Billjim had resigned himself to that.

Yet the anger when he heard the brass hats were planning to sell the horses to the locals! He'd seen how badly so many of the poor animals had been treated. Mules beaten at the plough. Camels half starved. Donkeys weighted under loads till they almost collapsed. Billjim would rather put a bullet through Missy's head himself than leave her to that. Everyone felt the same.

Such fortitude! Missy had often carried him for two days in the saddle without water. It was nothing for her to bear 250 pounds weight forty miles a day over some of the hottest, most desolate country in the world. Didn't the brass hats know what they'd got?

Round the next bend and into the back straight. The horses were stringing out now. Sweat glistening and eyes alight. Billjim looked around. The chestnut without a mane was still up with him, going flat out. Hooves dancing over the sand.

He exchanged glances again with the red-and-white rider. Their thoughts were the same. Both slackened the reins a little, and pointed their horses for an opening on the inside.

Go, Missy! Just like we did in Sinai. Enemy machine guns giving more speed to your heels. Outrun those swooping aeroplanes.

Rhythm of galloping horseflesh over the earth, the steeds and their riders as one.

So the brass hats knew, from General Harry Chauvel no less, they'd have a brawl on their hands if they sold the Walers to the locals. But they still couldn't come home. And they couldn't all be absorbed into the rest of the Imperial army.

Thus, only a week ago, when preparations were in full swing for the race, came news that all AIF horses in Egypt and Palestine were to be classified. Young and fit horses at Tripoli would go to the relieving British and Indian Cavalry. But the sick and those aged over twelve were to be shot, their hides tanned and bodies burned.

Trooper Billjim crouched low in his saddle. He gave Missy a kick (not that she needed it) and headed for the home turn.

How he remembered the emotions of this last week. For days, the veterinary officers had been inspecting thousands of horses and mules camped with the brigades at Tripoli. Billjim waited beside Missy, his heart drubbing, to learn her fate. She was ten. She was in good health. The relief that she wouldn't be shot.

But the others . . . Trooper Billjim had seen the tears in his mate's eyes only yesterday when Starlight was marked for destruction. His horseshoes were removed – such petty economies. Starlight's mane and tail were cut off, to make him easier to identify. Today, the Walers were being taken for a last race. And tomorrow . . . ?

Tomorrow the horses being transferred would go to their new units, Missy among them. But Starlight, and all the others without manes and tails, would be led to the plateau outside camp and killed. It would be humanely done, under the supervision of the vets. Even so, some men wouldn't trust their beloved horses even to that and, despite regulations, they would shoot their Walers themselves.

Turning now into the home straight. Hearts and hooves beating. Ground drumming beneath them, and the sand swirling.

Billjim heard the mob start to roar. Glimpses of red and white through the dust. The two were still side by side, racing with necks stretched out and every muscle straining. He gave the mare her head.

Go on, old girl! This is the last. Show them your best.

Going like the bloody clappers towards home.

Missy and the chestnut gelding with no mane or tail were stride for stride. Foam flecked. Their nostrils wide. The love of life and of battle shining in their eyes.

On! On!

And all at once Trooper Billjim imagined himself back in Palestine, at Beersheba. October 1917, and charging with his regiment towards the wells. The last successful cavalry charge in history, it would later be called. But then it was just a last throw, late in the afternoon, after two days riding across the desert and the horses needing water. If they didn't capture Beersheba by nightfall they'd be done for, with the Turks threatening to blow up the wells.

He could see again the squadrons in lines of three, breaking into a trot as they rode out of the gully and onto the flat, stony plain. The minaret of Beersheba was in front of them, the sun setting in their eyes. But before the town were the Turkish trenches, their riflemen waiting.

'Draw your bayonets, boys,' Billjim heard his sergeant cry. 'We'll water our horses in Beersheba tonight.'

They were into a canter. And then at the gallop. He sensed the rattle of machine-gun fire and caught glimpses of horses falling. Faster and faster they galloped across the plain.

'Charge!'

At full career. Sparks were flying. Billjim was yelling. The gunfire was thicker now, but not like he'd feared. Were the Turks waiting, thinking the horsemen would dismount to fight, as they usually did? Not this time, Jacko.

Closer and closer.

Go, Missy! Run for your life.

He had bent low over her neck, just as he was doing on the home straight. He heard the whine of bullets past his ears. Aha! Jacko had woken up at last. The man on his left went down with a sigh . . . but here on the racecourse the bloke in red and white was still there, the horses running neck and neck.

Nearer they charged the trenches, but the bullets had almost stopped. What happened? Did Jacko forget to change his rifle sights?

Here's the first trench coming up, Missy. Ready. Gather yourself and leap, old girl. Bayonets glint and thrust. But don't stop. Here's their second line of trenches. Up and over.

Other men have dismounted, but we won't. Not now. The town is just in front of us. Almost there, Missy.

The shouting and the tumult and the rush of it all. Just a bit more, great heart. We're nearly home. I can see the winning post . . .

But the bloke in red and white, on his chestnut gelding with the shorn mane and tail, has got there before us. Half a head, Missy. That's all. No shame in that. We've all run the race of our lives.

The horses began to ease up after their last charge home. Gallop slowed into a canter on the sandy track outside Tripoli. They pulled up, sweating and heaving and catching their breath.

Trooper Billjim and the chap in red and white were stretched low, arms around their Walers' necks, Missy and the chestnut gelding, telling them things that they wouldn't be able to say tomorrow. Not in front of others.

The two men sat upright in their saddles. They looked at each other. Grinned. And clasped hands.

'Good ride, mate.'

Then they turned the horses' heads, and slowly walked down the track to the judges and the officers to receive their prizes.

BULLET, TRICK AND NELL

On the morning of 3 May 1918, three eager Australian messenger dogs set out for a day's work with the battalions stationed just outside the French town of Villers-Bretonneux. One was a black setter called Nell. Another was Trick, something of a bitser with a fair bit of collie in him. And the third was an Airedale-cross called Bullet, who wore a message cylinder on the collar around his neck.

Alas, Bullet was about to bring disgrace on himself and the whole messenger dog service.

Messenger dogs and carrier pigeons were used by all armies during the First World War. Wireless was still being developed, and signal cables were often damaged in the fighting. But trained homing pigeons could fly military dispatches in cylinders attached to their legs, and dogs could run quickly from the trenches back to headquarters.

They faced the same dangers as men on the battlefields: the same terrors of bombardment and gas attack. Some animal heroes were so frightened they strayed – and who can blame them? Many were shot by enemy snipers.

Australian soldiers had long distrusted animals to carry messages. Generally, they preferred to rely on signallers and runners. During the later stages of the war in France, however, they carried out trials with pigeons and dogs. The birds worked well. But the dogs . . .

Like Bullet, Trick and Nell, they just weren't reliable enough. A dog that worked well one day might wander off the next. Even Trick, who was commended for fine work, tended to stray. One day he ran two miles in fifteen minutes, which was pretty good. Next day it took him twenty-three minutes – and the day after that, forty minutes. Men ran faster themselves.

And what about poor old Bullet?

The Airedale once took thirty minutes to run just over a mile. Two days later he did it in eight minutes. Great! But two days after that, Bullet had what his commander called 'a lapse'. It took him nineteen hours and ten minutes.

The dog didn't exactly live up to his name.

Nobody knows what happened. Perhaps he was dodging German bullets. At least one Australian war dog was shot by the enemy. Another bolted and was heard of no more. Perhaps Bullet found a juicy bone. Or maybe he caught the scent of an attractive French female dog, and enjoyed her company overnight. The historian Charles Bean said that was a problem with the war dogs.

Another was the fact that so many soldiers fed and petted them. For men so far from home and loved ones, it was an understandable thing to do. The dogs should only have been handled by their keepers, and orders were issued to that effect. But these orders were often ignored, and many good working dogs were ruined. One was so spoiled he refused to leave headquarters at all.

Australian signallers continued to use carrier pigeons but, after only a few months, the experiment with messenger dogs petered out. From the start of the final offensives in August 1918, there's little mention of them in the records.

Lovable as Bullet, Trick and Nell were, the soldiers found their four-legged friends were never reliable enough to replace the wireless message, the telephone cable, the dispatch rider on his motorbike, a pair of pigeon wings – or even a human being running on just two feet.

BILLY BANTAM

And other game old birds

Billy Bantam was the mascot of the 13th Battalion: one of the gamest little fighting birds the men ever came across. Whatever we may think of cockfighting today, we can acknowledge Billy's courage. During the Great War, he would take on anything, and not just bantamweights. He fought roosters of the largest heavyweight division – and usually came off best.

In 1916 Billy left Australia as a young bird with a detachment of reinforcements and joined his battalion in Egypt. They went to France soon afterwards; and at their very first camp, Billy showed them what he was made of.

He tackled four roosters in a neighbouring farmyard, one after the other, and cleaned them up in less than half an hour. According to Tom White, who wrote the battalion history, the smallest of them was at least eight times Billy's size. And that night, listening to the complaints of the losing farmers, 'the diggers learnt practically all the French swearwords in general use'.

Wherever the battalion went, the men always offered to pit Billy against the local champions. It rarely took him long to establish himself as the reigning cock of the walk.

Squawking, spitting, eyes flashing fire and claws extended, Billy would launch himself furiously against an opponent, in a hellfight that reflected the wider human conflict around him. The men no doubt picked up the remaining French swearwords from other aggrieved farmers. And they made their champion a medal, which he wore on a ribbon around his neck: *Billy Bantam, 13th Bn A.I.F.*

For three years, Billy fought for his unit in France. With the signing of the Armistice the rooster also called it quits and travelled back to Australia with the man who cared for him, Driver Tom Igoe, of the battalion's transport section.

Tom safely smuggled Billy ashore when their ship berthed in Sydney in June 1919. We don't know how he did it. Perhaps it was a version of the kitbag trick played with the silky terrier, Driver.

However it happened, Billy Bantam went home with Tom Igoe, and lived in his backyard chook pen for the next three years. Where first thing, every morning, the feathered veteran could be heard crowing of his exploits against the enemy in France to the entire neighbourhood.

JACKIE

Another rooster mascot from the First World War was Jackie, who liked to perch on the shoulder of Driver Walter Farrell of the 2nd Divisional Signals Company.

The transport drivers spent much of their time behind the fighting lines – and as they already cared for the horses that hauled their wagons, they generally looked after the regimental pets as well.

Jackie had been bought as a chick when the signallers were in Egypt in 1916. Like Billy Bantam, he also went with his soldiers to France. But unlike Billy, Jackie rarely fought other roosters. His opponents were of the human variety.

If any stranger or soldier unknown to Jackie dared enter his lines, the bird immediately attacked them. A flying missile of red and green feathers, shrieking, scratching, and ready to peck their eyes out. Men always swore he was better than any guard dog.

ROBERT

Shed a tear for Robert the parrot, one among the many casualties of war.

Robert had been acquired by the crew of the first HMAS *Melbourne* during one of their voyages to foreign ports, and he joined the various pets they always carried on board.

There were at least two dogs, and a fine black cat that was featured on postcards of the ship. But Robert was a particular favourite. He was musical, for a photo of him in the Australian War Memorial collection shows him sitting on the ship's drum. He'd squawk along whenever the band played; and every time the sailors sat down to mend their clothes, Robert entertained them with a tune or two.

He felt they so enjoyed his company, he'd tear the buttons off their uniforms with his powerful beak. The men would have to spend twice as long sewing them back on, and listening to his song!

Yet life on a warship had its limitations for a bird born to fly free in tropical jungles. Perhaps Robert sensed the faint aromas of home carried on the sea breeze. Perhaps the cat was after him. Or perhaps he'd just had enough. For one day, Robert was swept up by the wind and blown into the water – where he sank, singing a colourful lament, beneath the waves.

Afterwards, the crew printed a memorial photo of the bird sitting on his drum, below which somebody wrote his epitaph:

'ROBERT'
Drowned at sea 13 March 1916

No more will Robert's 'note'
Disturb our 'make & mend',
No more we'll scratch his head,
Whilst he our buttons rend,
With life on a 'man-o'-war'
He'd got 'fed up' – 'twas said,
Like us – he wanted a change
So – the-poor-old-bird-is-dead!

ROFF

Prisoner of war dog

At the very time that Bullet, Trick and Nell were being trained as messenger dogs at Villers-Bretonneux, another dog found its way into the Australian lines. At lunch time, two soldiers paused for a bite to eat in a dugout a mere kilometre away. The town had only recently been liberated from the Germans, and these 13th Battalion men had been hard at it all morning, forcing enemy troops opposite to keep their heads down.

The diggers had just opened a tin of bully beef, when they heard movement close by.

'What's that, Bob?' asked Corporal Mick Roach, listening intently.

'Dunno, Corp. I'll have a squiz. Cover me.'

Gripping his rifle and adjusting his helmet, Private Bob Conway poked his head above ground level, finger tightening on the trigger.

Then he stopped. And stared. His trigger finger eased. It was no German enemy he saw at the end of his rifle sights, but two pricked ears and a pink tongue panting in a tan muzzle.

'What is it, Bob?'

'A flaming dog . . . some sort of wolfhound. One of Fritz's messenger dogs, I reckon. Got a container round his neck.'

'Could be important,' said the corporal. 'Might be a top-secret message from a German general. We should get hold of that dog.'

Bob whistled softly. 'Here, boy.'

The big black, brown and tan dog moved closer. But as soon as the soldier tried to grab him, he backed away, growling.

'He's got a good set of snappers. Won't let me near him.'

'P'rhaps he's hungry. Try him with a bit of lunch.'

Mick Roach passed up a slice of bully beef and Bob held it out. The dog sniffed it and turned away in disgust at the salty, greasy stuff. It took several goes before the dog was tempted to eat – but then he wolfed it down. Lunch had almost disappeared before he let Bob take hold of his collar.

Suddenly, a shot rang out. They'd caught the eye of a German sniper. The bullet went wide however, spurting the dust. But both Bob and the dog were so surprised they tumbled into the foxhole, while Mick returned fire.

Neither were hurt. As the dog licked the last of the bully from Bob's fingers, the man opened the message cylinder on the dog's collar, and withdrew a note.

'What does it say?' asked Corporal Roach.

'I can't read it.'

'Give us a look.' Mick dropped back into the hole and took the paper. But he couldn't understand the German words either.

'This really could be some vital enemy plan,' he said again. 'Might bring the whole war to an end. You'd better run it back to headquarters in town.'

'Why me?'

'Because you've got faster legs. And get us some more lunch while you're there.'

Bob Conway put the message in his tunic pocket, climbed out and began running back to Villers-Bretonneux. He'd only gone a short way when a shell burst nearby. Bob redoubled his speed. *Two near misses!* In the dugout, the dog was so frightened he also leapt out and ran for his life.

'Hey, you,' ordered Corporal Roach, 'come back!'

But it was too late. The dog had gone.

He reappeared a few hours later, as Captain Robert McKillop was returning from the trenches for a meeting with his commanding officer. He'd just reached the outskirts of town when he saw a large dog bounding down the road towards him.

Captain McKillop reached for his pistol, wondering if it would attack him. But hunger, not aggression, was driving the dog. As he reached Captain McKillop the dog stopped, whined, and started sniffing his pockets for more bully beef.

The officer held him by the neck chain. He noticed a metal tag with the German word *Diensthund* [working dog]. The captain unbuckled the collar with its message container. It was empty. But his CO, Lieutenant-Colonel Douglas Marks, would certainly be interested. Telling a soldier to take the dog to the quartermaster for something to eat, Captain McKillop went into his meeting.

The two men were there to discuss the coming night's tactics: probing and infiltrating enemy trenches, slowly disrupting the German lines. But they spent the first few minutes talking about the *Diensthund*. Mick's vitally important message had already been sent to the intelligence officers, and the translation returned.

It was only a complaint from a German platoon, saying the men were tired and had received no food for two days. Their commander told them not to whinge. *We will send you food tonight. Give Roff any further messages; he does not complain.*

'That's not quite right,' Captain McKillop said smiling. 'The dog, Roff, has more than complained. He's voted with his feet and come over to us. He's a deserter. And now he's a prisoner of war.'

'We also know the enemy are tired and hungry,' Colonel Marks observed. 'A good time to attack, I think. About tonight's plans . . .'

They got down to business. Though as their meeting ended, Colonel Marks asked what Roff the POW dog was doing now.

'I imagine he's eating his head off,' said Captain McKillop.

'I'll go and have a look at him,' replied the CO, and he strolled off to the quartermaster's stores. Captain McKillop returned to his trench, but not before he'd stowed Roff's collar and message container with his kit. They'd be good souvenirs to take home.

It was as Robert McKillop supposed. When Colonel Marks saw the dog, Roff was stretched out in the sun noisily eating a bacon bone, surrounded by a group of soldiers admiring his strong build and handsome features. But when Colonel Marks said the dog's name was Roff, the men wouldn't have it at all.

'Beg pardon, sir. That might be his *Hun* name, but he's one of us now – and as of now, we're calling him *Digger*.'

So Roff became Digger, and entered the 13th Battalion. Like every fighting unit, the men had great fondness for all their pets. We've already met their mascot, Billy Bantam. So it's not surprising that Roff quickly found a place in their affections.

Douglas Marks was especially fond of him. Every day the young colonel took the dog out for walks to visit troops and inspect bomb damage around the town. Within a few days he was writing for advice as to whether such a 'fine specimen' could be sent back to Australia, and introducing him to distinguished visitors.

Even the great Australian general, Sir John Monash, wrote about Roff to a little girl at home: 'He is a beautiful Alsatian wolf-hound and is very friendly. He has learned to understand English, and is very faithful to us, and we all pet him.' (If Roff's English had been better, he might have told them that he was in fact a Doberman pinscher, a dog first bred in the 1890s for its strength and intelligence.)

Yet Roff *was* a POW. He couldn't sit around eating his head off and being petted. And a *Diensthund* has to work. So the battalion made him a cart and harness to carry supplies around camp. He was good at it. As the men moved forward with the flow of battle, the dog went with them. And after Monash's victory at Hamel in July 1918, they took a photo of Roff with his cart and a collection of other captured German war trophies.

Yet such constant attention began to affect Roff's temperament. Like Bullet, Trick and Nell, he lost interest in work. He even ran away in early August, as the great forward assaults were being launched, and was cared for by Private George Starke in a rest camp until 13th Battalion men arrived to claim him. Before they took the dog away, however, George slipped off Roff's metal chain and *Diensthund* tag, to keep among his own war souvenirs.

As for Roff, his behaviour got worse. He'd allow himself to be stroked and offered a titbit – then without warning he'd snarl and bare his teeth, and try to bite the man feeding him. Even Captain McKillop acknowledged that Roff had turned savage. Another good working dog ruined. The question arose: what to do with him?

To shoot Roff was more than Douglas Marks could bear. There was enough death on the battlefields that summer of 1918, and Roff was a fine dog. So Marks revived his idea of sending Roff to Australia.

As a first step, the dog went to England and into quarantine near Southampton. But out of sight, out of mind. As the Great War hastened towards its end, poor Roff was forgotten. After the Armistice men wanted only to go home as soon as possible: and nobody remembered a German messenger dog waiting for them.

Months passed. Roff's quarantine period ended, but nobody came to claim him. The cost of looking after him was rising, and there were arguments as to who would pay for it. Men, once back in Australia, seemed to disown the dog. And hopes of sending him there disappeared when the Australian Government banned any dog being imported from Britain, for fear of rabies.

Roff's last chance was to move into the family home of Mr Andrew Fisher, the Australian High Commissioner in London. But even that was denied him. After almost a year in quarantine, loneliness and disease took their toll. Roff lost weight. An abscess developed. His lungs became infected and, in October 1919, he died.

People who'd been dragging their feet when he was still alive suddenly sprang into action. The kennel bills were paid. Roff's body was mounted, sent to Australia and eventually exhibited at the War Memorial. Captain McKillop donated Roff's collar and message container. George Starke gave his neck chain and tag. The handsome dog was much admired, just as Douglas Marks said he would be.

Tragically, though, he never saw Roff again. Less than a year after returning home, Marks died aged only twenty-four while gallantly trying to rescue a drowning man. Yet his high opinion of the *Diensthund* POW has been amply justified by the years.

Roff was most recently on public display at the A is for Animals exhibition in Canberra in 2009, and his body is kept in excellent condition by the Australian War Memorial conservation staff. For

Roff still has many visitors. People who breed Doberman pinschers come from all over the world to see this early example of the dogs they love. They leave well satisfied with Roff. Full of praise. And there's a continuing nobility for him in that.

SANDY

The one horse that came home

In the late summer of 1923, an ageing warhorse called Sandy stood silently waiting under the gum trees in a Melbourne paddock. His eyesight was failing, and he couldn't keep pace with the younger horses as he once had. But his memories were stronger than theirs. He'd been places they knew nothing of.

Old soldiers still came to see him at the army's horse remount depot. So did a vet he knew, to check his tired bones. To stand in the shade, and feed him a sugar lump. And to say to the young men, 'This Sandy, you know, was General Bridges' charger. The only one of all our Walers who went to the Great War to come home.'

Returned men would pat the white star on his forehead and stroke his nose, remembering, themselves. For it was something, to come back alive.

Sandy had been in it from the beginning. He was seven when war broke out. As a patriotic gesture, a firm in northern Victoria bought him to serve with the Australian forces. So Sandy went to the Army Remount Depot at Maribyrnong, where the bay gelding was chosen by the AIF commander Major-General William Bridges to be his own horse.

He wasn't the General's only steed. Military commanders were allowed to have several chargers. One may have been more handsome than Sandy. Another more spirited. But there was something about Sandy's even temper that appealed to Bridges. He became a favourite. When the 15 000 horses were loaded into the ships carrying the first contingent to war, Sandy was among them.

It was an awful journey. Some horses died in the heat below decks as they crossed the tropics and steamed up the Suez Canal. Things improved, however, when they went into camp near Cairo. Most horses were tethered outside, but Sandy was comfortably stabled at the Mena House Hotel, where the officers lived.

Sandy always had a daily gallop with the grooms and sometimes carried General Bridges as he rode out to inspect his troops exercising in the desert. When, in April 1915, Australian and New Zealand forces left for Gallipoli, Sandy went with them.

Very few horses landed, however. The steep ridges were no place for them. Good for mules and donkeys. But the light horsemen fought in the trenches on foot, as they'd been trained, and most of the horses were sent back to Egypt.

Bridges soon followed his favourite charger to Egypt. On 15 May, the General was hit by a sniper in Shrapnel Gully, near the place where Jack Simpson would soon be killed. Bridges was carried to the beach and onto a hospital ship. But he died three days later, and was buried in the military cemetery at Alexandria.

Perhaps Sandy was at the funeral. It was customary for a charger to follow his master's coffin. When General Bridges' body was returned to Australia – the only Australian soldier to die in the First World War to be brought home – some said that Sandy also walked in his funeral procession. But it was another horse. Sandy stayed in Egypt, looked after at the Australian Veterinary Hospital.

Comparatively speaking, Sandy had a good war. Like all the Walers, he had a long time to acclimatise in Egypt. When the men

came back from Gallipoli and the light horse units were being read-
ied for the desert campaign, Sandy didn't join them. He stayed with
the vets, perhaps even going on inspection when the camel brigades
were being formed. Sandy was spared any fighting.

Some of the old soldiers visiting Sandy at the remount depot had
belonged to the Imperial Camel Corps, and they'd swap yarns under
the trees about their bad-tempered, evil-smelling *hooshtas*, as the
camels were called. They gave them names like Mange Dressing,
and Horace, and Barrak. 'The vilest, stupidest, craziest beasts,' said
the soldier-poet, Major Oliver Hogue, who wrote under the name of
'Trooper Bluegum'.

But oh, their courage. When the cameleers charged the Turks at
Gaza, three-quarters of them were hit. And their endurance. Camels
could carry a week's supply of food and water – whereas a light
horseman and his mount died after three days without a drink. Only
when the corps was disbanded, in 1918, did the men begin to appreciate the merits of a camel.

One of the vets who cared for Sandy was Captain Leslie
Whitfeld. He grew very fond of the horse, and when he went to
France in 1916 he took Sandy with him to the hospital at Calais.

Those northern winters were very different to Egypt. But at least
Sandy didn't suffer all the terrors of war in Flanders, as other horses
and mules did – hauling guns and supplies through the mud, often
sinking to their deaths, or being blown apart by shellfire and bombs.

General Bridges' favourite remained at Calais. And he was there
when, in 1917, the Australian Minister for Defence, Senator George
Pearce, had the idea of bringing Sandy home – as his master's body
had also returned.

Arrangements were made. Leslie Whitfeld certified that Sandy
was in good health and free of disease. The horse was labelled,

shipped to England with his groom, Private Archie Jordan, and spent some months in quarantine before he and Archie embarked for Australia. It was a more pleasant trip than the voyage out had been. Going home! They reached Melbourne two days after the signing of the Armistice, and went back to the remount depot.

It had been intended the horse would go to Canberra, and see out his days at Royal Military College, Duntroon. General Bridges had been the first commandant and his remains were buried there. But Sandy stayed at Maribyrnong, visited by the vets and returned horsemen who'd wait with him under the trees to remember the old days and the rides they'd known.

For just as the war ended, the brigades learnt their Walers wouldn't be coming home with them. The dismay was universal. Oliver Hogue – 'Trooper Bluegum' – wrote a poem, 'The Horses Stay Behind', that was published in the Desert Mounted Corps' own book, *Australia in Palestine*.

Perhaps this, and similar writings, were the source of a widespread belief in Australia that the 9000 horses left in the Middle East after the war were all shot. Many were. But it seems the majority, like the horses after their last race at Tripoli, were transferred to the Indian and other Imperial cavalry units. Their fate was not as awful as sometimes supposed.

Still, it's true that of the 135 000 horses who left Australia during the First World War, Sandy was the only one to come home. And as such, he assumed a significance that his lack of experience on a battlefield might otherwise have denied him.

The old bay gelding propped in the shade under the gum trees at the remount depot, that late summer of 1923, was the one who came to symbolise them. He remembered the past, without knowing that his future had already been determined.

Sandy was only sixteen – no great age for a horse today, but it was different then. Walers in Palestine aged over twelve and those in poor health were shot after the war. In this respect, Sandy shared their fate. He was becoming blind and debilitated, and as an act of kindness the vets eventually decided to put him down. This was done in May 1923, though even then Sandy didn't disappear from public view.

His head was mounted, dressed with a bridle given by Lady Bridges, and went on display. It's still preserved at the Australian War Memorial. Sandy's hooves were also kept: polished and mounted on silver, to serve as Defence Force paperweights. It seems a strange thing to do: even stranger, when apparently *five* of Sandy's hooves once turned up.

But his most lasting tribute is to be found elsewhere. When Web Gilbert came to design a memorial in Egypt to the Australian and New Zealand Light Horsemen, it is said he used Sandy's head as one of his models. Although the bronze sculpture was badly damaged in 1956 during the Suez conflict, the metal head is now at the Australian War Memorial, where it is the focal point of a powerful and evocative memorial designed by Steven Holland for the RSPCA to commemorate all the animals that have served with Australian forces in war. Set in the War Memorial's sculpture garden in Canberra, the head sits on a granite column resting on a base that reflects the shape of an eye . . . and of a teardrop.

COCKY

Goes to church

Cocky used to be a well-behaved bird. Polite. Genteel. And very nicely spoken. Until a mob of soldiers, convalescing from the First World War, taught him their wicked ways. Cocky fell from grace in their company, and became a very bad bird indeed.

He'd been born in early 1878, in a hollow tree on a fine property at Bonnie Doon, in central Victoria. As only a fledgling, the young sulphur-crested cockatoo had been found and taken in as a pet by the owner's wife, Mrs Anne Bon.

She taught him all his good manners.

He'd sit on his perch on the homestead verandah and say 'Hello' and 'Goodbye' to visitors, as a courteous cockatoo should. He'd say 'Good morning' and 'How do you do?' to Mr and Mrs Bon. 'Who's a clever boy then?' to the children and station hands. And if there was nobody else to talk to, he'd say 'Hello Cocky' all day long to himself – though we don't know what he said in reply.

Whatever it was, it would have been quite proper and correct. Mrs Bon was that sort of woman. Cocky never swore. He was never vulgar. He never danced up and down or made fun of the visitors. He never cheeked the clergymen who came to tea. He never tried to escape. He never ripped up the furniture or shredded the household books.

No. Cocky was a good bird. A model of his kind. Something of a prig, perhaps: and even, one suspects, a little bit of a bore.

Then, in 1914, came the Great War. Like Australians everywhere, the patriotic people of Bonnie Doon rallied round to do their bit for king and country. Men marched off to fight at Gallipoli and on the battlefields of France. They went with high enthusiasm at first, though that was to change as they realised the dreadful human cost of the conflict. Two out of every three Australian soldiers who went to that war were killed or injured. Scarcely a family was untouched by it. And those men who'd been so badly wounded by bullets, shells or poison gas that they could fight no more came home to recover as best they could in repatriation hospitals.

It was then that Mrs Bon decided to *her* bit for king and country. In 1917, she lent Cocky to Wirth's Park No 1 Rest Home, in Melbourne, to help entertain and cheer up the soldiers convalescing there. The home – just across Princes Bridge, where Wirth's Circus used to be and the Arts Centre now flourishes – was run by Red Cross nurses, as a place for returned servicemen to regain their strength and get ready for civilian life once more.

So Cocky took up his daily perch in the front foyer of the No 1 Rest Home, outside a little hall that was used for evening concerts and Sunday church services.

No doubt, as a well-bred and dignified cockatoo of thirty-nine years, it was hoped he'd give a certain 'tone' to the rough-spoken soldiers. Alas, it wasn't to be. As so often happens, far from raising men to his level of refinement, the soldiers reduced *him* to theirs! In a few short weeks, Cocky's language sank to the lowest depths.

As they passed through the foyer on their daily rounds, men would repeat every swearword they'd learnt in the trenches – including quite a few German ones. Cocky was a quick learner. All the good manners Mrs Bon had taught him went straight out the window.

He'd sit on his crossbar in the rest home, and to everyone who came in the front door Cocky would shriek, '*!@*$#!'

As people passed his perch he'd scream, '@^!*#%!'

If somebody were performing a song at a concert in the hall ('O For the Wings of a Dove' for example), Cocky would accompany them by singing out in a raucous voice, '^%@*#!'

And on Sunday mornings, the minister conducting the church service could barely make himself heard above the cockatoo screeching '*!@&‡!' during the sermon.

Cocky's language was shocking! Even years later, the nurses couldn't bring themselves to repeat it. Though for the men, of course, it was vastly entertaining. Cocky certainly cheered them up.

He even learnt a few tricks from army life.

Whenever a soldier went out the front door, Cocky would shout at him, 'Show us your pass!' Just like a military policeman.

Men who were used to him took no notice, and kept on going. But newcomers would stop and fumble in their pockets, looking for a non-existent scrap of cardboard giving them leave to go out.

Cocky thought this was great fun. His sulphur-yellow crest would spring erect, and he'd dance up and down on his perch, squawking with laughter at the man he'd just caught out.

And when the soldier, feeling rather foolish, came over to remonstrate, the bird would fix him with a steely eye and say, 'Go on, you're a German!'

And shriek again.

'@^!*#%!'

To be sure, the clergymen who came to the No 1 Rest Home did try to reform Cocky from time to time, and lead him back to the straight and narrow path of good behaviour from which he'd sadly strayed. But Cocky wasn't interested in religious salvation. Not yet. He was having too much fun.

So his fall from grace continued. If anything, his language got worse. And on Sunday mornings, it wasn't just the minister's sermon he interrupted with his swearing, but the whole church service.

During the hymns and prayers, and all through readings from the Bible, Cocky could be heard screeching his own unauthorised version just outside the door. While inside, the congregation did its best not to laugh – all except for the clergyman, who became ever more red in the face with anger, shame and embarrassment.

On more than one occasion the minister asked if Cocky could kindly be moved away from the foyer, at least on Sunday mornings. But the men wouldn't hear of it. Nor would Cocky, who said what he thought in no uncertain terms.

'*!@*$#!'

And '*!@*$#!' again.

Then the cockatoo did something really dreadful.

One Saturday evening, after the usual concert in the hall, instead of Cocky going to sleep on his perch outside the door, somebody let him off his leg chain and shut him *inside* the hall. Whether it was an accident, or whether it was deliberate, who can really say? Perhaps somebody thought that if Cocky spent a night meditating by himself in the House of the Lord, he might repent of his blasphemies and attend church on Sunday morning a reformed bird.

If that was the idea, it didn't work. Cocky trashed the place.

Alone in the darkness, he got down to business. He hopped onto the wooden rack at the back of the hall where the hymn books were kept, and threw them to the floor. One by one, he started tearing them up with his fearsome beak.

Rip! Through the pages of 'All Things Bright and Beautiful'.

Rip! 'All Creatures of our God and King' lay in shreds.

Rip! 'Each little bird that sings' fell scattered on the carpet.

The hymn books disposed of, Cocky turned his attention to the prayer books and Bibles.

Rip!

'And God said, Let the waters bring forth abundantly the moving creatures that hath life, and fowl that may fly above the earth in the open firmament of heaven.'

Rip!

'. . . and God saw that it was good.'

Rip!

If God had looked down and eyed Cocky's handiwork when the bird had finished that night, He would not have thought it was good. He'd have been mighty displeased. Cocky had created an unholy mess.

When people arrived for the church service next morning, shredded hymnals and testaments were strewn from one side of the hall to the other. Little drifts of torn paper fluttered like early snow. And whatever God and the clergyman may have thought, the cockatoo himself sat on the pulpit rail, his yellow crest snapping open and shut like a fan, shrieking with delight.

'Hello Cocky! Who's a clever boy then?'

'@^!*#%!'

You might have thought such a disgraceful episode was enough to have Cocky banished from the No 1 Rest Home forever, but it wasn't. The soldiers had taken the bird to their hearts. He was one of them! And they gathered around his perch in the foyer, feeding him dainties, teaching him new words and resisting any attempt to send him away.

The end, when it came, was quite different. One of the men had become so attached to the bird that he'd take him for walks through the streets of Melbourne – Cocky perched on his shoulder, or even his head, the better to view the world. But the walks went so far, it was feared that Cocky might fly off and not be found again.

So, with some reluctance, Matron Anderson wrote to Mrs Bon, and Cocky went home to Bonnie Doon. Where, with the war over and far from the wicked influence of returned soldiers, the bird (more or less) resumed his old ways of polite gentility.

Eventually Cocky went to live with members of Mrs Bon's family in Melbourne, where he's said to have 'terrorised' the youngest child. Still, when the director of the War Museum, John Treloar, visited Mrs Bon at the elegant Windsor Hotel, he was so impressed with her account of Cocky's sterling war service at the rest home, he suggested the War Museum should care for the old bird for the remainder of its life. And after he died they'd have the cockatoo's skin preserved and mounted for public exhibition – just like Driver and Roff.

'I can assure you we would take the greatest care of it and carry out any wishes concerning it you may express,' Treloar wrote to Mrs Bon.

But the good woman would have none of it. She offered the Museum certain other war relics, but as to her friend, she replied, 'I cannot think of parting with Cockie, but will give you a very nice photo of him.'

Still, when at last the bird went to his maker in July of 1925, at the relatively early age (for a cockatoo) of forty-seven years and six months, a journey to the taxidermist is precisely what did happen to him. Mrs Bon even sent a car to convey his remains to the Museum of Victoria in a box lined with blue padded silk.

And today, if you visit the Australian War Memorial whenever Cocky is on display, you can see him perched on his stand, a chipped blue enamel water can by his side, sulphur crest erect, feathers preened, a wicked glint in his eye and beak half open as if about to speak . . . But alas, there's never a '@^!*#%!' anywhere to be heard.

As for Mrs Bon, she lived for another eleven years, and her compassion for the welfare of those soldiers wounded in the Great War never ceased. Every year from 1919 until her death in 1936, aged ninety-eight, she gave each Victorian soldier who'd been blinded in the conflict a gift of twenty pounds. Equivalent to a couple of months' wages at the time.

Even Cocky would have praised the Lord for that.

World War II

1939–1945

The Second World War began when Nazi Germany invaded Poland on 1 September 1939. The major Allied powers were Britain and its Empire, France, later the United States and the Soviet Union, opposing the Axis of Germany, Italy and Japan.

Australian forces first fought in the Middle East, North Africa, Greece and Crete. Most returned home as Japan threatened to invade Australia. Darwin and some other northern towns were bombed. Nearly 15 000 Australians were among the 125 000 Allied troops captured when Singapore fell.

Thereafter, Australians fought mainly under overall US command in New Guinea, Indonesia (as it now is), South-East Asia and the Pacific islands. In Europe, the war ended with Germany's surrender in May 1945, but fighting in the Pacific continued until August 1945, when atomic bombs were dropped on the Japanese cities of Hiroshima and Nagasaki.

HORRIE

The twist in the Wog Dog's tale

Of all Australia's animal heroes during the Second World War, none was more famous than a small white Egyptian terrier called Horrie. 'Horrie the Wog Dog' his soldiers dubbed him: a derisive term to start with, though it came to be a name spoken with much pride and affection. And also with quiet laughter, by those in the know.

Most people thought Horrie was destroyed by quarantine officials three years after he came to Australia. That was the story. But it seems there was another end to it – a secret twist in his tale – that was revealed in the first edition of *Animal Heroes*. Since then a little more has been added to the telling, and Horrie is now a true public figure.

Horrie was a lost and hungry pup when he was found in early 1941, chasing lizards in the desert out from Alexandria. It was Private Jim Moody, a motorbike dispatch rider with the 2/1 Machine Gun Battalion, who saw him. Picked him up, tucked him into his jacket, and rode back to his mates with the signal platoon.

There were rules in camp about 'no pets'. But they didn't mean much to these signallers. As a group, they were known as the 'Rebels', for one of them was always in trouble with the officers.

Anyway, rules didn't apply to Horrie. He quickly endeared himself to the whole battalion, and from the photographs we can see why. His bright eyes and grinning face speak of an engaging personality.

Here was a dog who knew everything. Who knew everyone. Horrie was soon strutting at the head of every route march, and accompanying the CO on parade. He once cocked an excited leg against a corporal's shiny boots, to everybody's delight (except, presumably, the corporal in question).

He was himself promoted to corporal for fun, and given a made-up service number, EX1 ('Number One Egyptian soldier'). He took his turn at sentry duty, barking at any thieving stranger. And when the men went to Greece with the forces trying to halt the Nazi invasion, Horrie went with them, hidden in Jim Moody's kitbag.

Like all dogs, Horrie had acute hearing, and he became a brilliant early air-raid warning. During the bitter retreat from northern Greece, he heard the Luftwaffe long before human ears. He'd tilt his head, staring at the sky. Then he'd start to bark and growl. And as soldiers cried 'Enemy planes!' Horrie led the charge for cover.

Hundreds of people owed their lives to him. As Jim said, the 'Wog Dog' became a war dog, and grew very dear to them.

There was more war to face. They were bombed leaving Greece, and Horrie was dropped from his sinking ship onto a waiting destroyer. He was almost killed when two lifeboats crashed together.

On Crete, he became a messenger dog. Dispatches from outlying patrols were tied in a handkerchief around Horrie's collar, and he'd race down the rocky hillsides to Jim waiting in the olive groves below. During the evacuation, Horrie was wounded by shrapnel, which the men removed with a pocket knife.

Things improved when they got to Palestine. There was time for sightseeing in Tel Aviv. And Horrie met the love of his life: another white Egyptian terrier called Imshie, the mascot of 2/1 Anti-Tank Regiment. But they were separated too soon, when the machine-gunners were sent to Syria.

The mountains were freezing in the winter snow. The men made Horrie a jacket from a khaki greatcoat (the buttons snipped from Corporal Featherstone's own coat), but it wasn't warm enough. Horrie took to his bed. Daily bulletins were issued. 'The condition of Horrie continues grave. He accepted only a little warm porridge during the morning . . .'

Men spoke in whispers, afraid their mascot was dying, when Imshie unexpectedly arrived with her regiment. She was taken to see the stricken Horrie, and licked her hero on the nose. His eyes opened. He leapt from his bed. And pranced around Imshie with his stub of tail wagging. The little malingerer!

Then, in February 1942, came news of the fall of Singapore and the first Japanese air raids on Darwin. Diggers serving in the Middle East knew they'd soon be heading back to defend their homeland. The problem was, what to do with their pets and mascots? Orders were very strict. Animals were to be left behind: destroyed under Australian quarantine rules, if new owners couldn't be found.

Now, Jim Moody and his mates knew the importance of keeping rabies and other diseases out of the country. So they took Horrie to a vet in Tel Aviv, who kept the dog for a week and gave him a clean bill of health. That done, the Rebels developed a daring plan to smuggle Horrie home, hidden in Jim's backpack.

Moody was a fine dog trainer, and Horrie a quick learner. It didn't take long to teach him to sit very still and quiet for hours inside the specially fitted pack as the soldiers journeyed to Suez. Indeed, the pack was often carried in the heat by Moody's best mate, Don Gill, with Jim marching behind, wetting his fingers from a water bottle and letting Horrie lick them through a breathing hole.

The dog was smuggled aboard ship in the pack, and hidden in the Rebels' cabin. Somebody stayed below with him at all times. The cabin door was kept locked, and opened only after a coded knock. If any officer came on inspection, Horrie jumped into the pack and was covered by Jim's clothes.

Such precautions were necessary. On board another ship, Imshie had been found and killed. Only a day out of Fremantle, a mascot cat called Hobo, who'd been born at Dunkirk, was ordered to be handed over to the captain of Horrie's ship. The men held out for twelve hours before giving way – and the captain flung Hobo into the sea to drown.

Thus, the veils of secrecy were drawn ever tighter around Horrie, and he was never discovered. When they arrived at Adelaide, the dog was smuggled ashore in the backpack and eventually travelled to Melbourne to live with Jim's father, Henry Moody.

For the next three years, as Jim served in Australia and New Guinea, Horrie lived a quiet suburban life. But when Jim was discharged in February 1945, things began to go wrong. Horrie suddenly found himself in great danger from the authorities.

The author Ion Idriess was writing a book about Horrie's adventures, based on Jim's diary. An article appeared in the newspaper. To further the publicity, Jim offered his dog to the Kennel Club to raise funds for the Red Cross at its Easter Show.

No doubt Jim thought it would be safe after three years. But it wasn't. The article was spotted by the Commonwealth Director of Veterinary Hygiene, Mr R N Wardle, who ordered his officers to make investigations. It was a breach of the Quarantine Act to smuggle a dog into the country, whether it was healthy or not.

By that time, Jim and Horrie had moved to Sydney, where they were staying at Don Gill's family home, and it took the officers a couple of weeks to track them down. Jim went to see the officials – without Horrie. He said the dog had been sent back to Melbourne, but he wasn't believed. The officers thought Horrie was being hidden, and in this they were undoubtedly correct.

In any event, Jim agreed to return with his dog a week later. Which he did. But the animal was immediately seized and taken to the quarantine station. The officers were upset at what they'd been told to do, but orders were orders. 'I'm sorry mate, it's my job.'

Jim, too, was close to tears. In a kindly gesture, remembered from the visit to the vet in Tel Aviv, Moody left one of his socks with the dog, so it would know his master's smell and not fret. Jim went to visit him that Sunday, and found him lying happily with the sock.

Moody had already written to Mr Wardle, pleading for Horrie's life. It cut no ice with the officials, who saw it as proof the dog had been smuggled back as 'an object of financial return'. And although Jim claimed the quarantine officers told him Horrie wouldn't be destroyed if he was found to be healthy, this was denied.

At 4 p.m. on Monday 12 March, the dog was given a lethal dose of hydrogen cyanide (HCN). A message was left for Jim Moody five minutes before.

Public outrage at news of Horrie's death was swift and savage.

Legal Murder of War Dog
EXECUTED BY RED TAPE

shrieked the headline in the *Truth* newspaper. And it published a photo of Jim and a friend taking Horrie to the quarantine office 'little dreaming that their canine hero was going to his doom'.

Letters poured into government departments and the newspapers. Jim's old platoon sergeant, Roy Brooker, was staying with him, and wrote to say he hoped that those who ordered Horrie's destruction would spend the rest of their days as sleeplessly as he had. This was mild. Other letters accused the officials of being cowardly, arrogant and power-drunk.

A public meeting was held, where Jim said the dog's death was 'a malicious and deliberate act of cruelty'. The prime minister was petitioned. Questions were asked in parliament. Politicians and their staff found themselves abused in the street.

Jim's father, Henry, gave interviews about how much Horrie would be missed, and wrote a consoling letter to his son when he got news from Jim confirming Horrie had been killed.

On Anzac Day that year, a wreath was laid on the Cenotaph, 'In memory of our pal, Horrie the Wog Dog.' People sent condolence poems to Jim Moody, trying to express their feelings in verse:

His life is done, they blew him up,
And never more we'll see our pup.

The RSPCA collected funds for a memorial to Horrie. It wasn't built, but the Society issued statements calling for all animals to be quarantined however they entered the country, and released to their owners if free of disease. Nothing doing. There was a total prohibition on importing any animal from the Middle East and the authorities felt it was 'beyond all reason' that mascots should be an exception. If Horrie had been allowed to go free, they argued, other soldiers would have an incentive to do the same as Jim Moody.

In other words, Horrie was made an example. Mr Wardle admitted as much in letters to an army colleague. 'As you will fully appreciate, the dog was, of course, by this time of no risk of being infected with rabies, but action was taken in order to uphold the control under the Quarantine Act.'

So Horrie was to be destroyed as a bureaucratic gesture. And when Ion Idriess published his book *Horrie the Wog Dog*, the last page carried a short tribute.

EPITAPH

Well, Horrie, little fellow, your reward
was death. You who deserved a nation's
plaudits, sleep in peace. Among Australia's
war heroes, we shall remember you.
Under Quarantine Regulations, Horrie
was destroyed on 12 March 1945

Yet that wasn't the end of the tale. It now appears there was a secret, shared by only a few trusted people who said nothing to those outside the circle for nearly sixty years. Jim Moody and his Rebel mates planned to have the last laugh on bureaucratic authority.

HORRIE AND THE FIVE BOB DOG

Almost a year after his dog's death, Jim Moody went south to Wollongong to photograph the city and nearby coast. He struck up a friendship with a young cadet journalist, Norma James, and naturally they talked about Horrie. Norma observed what a shame it was the dog had died because of the government.

'I'll tell you something one day,' Jim said. Then, taking her reporter's notebook and pencil, he wrote a few sentences.

Horrie is not dead. He never died.
But if you tell anyone I'll deny it.

He tore out the page and gave it to Norma. Over the next few weeks, Jim revealed an extraordinary story of how he and his friends had devised a plan to save their dog.

'You don't think an Australian soldier would leave a mate like that, do you?' he asked.

Indeed not. For when the quarantine inspectors started asking their questions about Horrie, Jim was well placed to do something about it. He was staying at Don Gill's house. Sergeant Brooker had come to visit, and a photo of them had appeared in the newspapers. There was quite a network of family and friends able to outwit authority – and these Rebels were used to doing that.

By Jim's account the first thing they did was to whisk Horrie away from Don Gill's home in St Peters. The dog was smuggled from one safe house to another while arrangements were made to find him a more permanent home. Eventually he left New South Wales altogether.

As the storms of controversy broke around unhappy government officials for their 'legal murder' of Horrie the Wog Dog, the real Horrie was apparently settling into a farm in the Corryong district of northern Victoria where one of Jim's friends lived.

Moody seems to have decided very early on to make a switch – to substitute another dog for Horrie, and to hand that one over to the authorities instead. It was an obvious thing to do. But it took him some time to find the right dog in a Sydney pound: a small white terrier that not only *looked* something like Horrie, but also one who, as Jim told Norma, had no hope of being saved.

He was a man who loved dogs. He was rarely without one all his life. Even during the Horrie crisis, Jim had a white West Highland terrier he named after Imshie of fond memory. When he handed over the Horrie substitute to the quarantine inspectors, the emotion was not all pretence. Moody felt deeply enough about the dog whose life was to be sacrificed that the war mascot might live. He even went to see him that last Sunday, to say goodbye.

So he visited many pounds looking for the right animal. It helps explain why Jim sought – and was given – an extra week from the quarantine officers to bring in his dog. Perhaps they were even giving Jim a chance to pull such a stunt. Who knows? They'd have seen the newspapers and read the official correspondence. They'd have known, after three years, that there was no risk Horrie had rabies. They didn't like what they'd been told to do. If the officers were *that* serious, why didn't they go hunting for Horrie, rather than wait for Jim to bring the dog to them?

However that may be, at last Jim found an appropriate substitute and bought it for five shillings. Five bob. Fifty cents. The small white dog was taken home, fed, and seen by a vet who declared, like Horrie, that he was free of disease. On Friday 9 March Jim took the dog to the officials, who seized it. And the rest, as they say, is history.

Jim Moody and his Rebel mates maintained the deception to the end. Sergeant Brooker's letter about his sleepless days . . . Jim's angry words at public meetings . . . the staged photo taking Horrie to his 'doom'. . . the epitaph about 'a nation's plaudits' in the Idriess book . . . acres of newspaper space devoted to the fate of Horrie the Wog Dog executed by red tape . . .

All these things, to those in the know, were a charade. A blind. Necessary to protect the real Horrie. But a fiction, nonetheless.

As Jim told the story, it was another dog to whom he said goodbye that Sunday. Another dog who should have been honoured by the wreaths laid at the Cenotaph on Anzac Day that year, and for many years to come. A five bob dog who deserved a nation's plaudits. Who, all unknowing, became one of his country's animal heroes and the recipient of a remarkable outpouring of public grief in wartime.

HORRIE IN RETIREMENT

As for Horrie, never did one small dog have such a long tale.

Like all good stories there's an element of mystery: but it's said Horrie lived out his remaining days in the countryside around Corryong in relative obscurity, though Jim Moody came to visit and Horrie may even have sired several litters of puppies, perhaps with Jim's new dog, the westie Imshie II. 'Horrie lookalikes,' Jim often called them. 'The authorities couldn't tell which one was him, even if they came searching.' But still, it was all very hush-hush, for official nerves on the subject of Jim Moody and Horrie the Wog Dog were still extremely raw.

Yet in the decade that followed the first publication of this book, Horrie's story and his public reputation have continued to grow wonderfully. New leads have come to light as to where he might have gone, the family who looked after him, and the manner of his death. Roland Perry wrote a new book about him. And a bronze statue of Horrie has been erected by the local Tourist Association in the RSL memorial park at Corryong. Horrie the Wog Dog is now well and truly out of hiding.

It began in 2013 with an article by Andrew Rule in the Melbourne *Herald Sun* based on an interview with me. The piece was read by Ted Bennetts of Wodonga, and it began to ring a few bells in his memory. His family had run a dairy herd near Selsey Station at Cudgewa, not far from Corryong, and there was something about a small white dog in the years just after the war. The question as to whether it might have been Horrie kept nagging away . . .

'I rang Mum,' Ted says, 'and asked her if she didn't have a little white terrier dog at the time? I remembered the story because Dad normally wouldn't keep dogs . . . said they stressed his cows. Well, Mum said that yes, she did have a little terrier then. "Where did you get it?" I asked. "I don't know," she said, "it turned up and your father said I could keep it and look after it." That was strange in itself. Dad didn't want dogs around the cattle, although I know he would always look after a mate. And Mum said the dog was unusual for a white terrier. There wasn't another like it in the district. In fact Mum said she had a photo of the little dog and would get it out for me, but I've hunted high and low and I can't find it . . .'

Ted's mother has since passed on. The family album was certainly with her things, but several photos are missing and it seems it will now be almost impossible to compare her picture of the little white dog with the many photographs of Horrie. Ted wonders whether his mum took the photo of her white terrier out of her album, put it in one of her puzzle books to keep it flat and, being elderly, forgot about it. So that it was eventually thrown out after she died. It's the sort of casual, everyday occurrence that can make historical research so frustrating – and so very rewarding if, perchance, the lost scrap turns up again. As the echo of a recollection did for Ted Bennetts. Perhaps the missing photo will surface as well.

Now, Ted's the first to acknowledge he can't say one way or the other whether his mother's terrier was in fact Horrie. But there are several pieces of circumstantial evidence that suggest the Bennetts family might well have homed the dog, who was known to them as Benji. Jim was in fairly regular contact with them.

Ted's father, Edward Bennetts, left Australia with the 2/1 Machine Gun Battalion (Moody's unit), and later served as a driver with the 2/1 Anti-Tank Regiment in the Middle East in 1940–41. This was the same unit whose mascot was Imshie, Horrie's devoted girlfriend.

Eddie Bennetts and Jim Moody certainly knew each other and kept in touch. Eddie was discharged at the beginning of 1944 and returned to his parents' dairy farm. But he would go to Melbourne each Anzac Day to march with the 2/1 Machine-Gunners, meet up with Jim Moody and many of the other Rebels – and often spent the night with them at a hotel or boarding house.

'My Uncle Wally sometimes went with Dad,' Ted recalls, 'and one time he remembers Jim going in and out of the place during the night. In the morning they saw that Moody had a female dog in the back of his car, who'd just given birth to pups. He'd apparently been attending to her.'

There are several studio photos taken of Imshie with three small white pups, each with a tartan bow around its neck in homage to the West Highland terriers. According to Jim's daughter Leonie, Imshie had at least two litters, each of three or four pups – possibly with Horrie, though whether these are Horrie's offspring cannot now be verified. And Betty Featherstone, whose late husband Brian was the Rebels' corporal, remembers Jim saying he used to visit Horrie in the Corryong district – but not too often, in case it aroused suspicion.

The uncertainties surrounding Horrie's later life were very much part of the need to keep his whereabouts secret – not just for his sake, but also for those who hid him. They'd still be liable to prosecution by an angry officialdom. Ted Bennetts says that while his father mentioned Horrie and knew that Moody had smuggled him back to Australia, he never said anything about having kept the dog at Cudgewa. But then, of course, he wouldn't.

The circumstances of Horrie's death are just as mysterious. If the Bennetts' dog was Horrie, it appears he was killed some time before the family left Cudgewa around 1948 to take up a soldier-settlement block at Dederang in the Kiewa Valley. Ted's older sister has no memory of the dog having been there, and Ted himself wasn't born until 1954. Ted asked his mother what had happened: she'd been visiting her parents at Log Bridge, down the road from Cudgewa, when 'some bastard' in a car came down the hill and ran the dog over.

Another version of how Horrie died is given by Garry Power, who knew Jim Moody at Portland, in southern Victoria, during the 1970s. And Garry says Jim told him that Horrie died of snake-bite – where and when he did not say.

In either case, it was scarcely the most valiant end for a little dog who had faced, undaunted, the onslaught of German Messer-schmitts in Greece, a bombed troopship, the invasion of Crete, the risks of a smuggling pack and all the terrors with which Australian bureaucracy could threaten him.

RIP indeed. But that still wasn't the end of Horrie's tale.

HORRIE CAST IN BRONZE

Intrigued by what his mother had to say about the little terrier Benji she'd looked after on the dairy farm, Ted Bennetts passed her story to the journalist Andrew Rule. In turn it found its way to Roland Perry, who incorporated it at the end of his 2013 book *Horrie the War Dog*. In fact Perry seemed quite certain that Horrie *had* ended his days on the Bennetts' farm.

In any event, the story spread until it reached Sandra and Richard Hubbard, who live in Corryong and are active members of the local Tourist Association. They looked Horrie up on the internet and read the books.

'Our idea is to get as many things locally as we can to encourage tourists into the town,' Sandra says. 'We've done a lot with Jack Riley and *The Man from Snowy River*, but until someone spoke to us we'd no knowledge of Horrie and his connection with the district. The Tourist Association had some funds, and we decided it was worth getting a statue of the dog commissioned.'

They got in touch with a firm that had business with a foundry in Thailand that can model a statue from a photograph and cast it in bronze. So they selected a snapshot of Horrie in the Middle East, standing on a fuel can. They found a similar can at the local museum, took photos of its dimensions, and sent everything off. A Buddhist monk apparently made the clay model, using the proportions of the fuel can to sculpt the dog. It was then cast at the foundry, and the finished statue returned to the Australian firm at Ballina in northern New South Wales. It was put on display and a number of people came to see it, including a man aged ninety-two who had known the young Horrie in Egypt. At last it was brought back to Corryong, mounted on its plinth in the memorial park near the RSL, and unveiled on Anzac Day 2016.

'The response has been fantastic,' Richard Hubbard says, 'especially from the older generation who remember the war and Horrie's story. They were absolutely thrilled. It's been very well received. It cost all up about $7500 and we think it's worth every cent.'

There was something of a contretemps over the plaque. It was originally proposed that it would read 'Horrie the war dog', but the RSL and the town elders insisted on 'Horrie the Wog Dog'. That's what he was called in life – no doubt in a derisory way to begin with, though for everyone who knows his story (other than government officials perhaps), it turned into utter admiration.

So there Horrie stands today, permanently and prominently in the main street of the town and district where he's thought to have finished up. For years his presence was kept a deep secret, known only to the chosen few, and even now the real story remains inconclusive. But bronze Horrie is up there on his fuel can at Corryong in full public view, wearing his jacket and corporal's stripes with the same military pride he always did. A grin on his face, eyes wide awake and ears at full alert as sunlight and shadow play on his body. Sometimes you think he might even be about to move . . . until you remember how still Horrie was taught to remain, hidden in the smuggling pack.

'Australia's Most Famous Dog', Horrie has been called. Perhaps. He is certainly the one with the longest tale. And even now another question remains to tease: if Imshie's pups were indeed fathered by Horrie, whatever became of them?

PIGEON VC

Feathered heroes

A retired army captain stood looking at a display of carrier pigeons at the Australian War Memorial. Two glass eyes stared back at him from one particular blue-grey bird. Its breast feathers were tinged with pink and green highlights, and a metal canister was attached to one leg.

Nearby was a scrap of message paper. And as he read it, the captain felt himself back on Bougainville Island. 1945. His patrol was pinned down by Japanese troops. Wounded men lay bleeding. The radio was dead. No runner could get through to headquarters. His only hope of rescue lay with a pair of homing pigeons the patrols always carried with them, tucked in their cardboard boxes.

Quickly, the captain wrote a message calling for help. 'Situation grim.' He gave his position, date and time, and rolled it up. As one of his men gently held a bird, he slipped the paper into its container, and said a silent prayer.

Please God, don't let it be shot by a Japanese sniper.

'Release it.'

The bird fluttered its wings. Hovered a moment. Then, with gathering strength, it flew up through the canopy of trees to the clear sky beyond.

Such powerful recollections gripped the man that day. He was living it all over again. Then, with a smile, he turned to his companion and said, 'I owe my life to these feathered messengers.'

He was speaking no less than the truth.

During the war thousands of birds worked with the pigeon service, attached to the signal corps. When it was feared Australia would be invaded, breeders donated a whole network of pigeons around the country to carry messages in case radio contact failed.

As the tide of war moved to New Guinea and the nearby islands, it was realised the birds also had a role there. They could fly over mountains and jungles, weather tropical storms, and go places where other military communications were impossible.

Racing pigeons fly across known territory, to fixed lofts. But it's different in war. Armies are constantly moving. So the pigeon service started breeding and training young birds to 'home' to *mobile* lofts that followed the troops.

At four months old, the pigeons were ready for work – and they performed some extraordinary feats. All they had to guide them was an innate sense of direction and a need to find the shape of their mobile loft roof, hidden somewhere in the jungle, with a handful of feed waiting for them at the end of the flight.

The number of lives saved by the messages they carried is incalculable – as is the number of pigeons lost in the line of duty. But not once, it is said, did a message fail to get through.

After the war, two birds were given the Dickin Medal for gallantry. Awarded in Britain by the People's Dispensary for Sick Animals, the medal is regarded as equivalent to the Victoria Cross for valour. Bravery of the highest kind. These two pigeons were the only Australian animal heroes to win a Dickin Medal.

They were posthumous awards, however, for none of the pigeons came home alive. Quarantine regulations, again. But the medal-winners' bodies were preserved, and are still in the repositories at the Australian War Memorial, with their medals, ribbons, certificates and their stories.

PIGEON 139 DD 43 T

It's not much of a name to be remembered by – especially when you've won the equivalent of the Victoria Cross. A few numbers and letters stamped on a metal ring and slipped around your leg when you're only seven days old.

Yet we know a lot about this pigeon. He was a blue bar cock: a male, slate-grey in colour, with two dark bands across his wing. He was given the number 139 by the Department of Defence (DD) when he was acquired in 1943 (43) from Tasmanian (T) breeders. By July 1945, he'd flown more than a thousand miles on twenty-three missions.

At that time, his section was attached to a water transport company at Madang, on the north coast of New Guinea. They manned small ships, ferrying supplies to the fighting troops. The craft all had radio, but crews rarely put to sea without a pair of pigeons in a cane basket, as extra insurance. Wisely so.

On 12 July, an army boat left Madang with a cargo of stores and munitions. They were well at sea when a storm bore down and radio contact was lost. The wind howled, sheets of rain fell, and heavy seas pushed them closer to the shore of Karkar Island.

Suddenly, a huge wave broke amidships. The boat shuddered. Its engine stalled, choking like a drowning man, then died altogether. Helplessly, they drifted towards the beach, and felt a sickening lurch as the hull struck a sand bar. The vessel rolled, side-on to the waves. And as they stuck fast, it began to fill.

'The pigeons. Get the pigeons!'

A crewman hurried below to the wicker basket. He drew out the blue bar cock known as 139 DD 43 T and carried it to the wheel-house where the master was scribbling his message.

Engine failed. Washed on beach at Wadau owing heavy seas. Send help immediately. Craft rapidly filling up with sand.

The message was put into its capsule and the lid shut tight. The bird was taken onto the heaving deck and, with outstretched hands, the crewman launched it into the storm.

How the pigeon was beaten about by the tempest! It was forty miles to his loft at Madang. The bird's every instinct was to fly low, and find such shelter as he could from the weather. But too low, as he left the boat, and he'd be taken by the sea and drowned.

His wings beat furiously into the wind, trying to lift himself higher, away from the clinging salt spray. Ever more strongly he flew as the rain soaked his feathers and tried to drag him down.

At last, through the water curtain, the bird spied the shoreline and the fringe of jungle beyond. He couldn't see the foundering boat; but turning southwards he set course for home and dinner.

Lightning split the sky, and thunder cracked. Over land, the pigeon would be able follow his instinct and fly close to earth through the storm, but he had to cross more water before reaching the mainland – and it was some time before he found further pro-tection from the weather, and thus a little more speed for his flight.

Gradually, as the storm passed, the pigeon gained altitude. The sun came from behind the swirling clouds to dry his feathers. From this height, he could look down on the world: at the dark mass of the jungle, and the familiar blue and gold outline of the coast.

Travelling very fast now, the pigeon flew until he saw the roofs of Madang, the transport boats, and the welcome comfort of his loft.

Lower he dropped until, with a sure instinct, Number 139 landed safely home.

The pigeon service men had spotted his arrival. Hands reached out to hold him and withdraw the message from its cylinder. Only then was the pigeon released to his feeding tray and a handsome meal of wheat, rice and seed. Good bird!

As for the message, it was passed without delay to command. A rescue boat was quickly put to sea, and reached the stricken vessel an hour or two later. Fortunately the storm had passed; and although the engine and radio were damaged, crew and cargo were saved.

Pigeon 139 had flown forty miles in fifty minutes, through violent storm. A brave bird. True to his calling. And worthy of the blue, brown and green ribbon (representing sky, earth and sea) of the Dickin Medal for gallantry.

PIGEON 879 DD 43 Q

The second pigeon VC was won by a bird that flew through enemy fire, after his companions had been shot, to carry vital information back to headquarters and enable a patrol to be rescued.

Number 879 was only a year old when assigned to work with United States forces, during the struggle to recapture Manus Island from the Japanese in early 1944. The Americans had been much impressed by the Australian pigeon service. And this blue-chequered cock, his upper wings dappled with light grey feathers, was among the birds attached to the US 6th Army.

At the beginning of April, a reconnaissance patrol set out to investigate reports that enemy troops were massing for a counter-attack, near the native village of Drabito. It was a thirty-mile trek through dense jungle. The patrol took a radio with them and two pairs of pigeons.

They reached the outskirts of Drabito without trouble. From locals they learned that several hundred Japanese soldiers were concentrated nearby, with enough food for three weeks. It seemed the reports were correct: a major attack was being planned.

The men were getting ready to return when they were spotted by a forward Japanese patrol. Shots rang out. The Americans dropped for cover and returned fire. There was a sharp, hot fight. As the Japanese were calling for reinforcements, the US commander – an officer called Huffman – motioned for his men to withdraw deeper into the jungle and radio the information back to headquarters.

The trouble was, the radio had been hit by a bullet and was out of action. The only option was to use the pigeons. Huffman could hear the enemy searching, and it was vital his news got through. He wrote two identical messages, put them in containers carried by the first pair of birds, and released them.

Fly home, pigeons. One of you will make it . . .

But they didn't. The rising birds were seen by the Japanese. There was a burst of machine-gun fire, and tufts of slate-grey feathers drifted to the ground. Not only had both pigeons been killed, their presence had betrayed the American position.

Further the men drew into the jungle. Commander Huffman wrote his message for one of the two remaining pigeons. But again, as soon as it took flight the bird was shot down.

The Americans moved to new cover. Their situation was becoming serious. They could hear patrols beating through the undergrowth, anxious to find them and prevent intelligence of Japanese movements reaching US headquarters. It was essential for Huffman to send his message. But he had only one pigeon left.

He decided to harbour up for the night and wait. The Americans could hear drums and shots in the distance. Several times Japanese patrols passed close to them, but they weren't discovered.

The long hours passed. Morning came. At 0950, judging it was safe, Huffman took the one remaining bird from its cardboard box and wrote his message for a fourth time.

[. . .] Drabito could be bombed with good results.

The paper was rolled up tight inside the message cylinder and – with a wing and a prayer – Pigeon 879 was launched.

God speed, little bird. You're our last chance, now.

The bird beat his pinion feathers and flew up to an opening in the dark green shadows of the jungle canopy. Higher and higher.

Nearly there, pigeon.

But suddenly came the sounds of rifle fire. He'd been seen by a Japanese ambush. A bullet skimmed past him. Then another. He flew desperately towards the opening of light. Flying for his life.

And then the pigeon was through, into the clear, blue sky.

Instinct told him which way to fly, as high above the trees as possible, towards his loft. Thirty miles. Which he did in forty-seven minutes. By eleven o'clock, Pigeon 879 had finished breakfast and was getting ready for a snooze on his perch. Outside, headquarters staff were preparing to bomb Drabito. Japanese forces would be forced to retreat, and the US patrol able to return safely to base.

Some time afterwards, the chief signal officer of the American forces in the south-west Pacific sent a special message to his Australian counterpart, thanking him for having made the pigeon service available. 'The birds, equipment and personnel furnished from Australian sources have proved of the highest value . . .'

Indeed they had. Gallantry and a devotion to duty of a supreme order. Another Pigeon VC, though quarantine and logistic requirements meant that none of them returned to Australia alive. Some, including the two Dickin Medal winners, were mounted and brought home for display at the Australian War Memorial.

On 8 November 1945, the Sydney *Sun* carried this moving tribute to them:

> *Now fare you well my faithful bird,*
> *In war you were a wizard.*
> *So now your country honours you*
> *By taking out your gizzard.*

GUNNER

And his amazing ears

It all began on the day the Japanese first bombed Darwin: 19 February 1942.

Just after ten o'clock that morning, a black and white kelpie was having a scratch in the sun when he heard the low, throbbing sound of approaching aircraft. He didn't take much notice at first, for he was used to planes around Darwin airport.

But suddenly, these ones did something different. They swooped over the water, dropping bombs. The dog heard explosions down at the harbour. Loud and shattering. Columns of black smoke rose into the air, and he caught the oily stink of burning ships.

Modern warfare had come to Australian soil.

Sirens wailed. Anti-aircraft guns fired. The few defending Kittyhawk fighters were soon shot down. For forty minutes, Darwin and its port were under attack. The earth aflame. And the young kelpie fled to the sanctuary of bushland not far from the aerodrome and the nearby Royal Australian Air Force base.

He waited until the enemy planes had gone. Until it seemed safe to come out and sniff around the air force buildings for scraps.

But all at once the dog heard the distinctive sounds of the bombers again. His enemies were returning. The kelpie crawled under the long wooden building of the officers' mess and stretched out flat on the ground, head between his paws.

This was worse than before. This time the enemy wasn't down at the harbour but directly overhead, bombing the airfields.

The kelpie cowered in terror, his sensitive eardrums bursting, his nose burning with acrid smoke. An impact blast shook his whole body. The mess had been hit. There was fire and crashing timber, and the dog howled in pain as a beam fell across his leg.

He'd been lying in a shallow hole, and was able to free his paw. But the kelpie could only crawl to the end of the building and lie there, whimpering, until the bombers disappeared.

Still he hid among the debris, afraid to move until he heard voices and footsteps. The dog whined, and a man stopped. He looked under the building. And as the airman lifted the dog out he said, 'Hey, young feller, what have they done to you?'

The kelpie winced as he was held up, one white paw dangling helplessly. But his rescuer's voice sounded kind as he added, 'Look after him, Percy. He's got a broken leg. Better take him to the doc.'

The dog yelped again as he was passed over to Leading Aircraftman Percy Westcott. Percy had arrived from Melbourne to join No 2 Squadron only a few days before. He'd been unloading bombs at the ammunition dump when the raid started. As soon as it was over, he raced to the RAAF base to assist – and his job now was to get help for the injured kelpie.

Percy soothed the animal as he walked across the airfield. Planes were blazing on the runway. Almost every building and hangar had been damaged. Six men were dead, and many others wounded. Dr Lloyd-Jones was busy attending to them, and it was some time before he had a moment to look at the kelpie.

'What's the dog's name?' he asked.

'I don't know, sir.'

'His serial number?'

'I don't think he has one, sir.'

'I can't treat him without a name or number. We have to keep the military paperwork in order.'

'I see, sir. Well . . .' LAC Percy Westcott thought quickly. 'His regimental number is 0000. And his name is . . . Gunner.'

'Thank you. That will keep the clerks happy. Now, Gunner, let's see what we can do for you.'

Dr Lloyd-Jones expertly set the broken leg in plaster, and then Gunner was taken to the tent Percy shared with his mates. The dog was still badly shaken after the bombing; but he was only about six months old, and quickly responded to the men's attention.

Like most dogs, though, Gunner found the plaster a hindrance and kept trying to chew it off. This time the remedy lay not with the doctor but with the squadron cook, who sprinkled the plaster with mustard and cayenne pepper. Gunner soon left it alone, and spent next day with his tongue hanging out, drinking quantities of water.

A week or so afterwards, Gunner first demonstrated his remarkable hearing abilities.

His broken leg was mending well, and he was out with Percy and the men working on the airfield. Suddenly he stopped. His ears pricked up. Faintly – distantly – but quite unmistakably and getting ever louder, he heard the same droning engine pitch of the aeroplanes that caused him such terror on the day the bombs fell.

His enemies were coming back. Couldn't these men hear them? Were they deaf? For a dog, each sound is utterly distinctive. Yet these humans seemed oblivious to it.

Gunner started to whine, and to jump up and down. Still the men took no notice. The dog jumped again, trying to warn them another attack was on its way. It was nearly upon them.

'Look at Gunner, Perce,' said his mate, Lindsay Giles.

'He's just being a nuisance. Get down, Gunner.'

But a few minutes later a wave of Japanese raiders appeared in the skies above Darwin, bombing and strafing the town – though fortunately, for these men caught in the open, sparing the airfield.

Two days afterwards Gunner did it again: jumping and whimpering as soon as he heard enemy planes in the distance.

'That's good enough for me!' exclaimed Lindsay. 'I'm off.'

'What do you mean?' asked Percy Westcott.

'That's what Gunner did just before the last raid.'

Sure enough, not long afterwards came yet another attack.

It set a pattern for the months that followed. As soon as the dog started jumping, men knew what was coming and they'd head for cover in the slit trenches. Gunner began to run back and forth to the trenches himself, as a further warning. He couldn't get there fast enough. Percy even got a spare steel helmet – which he held over the dog's head during a bomb attack, just in case.

It was amazing. Gunner never performed when he heard the Allied planes taking off or landing: only when he heard enemy aircraft. And he was the only dog on the air base to do so.

Certainly, Wing Commander McFarlane made much fuss of his four-legged early air-raid warning. Gunner sat at his feet during meal times. And the CO allowed Percy to sound a portable siren whenever Gunner's jumping alerted him to a raid. Eventually, the dog was giving twenty minutes' warning: even before enemy planes showed up on the radar. It was enough time for anti-aircraft crews to man their guns and the fighter pilots to take off.

At first the Japanese flew low, to escape radar detection. But as the warning systems improved, of which Gunner was undoubtedly a part, their planes were forced higher and became more vulnerable.

It made no difference to the dog. He always knew when they were coming. Memories of his broken leg and the cook's mustard were fixed in his mind.

Between February 1942 and November 1943, there were more than sixty bombing raids over Darwin. No one can estimate how many lives Gunner helped save. Percy Westcott says that Gunner missed giving only very few advance warnings – and then, only because second attacks had followed hard on the first.

WHO-ARE-YOU

Gunner usually slept beside Percy's stretcher, under the mosquito net. Indeed, there was always much tangling of nets and abuse from other men whenever Gunner needed to go outside and lift a leg. But one poignant night, Gunner wasn't there.

A number of dogs from a nearby Aboriginal camp used to roam about the air base, until the CO gave orders to keep them away. Yet Gunner was a particular friend to one of them – a lithe, lean animal – a cross between a greyhound and a whippet, tall enough for Gunner to walk under his belly.

They went everywhere together, and most afternoons the two dogs disappeared to go hunting in the nearby scrub. Nobody knew the name of Gunner's friend. Men called him Spot and Jack, but the dog never responded. Until one day, during a card game, a new player looked at him and asked, 'Who are you?'

Immediately the dog's ears pricked up. He cocked his head expectantly. From then on he was known as 'Who-are-you'. He'd come bounding from a hundred yards away at the mention of his name.

Sadly, though, Who-are-you was bomb crazy.

Whenever the air raids were on, Gunner would huddle trembling in a trench, with Percy holding the helmet over his head. But Who-are-you would run in wild circles: howling, almost colliding with walls, and savaging anyone who tried to restrain him.

Of course the inevitable happened. Who-are-you was hit by a bomb, and had to be destroyed. It was the dry season. The ground was so hard men couldn't drive a pick into it to dig a grave. So they carried Who-are-you into the bush near the guard house and built a cairn of stones around his body to protect it from scavengers.

That night, they couldn't find Gunner anywhere. But at two o'clock in the morning Percy was woken by a sentry guard.

'Perce, you'd better come and get your dog.'

'Where is he?'

'I'll show you.'

They went out, and saw that the rocks around Who-are-you had been torn down. Gunner had uncovered the body of his friend and was dragging it down the bush track to be with him and to keep him safe. In the end they had to tie Gunner up until Who-are-you could be buried elsewhere.

Gunner was a lovely dog, Percy Westcott recalls. A faithful dog. A clean dog. Every day he'd join the men in the shower block and wouldn't leave until someone put a dab of soap on his coat. Then he'd shake himself dry all over their clothes.

Gunner went up with the pilots practising landing techniques – 'circles and bumps' – around the airport. And he'd sit with the men at the outdoor pictures, barking at the Metro-Goldwyn-Mayer lion.

He and Percy were best mates for a year and a half, until the man was posted south. Gunner stayed in Darwin. It was thought his health might suffer if he moved to a Melbourne winter. So Gunner lived with his second best mate – the RAAF butcher.

Percy Westcott didn't see him again. He often meant to go back, but didn't. Yet he never forgot his dog and the wartime service rendered the people of Darwin whenever Gunner heard the distant sounds of approaching enemy aircraft buzzing in his amazing ears.

REDLEAD

Redlead was a tabby grey kitten, the mascot of a very gallant ship, HMAS *Perth*. Like many animals, Redlead seemed to *know* when danger was coming – but unlike most cats, she went through all her nine lives in a week.

The kitten got her name not long after she came aboard *Perth* and knocked over a tin of red lead paint. Her fur was covered in it – which meant a scrub with turpentine, soap and water. Not the nicest thing to happen to a young cat.

She should have realised, perhaps, and tried to go ashore again. But she didn't. In fact, Redlead had a stroke of luck.

A little girl had given the kitten as a farewell present to Able Seaman Bob Collins, who sneaked her aboard under his jacket. Some officers didn't like pets on the ship, and Redlead spent her first few days hidden with the sailors below.

But the new skipper, Captain Hec Waller, was fond of animals. He'd kept a pet monkey aboard a previous ship. So one day, when Bob Collins was on duty on the captain's bridge, he took Redlead from his jacket and quietly placed her on the deck.

'What have we got here?' asked Captain Waller, as the kitten smooched against his leg.

'It looks like a kitten, sir,' replied Able Seaman Collins.

'Well . . . we'd better get her something to play with.'

He tied a wad of paper on a string. It made a good game, and the captain spent many happy hours playing with the kitten.

Thereafter, Redlead had the run of the ship, from the bridge to the engine room. The sailors even made her a traditional hammock in which to sleep. This cat was going to live as comfortably as possible.

Redlead had joined the ship in Sydney at the end of 1941. Two months later, HMAS *Perth* left Australian waters for the last time, to join a naval squadron trying to stem the Japanese invasion of what is now Indonesia. They soon saw action.

At Batavia (now Jakarta), *Perth* was attacked by enemy aircraft, but beat them off and wasn't badly damaged. Two days later, the squadron encountered a Japanese fleet in the Java Sea, and battle raged through the afternoon and night.

Big guns roared at close quarters. Shells and bombs whistled down. The ships shook with the force of human conflict. And huddled somewhere in a corner, a kitten called Redlead wished she were anywhere else instead.

If this was what being a warship's mascot meant, she wanted no more of it! She'd already used several of her nine lives that day. Of the eleven Allied ships in the battle, only *Perth* and the US cruiser *Houston* were still afloat. When fighting was broken off and they re-entered port, Redlead decided to quit. She'd had enough.

As soon as the ship tied up at the wharf, the kitten crept along the deck to the gangway. Surely everyone would be far too busy to notice her. But they weren't.

'Where do you think you're going?' cried one of the sailors. And he carried Redlead back on board.

The kitten waited awhile, as the crew took on fuel and stores, including some wooden life rafts. She tried to sneak ashore again. But once more, Redlead was seen and put back on the ship.

'She was slinking off. We need our mascot here, for good luck.'

Redlead stayed aboard until late afternoon, when *Perth* was getting ready to leave. Once again, the kitten decided it was time she also departed. She slunk up the companion stairs, across the deck, and along the ship's side until she reached the gangway.

For a third time, hoping that no one was looking, Redlead tried to make it ashore. But for a third time she was grabbed by a seaman, and held aloft in a pair of strong hands.

The kitten spat and howled and tried to scratch her captor. But it was no good. She was carried back to Bob Collins.

'She was trying to nick off again, Bob. Do you reckon Redlead knows something we don't?'

Perhaps she did. For in the official report on *Perth*'s last fight, it was noted, 'Redlead, ship's kitten, endeavoured to desert, but was brought back on board, despite vigorous protests.'

Perth and *Houston* left at seven o'clock. Four hours later, near the Sunda Strait, the cruisers came across a large Japanese invasion fleet. Although heavily outnumbered, they engaged the enemy, and for sixty minutes fought a running battle.

At last, with his ammunition running low, Captain Waller tried to force a passage through the strait. But just after midnight, *Perth* was hit by a torpedo. A second one struck, moments later. The captain ordered his crew to abandon ship. Men were diving into the sea, trying to swim to the wooden life rafts amid the shellfire.

Their ship was surrounded by enemy destroyers when she was hit by a third – and then a fourth – torpedo. Explosions rent the night. *Perth* shuddered. Her guns fell silent. She righted herself briefly. And then, keeling over to port, she sank. *Houston* and a

Dutch destroyer followed shortly afterwards. But it was said they took fifteen enemy ships with them.

Of the 680 men aboard HMAS *Perth*, half were killed in action. The rest, including Bob Collins, were taken as prisoners of war, and over a hundred of them later died in captivity – though Bob survived both Changi and the Burma railway POW horror camps.

Captain Waller went down bravely with his ship. He was last seen standing alone on the bridge. And Redlead . . . just before the end, she made it safely overboard in Bob Collins' arms. They floundered awhile in the sea, bobbing with other men and bodies, stinking of oil and debris, the scene lit by the glow of burning ships.

The kitten struggled and cried in the water. But just as Bob grabbed a passing float, Redlead was swept from his arms and carried away by the fast-flowing tide.

Bob held out a broken board, calling for his kitten to cling to it. Yet the current was too strong. There was nothing he could do but watch helplessly as Redlead disappeared into the darkness of the Sunda Strait.

She'd been quite right to try to leave her ship that afternoon. Call it an omen if you will. But this tabby grey kitten had indeed used every one of her nine lives in less than a week.

JUDY

The Changi dog

A brindle terrier called Judy ran up to her mistress, barking and wagging her tail, as she sensed they were nearing their new home.

It was a strange place, with high stone walls, a clock-tower, and iron gates. 'Changi Prison,' said the women with Judy. Not somewhere the dog knew. But the place offered them shade and rest after their long walk through the heat. Judy barked again, as if to hurry them up.

They were all exhausted. That morning, 300 women and children had been forced by their Japanese captors to stand outside for hours. And then, as the sun beat down through the day, they were marched eight miles from Singapore to Changi, past rice paddies and through native villages, carrying all they possessed in bags and suitcases. A few were pushing prams. Only the most infirm were driven in trucks. The rest sweated. Struggled. Shrivelled as Japanese soldiers drove past, laughing at them.

It wasn't so bad for Judy. The young dog was always able to run ahead and find a bit of shelter somewhere, waiting for them to catch up. No one, except her mistress, worried much about her. A few other village dogs even joined the procession, gambolling around. But the women and children were worn out. And many were already distressed at what had happened to their own dogs.

When Singapore fell in February 1942, British, European and Eurasian families of Allied soldiers and civilians were separated from the men and moved to hostels. Some took their pets, and one day Judy turned up to play with them. Nobody knew where she came from. But she stayed and attached herself to Mrs Freddy Bloom, an American journalist, recently married to a British army doctor.

A few weeks later, when the women and children were told they were going to prison at Changi, they were also told: no dogs. Most of their animals were shot. Some women even gave them a sleeping draught, so their beloved pets wouldn't suffer at the end.

Yet Judy was there that Sunday morning, keeping them company for the long march. Mile after suffocating mile. A few women even wore lampshades on their heads to keep off the vicious sun. Stumbling. Singing to keep up their spirits, for in the far distance they glimpsed the barbed-wire compounds of the Changi POW camp, where Freddy's husband, Philip Bloom, was already interned with thousands of British, Australian and other Allied soldiers.

During the last awful mile, Judy tried to hurry them up. They were nearly there. The stone walls of Changi Prison grew nearer. And taller. And finally, all-encompassing, as the gates slammed shut behind them.

They faced an inner courtyard with the clock-tower. On the right was a cellblock, already holding more than 2000 civilian men in a prison built for six hundred. Among them was an Australian mining engineer, John Allan, whose wife, and seventeen-year-old daughter, Sheila, had walked with the women to the jail that day.

The men and women looked at each other across the courtyard, but dared not speak. To do so would have risked a beating from their guards. Everything had to be said in those brief glances, before the women were led through a barred grille and up clanging metal stairs to their own cellblock, on the other side of the yard.

It was dreadful. Squalid and cramped. Privacy didn't exist. The cells each measured less than three by four metres, with a small, barred window high in the wall, an open lavatory 'squat' in the corner, and a raised cement slab in the middle, as a kind of bed.

The cells had been built to hold one person. Now, Sheila had to share with her Thai stepmother and another lady. Eventually, a fourth woman joined them. There was no furniture – though in time Sheila fashioned a table from bits of scrap, where she kept her few things: a book of Shakespeare, some poems, her father's dictionary.

The schoolgirl also had five exercise books, in which she wrote a diary of her imprisonment. But they were kept hidden, because diaries were not permitted by the Japanese. Her captors did allow Sheila to keep a lump of shrapnel. It had fallen on her pillow at home during a bombing raid, and might have killed her had she been sleeping there. To this day she keeps it, to remind her how precious life is.

Judy didn't sleep in a cell – not to begin with. The dog kept close to her mistress, and Freddy Bloom tried to avoid cells. She moved into an empty tool room with her pet and a few friends, and they stayed there until forced upstairs. Even then, Freddy spent much of her time camped on the verandah.

It was humid in summer, and sodden in the wet. But at least she had a *sense* of being outside, where the air could move freely and the wild birds sang. Sparrows sometimes fell into open drains, and were saved from drowning by the women. One bird, called Herbert, soon had the run of the place. He became so tame he didn't fly off, but stayed to chatter through concerts, peck at playing cards, and glean the few grains of rice left over at meal times.

Not that there was much for Herbert. Not much for anyone. Eventually, there was only one meal, at midday: a spoonful or two of powdered rice, cooked hard as rock, sometimes with morsels of meat or vegetables. A stale bun every other day.

Prisoners would retreat alone, to greedily eat with their fingers. Savouring every last skerrick. And they'd be just as hungry afterwards.

Judy was always there: the dog just watching them. When there was nothing more for people to scrape from the dish, they'd let their hands fall by their sides. And Judy would lick them clean.

The dog didn't beg for food. She merely sat and waited. Freddy Bloom and a few others saved some of their own meagre rations, and Judy scavenged anything else she could. But she grew ever thinner. Like everybody. Mere skin and bone. Without proper food, the dog's hair fell out – until in the end she had no coat at all. Which was a shock to those who'd never seen a naked dog before.

Even so, some still complained that Judy was eating too much of their food. Moves were made to get rid of her.

She wasn't the only dog in prison. Several others had come in with the women that first day and a few had already been living in the men's cellblock. There'd also been some cats, a goat and a hen – but they soon disappeared into somebody's cooking pot.

So a vote was arranged by the women, whether to keep the dogs or not. Judy seemed to know something was up. Everywhere she went, people came up to her, and stroked her, and said with tears in their eyes, 'Poor Judy, we won't let them hurt you.'

And women, who remembered their own dogs destroyed that day they'd marched to Changi, threatened to barricade themselves in with Judy if the vote went the wrong way. They knew what joy the terrier gave in return for the miserable portions of food she ate. A world that still had a place for dogs was not entirely black.

'I know there is no sense in getting sloppy about animals,' said Freddy Bloom in one of the unposted letters she wrote to her husband, as a kind of diary. 'But there is darned little to love in an internment camp and dogs are – dogs.'

The dogs won easily. More than 300 women voted to keep them, with only thirty against. They breathed a little easier – though the guards killed all but two, anyway. Only Judy and Nipper were left: Judy spending her days beside Freddy, as she sat at her worktable, except when the guards came banging round on inspections. At such times, Judy was nowhere to be found.

The women all had jobs. Some helped with the entertainment committee, organising concerts and even a pretend circus. Teachers arranged classes for the children (though history and geography were forbidden). Some worked with the doctors and nurses in the makeshift prison hospital. And Freddy Bloom, the journalist, sat with a typewriter scrounged from somewhere, editing the *Weekly POW-WOW,* a news sheet of Changi gossip and information.

Young Sheila Allan, who always wanted to be a writer, would visit her in the verandah office; and Freddy often talked of her own experience in the craft of writing. Sheila would show poems and stories of her own – but she never once mentioned the prison diary she was writing in those five hidden exercise books. That was a secret too dangerous to tell anybody.

There were so many difficulties of communication. From time to time secret messages could be passed between men and women in the prison. But what of those interned at the POW camp in the distance? How could you get news to them? Freddy once climbed on a stack of shelves to look through a high window towards the camp where her husband was held. Judy barked a warning, however, and risked giving the whole show away.

Then, some of the women had an idea.

A number of Girl Guides were taught to do patchwork in jail by their leader, Elizabeth Ennis. For a birthday present, the girls made Elizabeth a quilt out of cloth rosettes. The quilt was so attractive, it inspired the thought: why not have some of the older women make a similar quilt? It would give them something to do. If they were clever enough, and could send the quilt to the POW camp, it might be a way of getting messages to some of the men.

So that's what happened.

Each white calico bag of flour or rice that came into the prison was cut into small squares. Needles and threads were collected. Every woman who wanted to embroidered a square, later joined into a quilt, and put as much of herself as possible into the work.

Some remembered cherished symbols of home – England and Scotland, the flowers and tartans and regimental badges. Sheila Allan, who'd not been to Australia, nevertheless embroidered a map of her father's homeland, with a kangaroo in the middle. She signed her name, put the word Changi ('prison' wasn't allowed), together with a ship and a plane to show her determination to one day come to the country where her father had grown up. When she was free.

Some women, more skilled than others, embroidered pictures of their dogs: a pet Scotty, fondly remembered from that last day before Changi, and a couple of other dogs (perhaps even one was Judy). Freddy Bloom did a clock with wings ('Time flies'). Another woman embroidered a mother sheep and a lamb, with a blue ribbon around its neck, to let her husband know they'd had a baby son.

For they all signed their patchwork squares – and when the

war was over, discovered that many of the quilt messages had been received. They brought the first news to Philip Bloom of his wife, Freddy. He worked as a doctor in the POW hospital, and that's where the quilts were sent. Three quilts, altogether. One for sick Australian soldiers. Another for the British. And a third was made for the Japanese wounded.

Unlike many of the POWs, the quilts survived the war. Two are now at the Australian War Memorial. The British one is kept by the Red Cross in England. And Sheila has the Girl Guide quilt, given to her by Elizabeth Ennis, which she shows whenever she visits people to talk about those years as a girl imprisoned at Changi.

Because it was years. On the day the women and children were marched to the jail, they were told they'd be there for no more than two weeks. Instead, they were not released until September 1945, three and a half years later. Judy was not among them.

The dog had survived a great deal. The POWs vote to get rid of her. The Japanese purge of the pets. Having to be looked after by others, when Freddy Bloom was taken by the secret police and held for five terrible months. And, finally, the women's move from the prison building to a POW camp at Sime Road.

There, the women at least lived in leaking huts, not cells. Behind barbed wire, not stone walls. Sime Road had patches of ground to cultivate, not concrete yards and metal walkways. In one of her letters to Philip, Freddy Bloom spoke of Judy leaping delighted through tall grass, like a rabbit.

Her delight didn't last. Only a few months before the war ended, the dog was killed by the Japanese. They said no more food should be wasted on pets. And despite tears and pleading, Judy was led away with a rope around her neck. Probably she became a meal for the guards, herself.

'It's silly,' Freddy confessed to her husband next day, writing of friends who had also died, 'but all the tears that I didn't shed for Norman, Middy, and the sad state of the world during the last three years have now rushed out. It's all so inhuman, so evil.'

Yes. But not so silly to cry. Not when you weep for a dog who has given much; who lost all her hair, through hunger, to stay with you; and who asked for nothing in return except your affection.

'Judy made us think of what life was like before we were interned,' Sheila Allan remembered, nearly sixty years later. 'We shared our emotions with her. She was a link with normal life. A life that we *knew* we would go back to one day. Judy was our hope, and we all loved her.'

Surely there is still some good, even in a world wracked by war, where a dog can make you feel that.

Korea
& Vietnam
1950–1975

In the decades after 1945 Australians were involved in a number of limited conflicts between communist and other insurgent forces and the western alliance, including in Malaya and Borneo.

When communist North Korea invaded South Korea in 1950, Australia sent forces to help the South, along with other countries, acting under the command of the United Nations. Fighting intensified as China intervened on the side of North Korea. The conflict ended in 1953 along the demilitarised zone between the two Koreas.

Vietnam was also a partitioned nation. Civil war developed when regular troops from North Vietnam and local communist insurgents, known as the Viet Cong, sought to overthrow the government of South Vietnam and reunify the country. From 1964, forces from the US, Australia, New Zealand and some other countries were sent to help the South. But as opposition grew at home, all foreign troops were withdrawn by 1973 and South Vietnam fell in 1975. Australians served mainly in Phuoc Tuy province, south of Saigon.

THE DAWN DOG

Korea, 1953

There was a noise. A faint scrambling of footfalls and loose stones slipping down the slope. An Australian soldier, on dawn picket in a forward post on Hill 355, cautiously raised his head above the sand-bag parapet.

He didn't know what to expect. The post looked out across no-man's-land towards the Chinese and North Korean positions. Maybe the enemy was moving up for an early morning assault.

The soldier strained his eyes in the half-light. He sensed no other movement. And as his vision adjusted, he saw the culprit not three metres away: a large dog, sitting and staring at him. Like Roff on the day he joined the 13th Battalion on the Western Front, thirty-five years before.

Here in Korea, however, the soldier didn't tempt the dog with bully beef, but tried kind words instead.

'Come here, boy. Good boy.'

Yet the dog didn't move: a faint silhouette against the eastern sky.

'Who are you talking to?' asked the soldier's mate. And he, too, looked over the parapet, rifle at the ready.

'You ought to shoot that dog.'

'I don't want to shoot him.'

'You know what they say . . . It could be a Chinese attack dog.'

'Doesn't look as if he's going to attack us.'

'Could be an enemy patrol dog, pointing us out to an ambush.'

'They know where we are anyway. Come here, feller.'

He whistled, but still the dog sat. They called the corporal.

'He's a fine-looking dog,' said the corporal. For the dawn light was revealing a German shepherd, with a good strong head and sharp ears. 'Seems friendly enough.'

'Do you reckon he's one of theirs – or one of ours?'

'Dunno.'

Australian battalions in Korea had no military dogs of their own. Few diggers then had much regard for their abilities. But American and British forces used dogs widely in Korea for patrol and tracking work, and also minefield detection. Most of them were German shepherds, bred for their intelligence, stamina and aggression.

'The Royal Engineers' dogs sometimes slip the lead and go hunting,' the corporal went on. 'He could be one of them. But I tell you one thing, he can't stay out there.'

The corporal called gently, 'Come here, pooch. Nice dog . . .'

But the animal took no more notice of the NCO than he had of the diggers. At length, the platoon commander, Lieutenant Quinlan, arrived to take charge. He looked over the parapet at the dog.

'Come along, old chap.' The dog looked back.

After several more fruitless attempts at coaxing the animal, the lieutenant gave up. 'Do we have a man in this platoon who knows anything about dogs?' he asked.

'There's Lance Abbott, sir. He worked on a farm.'

Private Abbott was brought into the bunker.

'I'm told you know about dogs,' said Lieutenant Quinlan.

'Sheep dogs, sir. Not war dogs.'

'A dog's a dog, soldier. See if you can move this one.'

With much trepidation, Lance Abbott peeped above the sand-bags. It was a risky undertaking. The sun's first rays were already blushing in the east. With his head and shoulders exposed above the trench, Lance felt like a target down at the rifle range. If he didn't hurry up, it could well be *bullseye!* for an enemy marksman.

He glanced at the dog, still sitting with that expectant look on its face he'd seen a thousand times before on the farm dogs.

Without wasting another moment, Lance spoke with a strong, authoritative command in his voice, 'Come here!'

At once the dog rose, padded across to the bunker, jumped over the sandbags, and followed Lance into the trench.

Everybody was amazed. So *that's* how you did it. The lieutenant led the dawn dog away. Lance didn't see him again, although he probably ended up at the Royal Engineers' dog section.

Certainly Private Abbott's own reputation grew as someone who could control dogs. So that when, a few months later, the British were looking for Commonwealth soldiers to train as dog handlers, Lieutenant Quinlan said, 'I've got just the feller.'

BRUCE

Three diggers began training with the British Royal Engineers in Korea. It was the first time they'd done any sustained work with military dogs.

Lance Abbott's dog was a bit unusual. His name was Bruce and, unlike some patrol dogs, he was very friendly. He'd stand on his hind legs and put his front paws on your chest, asking for a pat. Nor was he a standard tan-and-black shepherd. Bruce was snowy white.

It was good camouflage in winter, when snow lay thick on the hills. And in summer, you couldn't miss Bruce if he took off to go hunting small Korean deer through the undergrowth. But a white dog wasn't much use on patrol, when you were trying to avoid being seen. They solved this problem by dyeing Bruce – with coffee.

The Royal Engineers would make a good strong brew, let it cool, then rub the coffee into his coat. Once dry, they'd rub in more cold coffee, until Bruce was as brown as the other shepherds.

Whatever his colour, Bruce was as alert and obedient as all the war dogs. Even so, few Australian troops took the dogs seriously as allies that could help save lives on a battlefield.

Lance told of one exercise, organised by a company commander in Korea, to test the dog's worth. It was nothing like the real thing. The sections were too close together. Men wandered about, laughing and talking, as if they were going to the canteen. As an example of a patrol in action, it was a joke. And Bruce knew it.

'He just stopped and looked at me,' Lance recalled. 'And Bruce made it quite clear, "This is bull dust."'

EROS

Australian soldiers might have been more quickly persuaded to treat the dogs seriously if they'd had much to do with the animal given to Lance's mate, Corporal George Gray, in Korea.

This one was a genuine German shepherd – from Germany. George's first job was to teach him commands in English. He was a military guard dog, a real trained killer. And his name was Eros, after the Greek god of love. Love? Eros not only bit other people, he also bit the hand that fed him, as George always remembered.

'Eros was a top dog, but he was like any other soldier. You had to treat him with a bit of respect and then he'd work for you. I had to convert him from a guard dog into a patrol dog, teaching him to track on the lead. But if I took my mind off him, or did something silly, he'd just grab my hand and bite it. They'd trained that dog so hard in Germany, Eros was crooked on everybody.'

The dog had another reason for feeling crook. Just before George took him over, Eros had been injured on patrol at the frontline. An enemy grenade exploded near him. Eros lost part of two toes on one of his paws, and a small piece of shrapnel lodged in his back. The vets operated successfully, but for a while Eros was among the walking wounded. He had to go over the training jumps on only three legs. Both his ears hung very low.

Then, as his wounds began to mend, one ear pricked up. As his foot healed, the other ear righted itself. And before long Eros was doing the assault course all by himself.

George only had to show Eros the training ring and the dog would go around it on his own: up and over the jumps, crawling through tunnels, and then come back to sit in front of his handler.

Once trained as a patrol dog, Eros could sense any hostile force. He'd sit and point with his head directly at an ambush. George only had to get behind the dog and look between his two pricked ears, to see exactly where the enemy might be hiding.

Some Australian troops may have scoffed at the dogs, but the authorities were taking notice. As the war in Korea ended, the handlers who'd trained with the Royal Engineers were posted to a new war dog course at the School of Military Engineering in Sydney: the first time that Australian working dogs would be trained in modern battle skills.

PRINCE

A couple of years had passed. The war dog school was working well. George Gray and his new dog, Prince, were in Canberra, demonstrating just what they could do to the officer cadets at Royal Military College, Duntroon.

Darkness had fallen. They were out on a night ambush exercise in the scrub. One group was the 'enemy', bunkered down on a hillside, with forward sentries dug into foxholes, watching for Prince and George trying to track them down with the second group.

'The dog will find them, no trouble,' George told the soldiers. 'He knows his job. Your job is to move in silently, and put those sentries out of action. The most important thing is to gag them straight away, before they can yell out and raise the alarm. That's the first lesson we learned in Korea.'

The officer cadets nodded their heads. They'd been impressed by the war dogs' work over the past couple of days. Especially, they liked the way a little bitser called Tiger was able to find his way through a dummy minefield.

Tiger had come from a Sydney dog refuge, but he could sniff his way through any minefield like an expert. As soon as he found one buried in the ground he sat beside it, while George placed a marker. Sometimes he sat where the men knew no mine had been planted. But when they dug down they'd find a broken plate or a box of old fencing staples, left from the time Duntroon had been a sheep station. Always there was something.

Prince, on the other hand, was no homeless mongrel. The German shepherd had been a champion show dog in his day. But he'd bitten a judge and been banned from the ring. He was one of several such dogs bought for the school. Aggression was a useful trait for the army; and in any case, biting judges didn't affect Prince's nose.

Tracking down an ambush was his speciality, as these Duntroon soldiers would find out. Many of them would soon be going to Malaya with the war dogs, joining Commonwealth forces fighting communist insurgents. Before going into the jungle, it was essential men understood how the dogs could help them. So, now, the night patrol exercise in the Canberra bush.

Stealthily, in the darkness, George Gray moved forward with Prince. Once into his breast harness, the dog knew he was at work. The rest of the patrol fanned out behind him, faces blackened, weapons at the ready.

'Watch every step,' George warned them. 'Make no noise. Not a twig breaking, or a leaf rustling. Keep your eyes on Prince and my hand signals. And remember, when you spring their sentries, gag them at once. Don't give'em time to yell out.'

He turned to Prince. 'Seek,' he commanded. 'Seek on!'

They moved cautiously up the hillside through the scrub. The moon hadn't risen yet, so there were no shadows to worry about. Steadily. Carefully. Watching for fallen branches and rabbit holes.

Prince moved at an easy pace, nose twitching, alert for any hint of an enemy's trail. Handlers say that a dog's nose is thousands of times more sensitive than a human's. Certainly, nobody teaches a dog how to track. All we can do is learn how to control and read the animal's behaviour.

Suddenly, Prince slowed. His whole body stiffened. He'd picked up a scent. Tension ran down his spine, from his nose to the tip of his tail. George motioned to the patrol to keep up, as Prince started his track.

Quickly now, through the trees, the dog's nose bent to the earth, then lifted to sniff for any trace of human odour on the surrounding leaves and grass, or drifting in the air. Then head down again. Up the steep hill.

All at once, he paused and pointed. Then Prince began to tug strongly on the lead, trying to make for some low bushes a hundred metres away.

There. That's where they're hidden.

It was all a game to Prince. He'd been trained to get a bit of meat from the ambush, once he found them. But this wasn't playtime. George pulled the dog back. 'Leave,' he whispered. 'Heel. Sit.'

He motioned the patrol leader forward and pointed.

The leader gave thumbs up. He signalled orders to the patrol. As his men crawled on their bellies around the ambush to attack, George and Prince retreated quietly behind a log to watch. The dog's eyes didn't once leave the hide.

Minutes passed. Then, through the darkness, they heard a *thud* as the patrol tackled the sentry. But they forgot to gag him quickly enough, for they also heard the sentry yelling, 'Stand fast!'

Strictly, he should have called 'Stand to!' But it made no difference. The place burst into action. Flares lit up like noonday. Men were shouting. Running. And down the hill came the rest of the ambush, spoiling for a fight. Explosions went off. Blanks fired.

None of which bothered Prince, who was used to the noise of war games. He just sat behind the log with George, quietly expressing his contempt. He'd done his bit. Then these humans had mucked it up.

Afterwards, the officer cadets gave Prince a friendly pat. 'Sorry, old feller. We forgot. Always silence the sentry immediately.'

It was a lesson well learned. Something they'd remember next time – when it was the real thing, and they were stalking an enemy bunker with the dogs and live ammunition, in the jungles of Malaya.

PEDRO

And the aniseed trail
Malaya, 1957

The signal from the police chief on Penang Island came through late one afternoon: *Urgent send best available war dog and handler.*

When Corporal George Gray, in charge of the dog platoon, was called into the orderly room and shown the cable at 2nd Battalion the Royal Australian Regiment (2 RAR) headquarters in Malaya, he knew something big was on.

'They've set a trap for a couple of insurgents,' said the duty officer. 'Couriers, probably, for the local Communist Party cadre. The police need a good tracker. Who'll you send?'

Corporal Gray cast his mind over the possible dogs.

'Prince is away up country,' George said. 'He's the best. But Pedro's here, and he's pretty good. We've worked together on Penang before. I'll take him across myself.'

'Good-oh. Truck leaves at first light tomorrow.'

George saluted, and went off to the kennels in the lines at Sungai Siput, the mainland town where Australian troops were based as part of the Commonwealth forces fighting communist terrorists (CTs as they were called) on the Malay Peninsula. It was known as the Emergency, but in truth – for soldiers and civilians alike – it was a protracted, vicious guerrilla war. Ultimately the mainly Chinese insurgents were defeated: cut off from supplies and local support.

George Gray had taken eight war dogs to Malaya with 2 RAR, the first Australian-trained tracking and patrol dogs to serve overseas. They were all German shepherds, apart from a British-trained Labrador called Stamford, who was brilliant at following complex trails through village streets. Oh, and a black and white spaniel-cross called Wild Dog, who wasn't much good for anything except affection and being the battalion mascot.

One war dog and handler were attached to each battalion company, but others came and went from Sungei Siput as they were needed by troops in the field.

Prince, who we met in the previous chapter, had been trained by George and was clearly his favourite. They'd once tracked a party of CTs to their hideout deep in the jungle, where whole families had been living. The terrorists had vanished, yet Prince kept pawing at a pile of leaves. Afraid it might be a booby trap, George carefully uncovered it – to reveal a Chinese baby hidden underneath. The infant was taken to Singapore and adopted by a British family – another life saved by Prince's quick instinct.

Yet Prince was away this time, leaving Pedro as the next best dog for George Gray to take to Penang.

The powerful, strong-willed shepherd was lying in the shade of his kennel, trying to escape the tropical heat, as George approached. He eyed the man cautiously, as if wondering what was going to be asked of him and whether he'd bother to do it.

Pedro sat up and took the biscuit George offered. He even allowed himself to be patted, though he didn't show many signs of returning any affection. He rarely did. George was one of the few people Pedro would work for. Other handlers couldn't manage him properly. Some even seemed afraid of him, especially when he showed a bit of aggression.

'Pedro's his own man,' George used to say, unconsciously reveal-ing the depth of the bond between them. 'He's full of himself. Got a fair bit of spirit, like anyone who's good at their job. That's why he has a high opinion of himself – and why you've got to keep the discipline on him.'

George's discipline and lack of fear were something to which Pedro did respond. The dog stood up as Corporal Gray scratched the back of his ear, and gave him instructions for next morning.

'We're going back to Penang, boy. Remember our last track into the hills, and we spotted the disappearing leg? Well, the police chief's got another job for us. We leave first thing. Okay?'

Pedro's tail wagged slightly. Even as George gave orders for Pedro's tracking harness and gear to be packed ready, the dog had already come to the conclusion that, whatever his first inclinations, he might as well do what the man asked.

The truck left just as dawn was breaking, for the trip to the coast and the Penang ferry. It was a journey of several hours, depending on the weather, the state of the roads, and the hostile activities of the local CTs.

George and Pedro travelled in the back of the covered truck: the dog lying on the floor, head between his paws; the man trying to doze against the canvas sides. They had a long day or two ahead of them, with not much chance of a decent sleep. But it was difficult to nod off, what with the racket of early morning birds and monkeys in the jungle outside, and the jolting inside the truck. George's mind kept going back to the last time he and Pedro went to Penang.

The British, as the colonial power, had a good network of informants among the Malays. They'd heard that a communist district committeeman and his bodyguards had been active in the kampongs (as the local villages are called), gathering money for the party. There was nothing voluntary about these donations. Any resistance and you could have your throat cut as a warning to others, or your teenage sons kidnapped and taken into the hills to join the terrorists. The money itself was taken to the mainland and carried by a chain of couriers to the party leader, Chin Peng, at his headquarters near the Thai border.

Thus, it was important to stop the flow of funds at the source. George and Pedro had been called in after a tip-off that the party committeeman and his thugs were hanging around the much-revered Snake Temple in the hills.

It was a hell of a track. Pedro had picked up the scent quickly and went bounding up the steep jungle slope, the rest of the patrol having to follow at double their normal pace. They were exhausted when they reached the temple at the top – but there was no stopping to catch your breath, for Pedro kept on going down the other side. Down into a gully, where the trail seemed to peter out.

Pedro cast around, anxiously trying to find the trail. But there was nothing – until, suddenly looking up, George glimpsed a human leg disappear behind an outcrop of rock on the hillside.

'Is that one of your men up there?' he asked the patrol leader, a British Army officer, Lieutenant Ian Hyde, attached to the Penang police field force.

'Where?'

George pointed.

'No. My chaps are all down here. You wait with the dog, and we'll have a look.'

George told Pedro to 'leave off'. They sat together to watch as Ian Hyde and his men climbed up to the rock face.

There was a gap behind it – a crevice opening into a cave. It was far too dangerous for the patrol to enter if there were armed men waiting for them. Ian Hyde fired a few warning shots and called on those inside the cave to come out.

Nothing happened.

George asked himself if he'd imagined the leg. But it seemed real enough. And it was made manifest a few minutes later, when Ian Hyde tossed a couple of phosphorous grenades into the cave.

There was much coughing and retching through the smoke billows. Two men came out with their hands up, followed by a woman and a young child. They were taken into custody, though the communist committeeman had made his escape.

Curiously, however, the phosphorous also dislodged a fat twelve-foot python. It came, unwinding itself from the cave in something of a stupor, and was immediately seized by some Chinese patrolmen. They lashed the python to a length of bamboo with their bootlaces and, so trussed, they carried it back up the hill to the Snake Temple and presented it to the old priest there. It took up residence with the other pythons that lived at the temple, and brought much good luck to the worshippers and mahjong players.

Jolting with Pedro in the back of the army truck down to the Penang ferry, George Gray wondered what this new job would be like. You could never tell: with counter-terrorist soldiering nothing was predictable. Every mission had its own unique circumstances, as women and children in the area could also become implicated. Indeed, some of the women were armed as well. You always had to be careful. But it was no doubt going to be interesting, for otherwise the police wouldn't have called them down so urgently.

They reached the ferry, near the RAAF bomber base at Butterworth, about mid-morning. It was a vehicle ferry, and they rolled on board for the short trip across the strait to Penang. Orders were to leave the truck when they berthed at Georgetown, where George and Pedro were met by their old mate, Ian Hyde.

'I'll take you in the car up to the chief's house,' Lieutenant Hyde said. 'He'll brief you on the job and we'll stay there for the afternoon, out of the way. Don't want the locals knowing we have a war dog with us. Word passes very quickly to the CTs.'

The intelligence networks were everywhere. Chin Peng's own father ran a bicycle shop in Georgetown ('That's a bad boy of mine,' he'd say to visitors). Though the British spies were just as active – as George found out when he spoke to the chief.

'One of the locals at the other end of the island got in touch with us a day or so ago,' the superintendent told him. 'A terrorist had given him a sugar bag, and told him to fill it with medical supplies . . . bandages, thread for sutures, anti-malaria pills, that sort of thing. They even wanted "morning sickness" tablets for their pregnant wives. He was to steal them and leave the bag under a certain tree just outside his kampong. Well, he came to us. We've given him what he wanted, and he's planted the goods, just as he was told. The pick-up is tonight. Reckon you and Pedro can follow their trail?'

'It shouldn't be too hard, sir,' George replied, patting his dog. 'This fellow likes a good fresh track.'

'Thought so. In fact, we've given him a little treat.' The super paused for effect. 'We put a few drops of aniseed in the bottom of the bag. Not too much, mind. But just enough to help things along.'

'You couldn't have done anything better!' George laughed.

And indeed they couldn't. There was nothing Pedro loved half so much in this world as the pungent, bittersweet, liquorice scent

A very fine specimen: Bushie, Australia's first official war dog, painted by Wollaston J. Thomas in 1900. *Postcard photo by Anthony Hill.*

ᴏᴠᴇ: The puppy who went to war: Driver as is today. *RELAWM09411.*

ʜᴛ: The Sudan donkey with a group of dentified men at Duntroon, c. 1910. *to courtesy Army Museum of Officer Training, 'C Duntroon.*

Jack Simpson and his donkey carrying a wounded soldier at Gallipoli, 1915.

Photo National Archives of Australia 11405235.

TOP LEFT: Sandy's shattered bronze head, centrepiece of Steven Holland's memorial to all animals in war at the Australian War Memorial. *Photo by Anthony Hill.*

TOP RIGHT: Reproduction in Anzac Parade, Canberra, of Web Gilbert's original monument (destroyed at Suez) to the Australian and New Zealand Light Horse. The head of the horse on the right is modelled on Sandy, the other on an NZ mare called Bess. *Photo by Anthony Hill.*

BOTTOM: Great hearts – the Australian Light Horse in 1914. Trooper Woods (centre) was to die at Gallipoli. *Photo AWM J00450.*

Horrie in the streets of Tel Aviv with
Jim Moody (left) and Don Gill (right).
Photo courtesy Ian and Leonie Moody.

TOP: Horrie in Jim Moody's arms, rescued at sea, 1941. *Photo courtesy Brian and Betty Featherstone.*

MIDDLE: A tubby Horrie home in Melbourne with the smuggling backpack – note the slit for a breathing hole. *Photo courtesy Ian and Leonie Moody.*

BOTTOM: Out of hiding: the bronze Horrie in the memorial park at Corryong, wearing his jacket with the corporal's stripes. *Photo by Anthony Hill.*

Cat in the gunsights – a tabby mascot aboard HMAS *Encounter*.
Photo AWM 304910.

TOP: Australian pigeon VC: the blue-chequered cock 879 DD 43 Q, mounted with his Dickin Medal. *Photo AWM 134260.*

BOTTOM: Not a swearword any more to be heard: Cocky perched on his stand, as he was when cheering up wounded WWI veterans. *RELAWM08024.*

Canine early air-raid warning: Gunner and his amazing ears with Percy Westcott, Darwin, 1942. *Photo courtesy Percy Westcott.*

White coffee – Bruce relaxing with Lance Abbott. *Photo courtesy the late Lance Abbott.*

Crooked on everybody: the Korean War dog, Eros. *Photo courtesy the late George Gray.*

The bond between dogs and their handlers – on the left Denis Ferguson with Marcus, on the right Peter Haran and Caesar. *Photo courtesy Peter Haran.*

War dog school – Prince with George Gray in Sydney. *Photo courtesy of the late George Gray.*

Snappa. Beware the smile on the crocodile. *Photo courtesy Bob Flemming, Billabong Sanctuary, Townsville.*

Roaring into life – the mascot tiger Quintus Septimus. *Photo courtesy 5/7 RAR.*

LEFT: On parade: Stan the Ram V and his handler. *Photo RAINF Sergeants' Mess, by kind permission Department of Defence.*

RIGHT: On guard: Warrant Officer Class 2 Courage perched on the gun barrel of a tank. *Photo courtesy Lance-Corporal Joseph Blundell and 2nd Cavalry Regiment.*

One of the pig mascots of 5/7 RAR, known as 'Willis Secundus', at peace with the world. INSET: Pig mascot sticker. *Both photos courtesy Dave Willis.*

LEFT: 'Mister! Mister!' Lee Doyle with Sandra and her elder sister, Dili 1999. *Photo courtesy Lee and Deanne Doyle.*

BELOW: Home: Lee Doyle and Boris in Queensland. *Photo courtesy Lee and Deanne Doyle.*

Dolphin carrying the marker buoy attachment on his nose – a real Marine Mammal System at work. *Photo Barcroft Media/Getty Images.*

Simpson, Murphy, Roy and HG with the SAS in the Afghanistan mountains. *Photo courtesy SASR by kind permission the Department of Defence.*

Absolute trust: David Simpson and Sarbi taking a moment to relax in Afghanistan. *Photo courtesy David Simpson, by kind permission the Department of Defence.*

ABOVE: Sarbi in Afghanistan with her red booties. *Photo courtesy David Simpson, by kind permission the Department of Defence.*
LEFT: Ace on his first day of training in the EDD search house. *Photo by Anthony Hill.*

DEDICATED
TO THE EXPLOSIVE DETECTION DOGS
WHO HAVE PAID THE ULTIMATE SACRIFICE
SO OTHERS MAY LIVE

My eyes are your eyes,
To watch and protect yours,
My ears are your ears,
To hear and detect evil minds in the dark.
My nose is your nose,
To scent the danger of your domain.
And so you may live, my life is also yours.

ᴘ: Elevation of the Senses: Ewen Coates' evocative statue at the Australian War Memorial of an ᴘlosive detection dog and handler draped in red poppies. *Photo by Anthony Hill.*

ᴛᴛᴏᴍ: The ode on the Explosive Detection Dog memorial at the EDD section kennels, Holsworthy, ᴅney. *Photo by Anthony Hill.*

A soldier and his dog – Mick with Sapper Seamus Doherty at sunset in Somalia, 1993.
Photo Simon French by kind permission, courtesy Seamus Doherty.

and taste of aniseed. Like many dogs, if Pedro was ailing and off his food, a little essence of aniseed on his plate was enough. It made him ravenously hungry. He'd wolf it all down and beg for more. Pedro would indeed go anywhere and do anything for a whiff of aniseed. Tonight's track was going to be fun!

As dusk fell, George and Pedro were driven by car to the police barracks, ready for a quick departure with the patrol as soon as word came through the aniseed bag had been collected.

'I've made an empty cell available for you to rest in,' said Lieutenant Hyde. 'I hope you don't mind, but we've got to keep the dog hidden from snooping ears and eyes.'

That was fine. They had something to eat, and George even tried to snooze on the hard prison bunk. It was bloody uncomfortable. At one stage, during the dark hours, George got up to stroll around, leaving Pedro alone in the cell. Unfortunately, a couple of Malay police came in to see how things were. Pedro was up and at them at once, barking loud enough to bring down the barrack walls. If snoopers hadn't seen him by now, they'd certainly have heard him!

It was after four o'clock in the morning when Ian Hyde came to the cell door.

'You awake, George? We've had contact. The bag's been picked up. We're leaving shortly.'

'Now? It's still pitch black. We'll get a face full of lead if we go out there now!'

'We don't want the track to go stale on Pedro.'

'Stale? With aniseed in the bag? You'll be lucky to keep up with him!'

By the time they had a mug of hot coffee and a bite to eat, the silver edge of dawn was already slipping into the eastern sky. And as they drove in convoy to the southern end of Penang – George and

Pedro in the police car, the patrol following in a truck behind – the island slowly revealed itself in the strengthening light.

The phosphorescent blue on twigs and leaves, with which the jungle glowed in the darkness, began to fade. Dark masses on either side of the road turned into hanging fronds and vines, silhouettes of trees in the rubber plantations, and the thatched roofs of kampongs, the first inhabitants already astir for the coming day.

The morning heat was rising as well, shimmering on the road ahead. They stopped the vehicles a mile or so short of the target kampong. They'd go the rest of the way on foot, without alerting locals to their arrival.

Pedro would have preferred to stay in the car, curled up on the seat, for his skin was already starting to prickle in the steamy, humid air. Yet, like all war dogs, as soon as George put him in his tracking harness, Pedro's listlessness vanished. He was now on duty.

Where is it? Which scent do you want me to follow?

'Heel, boy. Your treat's coming!'

The handler and his dog dropped back as Lieutenant Hyde led them into the jungle to skirt around behind the village. There were ten in the patrol – mostly Chinese men, some of them former terrorists who had surrendered and been posted to the police field force.

They moved quietly in single file, fully armed. George with his submachine gun and Pedro on the lead. The patrolmen carried jungle rifles, all except the coverman behind George who had a pump-action shotgun, which made the hairs stand up on the back of Corporal Gray's neck. Ian Hyde had a sten gun hidden in a sack; he was wearing civilian clothes to disguise his military rank.

The dawn chorus of birds and monkeys was at a crescendo when they reached the kampong. Telling the others to find shelter, Lieutenant Hyde moved forward with his radio man to make contact with the village informant in person and report back to the patrol. But the screeching of the jungle animals was so loud that the patrol could barely hear the crackle when it came on their radio, with Hyde giving a map reference to the tree where the bag of medical supplies had been dropped. The patrol moved forward again. But a reference wasn't really necessary: well before they reached the tree, Pedro's nose had caught the scent.

Aniseed!

He tugged at the harness, dragging George forward in his eagerness to find the source of the delicious aroma. To die for!

'I think we're onto it, sir!' said George through clenched teeth, as Pedro pulled him past the officer. 'Not much mistaking this!'

'Right. The rest of you fellows – try to keep up!'

Pedro set them a cracking pace: straight to the base of the tree where the bag had been hidden. But finding it already gone, the dog set off in pursuit – his nose guided infallibly by the traces of aniseed adhering to leaves and grasses, brushed by the bag as the CT couriers made their getaway.

Through the scrub and along a jungle track until they reached a rubber plantation. There they were, weaving between the trees, sentinel in the early morning, feet crunching on dry leaves . . . skirting beside the road until Pedro, with his nose lifted and scenting particles of aniseed hanging in the still, moist air, crossed quickly to the other side.

They plunged back into the jungle, sharp leaves and stinging vines catching them as they pushed through the undergrowth where ticks and leeches waited for them in the damp. Snakes, too, as the sun grew hotter. It was rough going for the men, though the dog took little notice of any of it. His mind was fixed on that wonderful smell clinging to the foliage, the perfume dancing before his nose!

It was too easy. Those CTs might as well have marked the trail with signs saying *This Way!*

At last, after an hour or so of this punishing pace, much of it up what seemed like a mountainside, the dog stopped for a break. He trotted up to his handler and shoved his snout against the water bottle, as he invariably did when he wanted a drink. Prince was the same.

George took the flask from his belt and, filling his floppy jungle hat with water, gave Pedro a drink. He took a swig of his own before squatting down in the dank, filtered light to recover himself and swat mosquitos, as Ian Hyde and the others caught up with them. Pedro stretched out beside him, pink tongue extended, resting a little to regain his strength for the last of the chase.

The patrol duly acknowledged their gratitude for his canine thoughtfulness. 'Good dog. Nice dog. Thank you Pedro.'

But they only stopped for ten minutes before Pedro was up and casting again, reinvigorated and ready to resume. Everyone scrambled to their feet and set off along the narrow track.

Another short burst and they crossed the summit. Although they couldn't see much in the dense jungle green, they sensed the track beginning to go downhill. And here, Pedro began to slow down. His nose twitching. Sharp ears pricked forward.

Not far, now!

George motioned to the others to go carefully, weapons at the ready. Stealthily. Warily. Alert for any sudden ambush. Every breath seemed to hang too loudly on the sullen atmosphere.

There was the sound of running water. They went a few yards further and the foliage opened a little to show a stream gurgling beside the path: eddying past stones and swirling through clumps of pale bamboo on either bank.

Pedro slowed almost to a halt, his nose rapidly scenting the air. He looked puzzled, and began to pull off towards the stream. Then he returned, and started casting back up the way they'd come. But he only went a few paces before he stopped, moved to his handler and softly started to whine.

'There's someone around here,' George murmured to Ian Hyde. 'I reckon they've doubled back in their own footprints, and the dog knows it.'

'I think you're right,' the lieutenant replied. 'I'm getting that certain smell of terrorists. Let's have a look round.'

But before he uttered another word, there was a shout behind him, and a CT dressed in working clothes leaped out of the bushes and began running up the track. George at once let Pedro go.

'Get him, boy!'

And with a flying leap, the dog brought down the man as he'd been trained, sharp teeth seizing him by the back of the legs.

As the patrol rushed to subdue the man, there was another shout and a woman ran from cover. She, too, was immediately seized; and although the woman was clearly pregnant, they found a Browning automatic pistol hidden in her sarong, and a grenade under each brassiere strap.

Fortunately for everyone, she didn't use the weapons. Nor was the man armed and, although they searched the area, Pedro found no other gun. No other terrorist. He did discover the sugar bag with the medical supplies, hidden in the bamboo. But great was his disappointment when the aniseed turned out to be nothing more than a few drops of essence on a hessian sack and some rolled up bandages. Nothing worth eating at all!

Yet the dog had his reward in the end.

It wasn't the handful of dry dog biscuits Corporal George Gray gave him, or the scratch behind the ears.

It wasn't the pat on the head and a 'Well done, Pedro,' from Lieutenant Hyde.

It wasn't the vote of thanks from a very happy police Chief Superintendent when they returned with the prisoners to George-town.

No. It was the large plate of prime steak and vegetables they gave Pedro for dinner that night. Topped with a few drops of aniseed.

Of course.

What else should it be?

STAN'S BAD HABIT

Stan the Ram had a weakness for tobacco. He didn't smoke the stuff or do anything really terrible like that. He didn't inhale. But he liked to chew tobacco, as if the ram thought himself a cow munching its cud. It was a bad habit. Stan should have known better.

In most respects, the purebred Australian merino mascot of the 9th Battalion Royal Australian Regiment was a model of the military virtues.

He stood firm and proud on parade in his fine woollen uniform, which he renewed every year after shearing. He had a thorough understanding of his weapons – in Stan's case, a large and dangerous pair of curled horns. He was aggressive in their use as a battering ram when provoked, and was once charged with striking a superior officer. Fortunately, the court martial did not record a conviction.

No buts about it, Stan was single-minded in his dedication to duty. Every year he was deployed to his home stud to help sire the next season's drop of pure merino lambs. It was exhausting work and Stan would return to battalion headquarters at Enoggera Barracks in Brisbane worn out.

The mascot was formally called 'John Macarthur', after the father of the Australian wool industry, when he first came to 9 RAR in 1971. Yet, in the way of soldiers, he was soon nicknamed 'Stan the

Ram'. It was a mark of his popularity, and there was much rejoicing when he was promoted to lance-corporal. More so when somebody put twenty dollars on the bar of the soldiers' canteen, known as the Ram's Retreat, to drink his health on that occasion.

Yet Stan's health was actually a worry, given his fondness for tobacco leaf. People tried to tell him that it was not good for him, but the animal never seemed to take any notice.

Whenever he saw a soldier take out a packet of cut tobacco and a cigarette paper, Stan would come across and enquire with a nudge and a wink if he could share in some of the makings. As you do with a mate.

If the soldier said he had nothing to spare, Stan would insist. A nudge became a gentle push. Push turned into shove. And if the mate still refused to share his 'baccy, shove developed into something more assertive. The mascot ram would go for his weapons – and this time there'd be quite a few butts about it.

Still, things usually didn't have to go so far. As a rule, most men were happy enough to indulge Stan's bad habit, and let him join them when they gathered off duty for a fag and a yarn. It's one of the things that so endear mascots to their soldiers: allowing the animals to share and in many ways parody the strict discipline of their military life. But playing the fool was to get Stan the Ram into a spot of bother.

One day a neighbour, who lived near the barracks, saw some men giving a plug of roll-your-own tobacco to Stan, who chewed it up and swallowed it with relish, as he always did. *More please.*

The neighbour was shocked. Didn't these soldiers know how dangerous tobacco could be to your health? Didn't they realise Stan could become a nicotine addict, if he wasn't one already? A forty-fags-a-day ram.

The neighbour rang up the RSPCA to report the incident. And to demand that the animal welfare body do something about it. The RSPCA took note, a veterinary inspector was despatched, battalion headquarters was notified. Word went down the line: produce Stan the Ram for a medical examination.

So the mascot was taken on sick parade. The inspector was thorough. He looked down Stan's throat and into his eyes. He took the ram's temperature and any number of specimens. He prodded and pushed and poked. He hummed and hemmed and hawed.

Finally the RSPCA inspector issued his opinion. 'If every animal was as healthy and well cared for as this one, I'd be out of a job.'

There was relief all round. At least the soldiers couldn't be charged with causing wilful damage to their mascot. And Stan could continue to enjoy his one bad habit. Indeed, as they left the sick parade that day, the mascot could be heard to bleat, expectantly, that he was quite free if anyone felt like going for a weed.

Stan the Ram remained a mascot for nine years.

When the 8th and 9th Battalions amalgamated to form 8/9 RAR in 1973, the merino soldiered on until, in the way of elderly NCOs, bad feet and worse temper began to take their toll.

At last, his keepers wrote to the CO saying that Stan had become 'impossible to handle'. A second ram took over his mascot duties, and after nine years in the job Stan was allowed to retire to an animal husbandry research farm.

Where he was sworn off tobacco, and lived out the rest of his days a model of self-denial.

CASSIUS

Vietnam, 1967

The dog collapsed without any warning. Cassius was like that. The black Labrador tracker had been out on a training run, going flat strap through the sand dunes at Vung Tau. No stopping to let the men in his tracking team catch their breath. Cass never did. He loved it too much.

For two hours he'd been going like the clappers in the morning heat. Head down, straining at the harness. When suddenly his whole body convulsed, and he dropped onto the burning sand.

'Oh, Christ!'

His handler, Lance-Corporal Norm Cameron, ran to the dog. Cassius lay there, barely moving. His eyes rolled upwards into their sockets, and white saliva foamed from his mouth.

'Help us! Quickly. He'll cook out here.'

The nine men in the tracking team gathered round. They lifted the animal and Norm carried him to the beach, just over the sand hills. They laid Cass in the shallows, letting the wavelets spill over his body and bathing his head.

The tropical sea wasn't very cold, but it revived the dog a little. His breathing grew stronger, and he began to stir.

'Come on, Cass. You can't stay out here. We've got to get you back to base – and then to the vet, as fast as we can.'

Norm stooped and the others laid the dog across his shoulders, body resting on his backpack, legs dangling in front. With Cassius in a kind of fireman's hold, and draped with wet cloths, the team set off down the beach to the Australian transport base at Vung Tau.

It was a three-kilometre hike. Far enough in that heat, without carrying an extra thirty-five kilos of dog: not dead weight exactly, though it soon would be if Cass didn't get help.

They'd only been in Vietnam for six weeks. Cassius and his mate, Justin, were the first two Australian tracker dogs to work with the task force out of Nui Dat. Neither the officers nor men of 7 RAR had been at all keen on them at first. Bloody dogs!

But Cass soon proved himself – leading a team to his first enemy kill and sniffing out a Viet Cong bunker system hidden deep in the jungle. Thereafter, the CO couldn't praise him enough, and even let the dog travel in his chopper with him on their way out to patrol.

Yet Cass wasn't getting enough exercise. He was a big dog, who'd been castrated when young as he was to become a seeing eye dog, and quickly put on weight. Sure, he went like a steam train when tracking. But there was a lot of hanging around as well, both on patrol and back in his kennels at Nui Dat. Nor was there anywhere safe at the Dat where he could go for a really long run. Hence, the CO had decently allowed them to go to Vung Tau for a week, to exercise in the dunes around the transport base, and get the dog back into top condition.

Then Cassius had collapsed.

It wasn't the first time. He'd done it once or twice before, while training with Tracking Wing at the Ingleburn Infantry Centre, near Sydney. But never like this.

Norm remembered picking Cass up from his first home. He was far too boisterous to be a seeing eye dog and lead the blind. So they offered him to the army, where those faults became advantages.

The dogs at Ingleburn were all Labradors or Lab crosses, with first-rate retrieving instincts. All were black, for better camouflage. And all had been given Roman names . . . Caesar, Juno, Marcian . . . Cassius loved it from the beginning. He once completed a three-day tracking course in less than one day. Within six months he was declared ready for Vietnam.

Now, in the sand at Vung Tau, the dog felt like a tonne weight on Norm Cameron's back, as they pushed themselves from the beach and over the dunes into the base camp.

Asking his team leader to arrange transport to the vet, Norm carried Cass into the lines, laid him on the tent floor, and began sponging him from a bucket of fresh water. It was only a twenty-minute ride to the American veterinary hospital. The trackers had no vehicles of their own at Vung Tau, and relied on the goodwill of people at the transport base. But it always took time to arrange – and time was one thing Cass didn't have a lot of.

Hurry. Hurry. Norm looked at his dog lying there half conscious. Funny, but Vietnam had been the making of Cass as a tracker.

His greatest fault in training was that he rarely pointed. In all his enthusiasm, he'd often bound up to the quarry and lick him in the face. Once he almost pulled Norm on top of a wounded Viet Cong soldier. Very dangerous. It was only after his first kill that Cassius learned.

A woman guerrilla had started to scream as she saw this black dog coming after her down the track. Norm quickly checked Cassius and pulled him back. The coverman and the rest of the team went into standard contact drill. There was a burst of automatic gunfire. Shouting. An explosion. It was over very quickly – though after-wards there were four black-clad guerrillas lying dead on the jungle track, and the smell of fresh blood in the air.

After that, Cassius always pointed. At least, he did in the few weeks that were left before they came to Vung Tau and this.

Time dragged. Two . . . three . . . four hours had passed since Cass had gone down, and still no transport came to take him to the vet. What were they doing? Didn't they realise?

Norm Cameron kept cooling his dog, though becoming more heated himself. It would have been quicker to carry Cass on his shoulders to the vet himself. Men asked what was happening, but always they were told to wait. Things took their own time in the army. There's a war to fight, feller, and what does a dog signify?

Cass was becoming more distressed. His tongue was hanging from his mouth, and darkening. Breathing shallow. Limbs stiff. And only a slight quiver from time to time showed he still lived.

The dog was sinking. Soon it would be too late. It was way too late, already. For when at last a vehicle did arrive and they got Cassius to the vet, it was five hours after the dog had first collapsed.

They put ice packs around him, to lower his temperature from forty degrees. But he only lasted little more than an hour and a half, and later that afternoon of 12 May, Cassius died. The autopsy showed many of his internal organs had indeed cooked in the heat.

Nobody can say now why it took so long to organise transport from the base for the short trip across Vung Tau to the veterinary hospital. But the memory of Cassius remains evergreen – not just with Norm Cameron, but with all who knew the Australian tracker dogs who served in Vietnam.

Cass was the first of them. As he was also the first Australian military working dog to die overseas – if not on active service, then certainly in the line of duty. An animal hero indeed.

TIBER

When Cassius died, he was replaced by a Labrador-cross called Tiber, sent from Ingleburn without a handler. And the brass said to Norm Cameron, 'Guess what? He's yours.' It was the last thing he wanted.

'I only wanted out. I'd just lost my best mate. I didn't want another dog. But what could I do? I wasn't going to say no.'

So Tiber tracked with Norm for the rest of the young soldier's year of duty in Vietnam. He was a good dog, if not up to Cass's manic standard.

Though there was one curious thing.

At that time, the dogs worked in pairs, one taking over partway through a track to give the other a rest. At least, they were supposed to. When Cassius was alive, however, Justin never led. He'd only go a few metres, then stop. Cassius was top dog, and he should lead. Yet as soon as Cass died, Justin became top dog and from then on tracked perfectly with Tiber.

Poor Tiber suffered more than his fair share of war wounds.

As each Australian battalion went home, new handlers from the incoming unit took over the dogs. Thus, Tiber was with 1 RAR when it was attacked at a fire support base, known as 'Coral', by Viet Cong and North Vietnamese forces in May 1968.

The dog was lying with his handler in a shallow earth scrape when they came under heavy mortar and rocket attack at half past three in the morning. The fury of battle was horrifying.

Tiber was usually pretty good in a fight. But this was different. The night was lit with gun flashes, exploding shells and automatic-weapon fire. A mortar platoon and a gun pit were overrun. And although the enemy retreated after three hours, nine Australians were dead and many others wounded.

Tiber had also gone.

A rocket-propelled grenade had burst only a few feet from his shelter. The terrified dog slipped his lead and fled into a nearby rubber plantation. An officer tried to stop him, but too late. Although Tiber returned the following afternoon, he was badly shell-shocked. Shaking and very nervous.

He also developed a peculiar characteristic. Every afternoon around five o'clock, Tiber put on a short display of aggression. He never attacked people or other dogs, but he'd grab a cushion or his own blanket, and give it a good shake for five minutes.

Tiber never really worked much after Coral. Other tracker dogs took his place . . . Janus, Julian, Milo, Trajan and the rest. Tiber spent most of his time at Nui Dat, becoming pretty much the task-force pet. Occasionally, however, he went out with men into the scrub – and it was there that Tiber was wounded. The enemy detonated a claymore mine and a bit of shrapnel lodged in his back.

Faithful Tiber was promoted to sergeant and retired from active service. In mid-1970 he was honourably discharged from the army altogether, and went to live with an Australian family, Ros and Gordon Selleck, attached to the embassy in Saigon. Their house had been burgled and they were looking for a guard dog. So Sergeant Tiber moved in, with two Vietnam service ribbons on his collar.

He may not have been the most assertive guard dog (apart from his five o'clock stunt with the cushions). He was friendly and gentle, slept on the family bed and had his shrapnel wound bathed with salt water. But there were no more robberies.

'Tiber was a dear, very much treasured family pet,' Ros remembers him. Sometimes he even went to play with old friends.

For the ten tracker dogs were all found homes with western diplomatic or professional families in Saigon. However much their handlers may have wanted to take the dogs back to Australia – whatever the public pressure to bring them home – neither the army nor the government seriously considered doing so.

It was to leave a scar on the memories of all who loved them.

MARCUS

'Have you ever seen a dog cry?'

Denis Ferguson's mind goes back to that day in 1970, when he walked to the Nui Dat dog kennels at the start of his second tour in Vietnam, and saw his mate Marcus, forlornly looking the other way.

'I gave *my* whistle. Marcus stood up. I gave him my whistle again. And he turned around. Have you ever seen a dog cry? Well, Marcus was crying. But so was I.'

Many handlers returned to Vietnam for a second stint, but it seems Denis was the only one to have the same dog both times. 1967–68. 1970–71. Forty-five years later, the emotion of their reunion is as palpable as the pain when they were forced to part again.

Denis took great risks to bring Marcus home. But no go. Like all the trackers, he stayed behind.

The champion black Labrador had once belonged to Sir Roden Cutler VC, Governor of New South Wales. But the dog, then called Tim, was rather stroppy with the Government House guests. So he was given to the army, renamed Marcus, and handed over to Tracking Wing because his retrieving instincts were so good. Denis first met him with Sir Roden in front of a television camera.

The two often trained together, and went to Vietnam with Caesar and his handler, Peter Haran. A Labrador-kelpie-cross, Caesar had come from a pound: the wrong side of town. He'd never *seen* Government House! But as a tracker, he was the best. Always

went at a steady pace – no bulldozing through the scrub for him.
And his point was unerring.

Every dog has its own signal or 'point' to indicate where the
quarry is hiding. Sometimes it's just a fleeting backward glance, but
always the handler *knows*.

Even Marcus forgot to point once, and Denis found himself
with an enemy rifle at his chest. The man with the rifle had just died,
otherwise Ferguson and half his tracking team might have died as well.
For punishment, he threatened to push Marcus from the chopper.

'If you fail to point again, you bastard, out you go!'

Perhaps Marcus liked riding in the helicopter too much: flying
above country, and the rush of wind as he was winched down to a
track. Whatever it was, Marcus never failed to point again. He'd
stop and turn to Denis, and the bond between man and dog became
instinctive.

When Marcus once kept pointing at a group of bushes, yet no
one was found behind them, Denis knew there had to be something.
Sure enough, several bamboo sticks poking up from the soil turned
out to be the air vents of an underground enemy hospital.

And when Marcus started zigzagging as he crossed open country, Denis realised the dog had tracked them into a minefield. The
enemy had known exactly where to step. There was nothing for it
but to stop. Turn around. Pick up Marcus. And for each man to follow his own footprints back to the road.

Afterwards, they learned it was one of the bigger minefields
found in the province, and a man had been killed clearing it. Though
as one section leader, Ian Atkinson, observed: the list of Australians
who died in Vietnam (some 521, in the end) would have been a lot
longer had it not been for the warnings of their tracker dogs.

Danger ahead.

A tracker team commander, Bob Bettany, once refused to heed Trajan's point and followed his enemy straight into a creek. Bob was out of there in a flash, and gave Trajan a little hug. 'I'm sorry.'

So the bonds grew ever closer. Often, back at Nui Dat, men went out of their way to walk past the kennels, to see the dogs. To pat them (though petting wasn't allowed in the field). To give them a biscuit (though only their handlers fed them outside). To hear them barking (though they were supposed to never bark on patrol). To get a sense of the normal again. Of home. After the day's killing.

So that when it was time to return to Australia, the wrench of parting from the dogs was acute. Many tried to persuade the brass to let the trackers come too. Always they were refused, though rarely were any substantial reasons given.

Official replies talked vaguely of the time and cost involved in sending the dogs to Britain for a year's quarantine. But when Garry Polglase, who handled Julian, was accidentally killed, and a public appeal raised enough funds to return all ten remaining dogs, the government still said no. There were hints the dogs might have some unknown tropical disease – though they were regularly treated for rabies and parasites, and went to the US vets for their health checks.

The decision appears to have been taken quite early to give the dogs to western families then living in Vietnam. The mindset was fixed against bringing any animal back from Australia's overseas wars; and it was all too much trouble to change it.

In Denis Ferguson's case, he coped well enough when he said goodbye to Marcus for the first time. But the second time . . .

'I went through the proper channels to bring him home. They said it would cost 700 dollars. I said, "Right, look in my pay book, the money's there." But the only answer I got a couple of days later was no. No explanations. It just came down to my sergeant saying,

"Your request is refused. The dog stays." '

Ferguson was so upset that shortly before his troopship sailed he found himself going up to unit headquarters with a loaded rifle. As if *that* would persuade them.

'Two military policemen had been forewarned I was on my way. One of them just grabbed my rifle, took the magazine off, slipped the round out, put an empty magazine on the weapon and said, "Go home, soldier." That was it. They put me on a chopper and flew me from Nui Dat out to HMAS *Sydney*. I thought I was going to get court-martialled. But I heard no more about it.'

Even in the army, understanding can take many forms.

But leave the last word to Peter Haran, whose book *Trackers* tells the story of Caesar, perhaps the most accomplished of all the eleven Australian dogs who served in Vietnam:

'He was a mongrel from death row. He was saved and conscripted to serve his country. He asked for nothing but was asked to give everything. To the soldier the Vietnam War was like all wars – mateship and loss. Australians died in Vietnam, but no man was abandoned there. Caesar and his mates were.'

WILLY'S CURRY DINNER

Willy was a very large, extremely well fed black pig, one of two animal mascots of the then combined 5th/7th Battalion the Royal Australian Regiment. Like all his kind, Willy was exceedingly fond of his stomach, adored by his soldiers, and was only too happy to repay their generosity to him with his overflowing bounty to their enemies, as this story will show.

The principal mascot of 5/7 RAR was a tiger known as Quintus Septimus (Latin for fifth and seventh), who originally belonged to 5th Battalion – always known as the Tiger Battalion. Willy, in one of his various incarnations, was the mascot of 7th Battalion – the Pig Battalion.

The way it came about was this. When the 7th Battalion was first raised at Puckapunyal in Victoria towards the end of 1965, during the Vietnam War, the men used to keep the boozer open all weekend and have their meals there. Apparently it became pretty mucky. The new CO, Lieutenant-Colonel Eric Smith, made a surprise inspection one Sunday, closed the boozer, and called a muster parade for the next day. Where, referring to the state of the boozer, those present heard him say, 'You're nothing but a mob of pigs!' From the rear rank came the sound of somebody uttering 'oink, oink!' And from then on the Pig Battalion it was.

It's a nice example of how spontaneously these things come about, strengthening that sense of identity and esprit de corps so necessary in any military unit. As it also reinforces an underlying spirit of egalitarianism within the group: the irreverent antics of an animal mascot provide an important safety valve for the disciplines of military life.

The men of 7th Battalion certainly took to their nickname with much affection, though for a while the representations of a pig were limited to cartoons, statuettes and even stuffed toys. Not until they went to Vietnam on their first tour of duty in 1967 did they acquire a live pig mascot, Willy the First. By happy coincidence it was presented to Lieutenant-Colonel Smith by the CO of 5th Battalion (Tiger Five), which the 7th was relieving, for the two were then separate. The mascot was a small Vietnamese piglet, on which had been painted black tiger stripes. It was a 'tiger pig'!

Well, the Vietnam War came to an end – though the fate of Willy the First is not recorded – and in 1973 the two battalions were amalgamated to form 5/7 RAR. Which is the unit that several subsequent Willys came to serve so loyally, and the time when this story took place.

The battalion was then at Holsworthy Barracks near Sydney and usually had a pig of one sort or another about the place. They became the special favourites of the transport supervisor, Sergeant Dave Willis. He was the last remaining man in the battalion who'd served in Vietnam, and had quite an array of little pig souvenirs in his office. He still does, in retirement at home.

Sergeant Willis liked to drive around in his Land Rover with a pig mascot looking out the window like a pet dog, to the consternation of certain regimental sergeant majors. Others were too large for that pleasure. One pig, brought from a nearby farm to counter the tiger at a special parade, was so vast its body spilled over the back of the Land Rover. And yet it's said that at the parade it sat politely to attention on its bottom, just like a dog, tethered to somebody's leg, while the tiger yawned in its cage at the other end of the parade ground (though it later roared into life when the regimental pipes and drums started up).

Dave even once had a cook, who'd been a tailor in civilian life, make a full regimental evening suit for a young ginger pig recently given to him from up country: black trousers with a red stripe (and hole at the back for the tail), red cummerbund, white mess jacket with two Korean ribbons, and a black bow tie. Thus attired, the pig was released at the end of a farewell dinner for a Commanding Officer. It ran across the room, behind the CO who'd just finished speaking, and pissed all over the floor. They say there wasn't a dry eye in the place.

Such was Dave Willis's attachment to the animal mascots that one particularly large black pig with a bit of Berkshire in him – for he had a white leg and a blaze on his shoulder – was nicknamed Willis Secundus (the second Willis) in a parody, perhaps, of the Latin moniker affixed to the tiger.

In 1986–7, however, there was no pig in the 5/7 lines. The second in command at the time was Major Peter Leahy, eventually to become Lieutenant-General Leahy and Chief of Army. Among his responsibilities at that time was to pay the public liability insurance and appearance fee to a zoo for the stand-in tiger Quintus Septimus, then the battalion's only living mascot. It was expensive for a beast that was hardly ever seen on parade – and even then he was doped up in a cage on the back of a Land Rover, certainly never wandering free about the barracks.

Anyway, it wasn't an entirely satisfactory situation; but Major Leahy had the chance to rectify it on a visit to one of the 5/7 RAR companies undertaking a course at the Tully Combat Training Centre in North Queensland. On the last day there was a route march along the river, back to base camp, where Peter saw Rodney the Pig, the camp's mascot. Nearby was a pen full of small black bush piglets, rounded up and ready to be destroyed, for a shooter had a licence to kill the wild pigs that abound near Tully.

'I thought to myself: the 7th is the Pig Battalion, it doesn't have a mascot, how good is this?' Peter Leahy remembers with much good humour. 'I asked the pig man if we could have one of the piglets? "Yes, sure, I'm only going to shoot them." So we got a little cage – a birdcage or something – popped a piglet inside, and went to board the C130 Hercules transport plane that was to fly us home.'

Unfortunately it caused an 'enormous hullabaloo'. For one thing, the piglet hadn't formally joined the army and all mascots have to be enlisted before they can fly on military aircraft. An arrangement was hurriedly made with the regimental clerk, the piglet given a number, and they tried to bluff its way on board.

Even then there was a problem, for the pilot didn't want to carry black pigs in his plane. 'It's not getting on *here*!' But it's such a little thing, the major argued, surely it couldn't do any harm? Yet it appears that some time earlier the pilot had been airlifting a large black tusker that was a gift from Vanuatu to the people of Papua New Guinea. It was given a dose of valium and strapped down in the back of the plane. Sadly the sedative wasn't strong enough, though the boar *was*. It woke up half way through the flight, broke free of its bonds, and began rampaging about the transport plane.

'They say blokes were hanging off the cabin ceiling as this thing was running around,' Peter goes on. 'So that the pilot, remembering the incident, said the piglet from Tully was not coming aboard. He relented at last however, and we brought the little animal back to Holsworthy. People said, "What are we going to call it?" But I answered, "Let's not bother. Something organic will happen within the battalion, as it should, and it will get a name eventually."

'One of the regimental policemen said they should take it to Sergeant Willis. And you know, within a day or two this piglet was known to everyone as Willis Secundus.'

Of course. Another Willy.

'It became part of the battalion's life. It's one of those things with mascots. It gives a spirit and a kind of larrikinism to the battalion that is really important. As a senior officer in a battalion it's the sort of thing you like to see. Willy gave us a sense of identity. That bird [the wedge-tailed eagle now known as Warrant Officer Class 2 Courage, who we'll meet a little later on] was with 2nd Cavalry Regiment up the road. Willy is over with us roaming around, and he's growing. And growing. He grew to the size of a table. It was huge. Well, it kept going up to the kitchen and the cooks kept feeding him.'

The wild bush pigs are sometimes known as 'Captain Cookers' in northern Australia – as they are in New Zealand. It stems from a belief they're descended from black Tahitian pigs that escaped from Cook's ship *Endeavour* when it visited these shores in 1770. Whether that's so or not, Willy certainly developed a close relation-ship with the cooks of 5/7 RAR. He had one wallow by a creek behind the battalion football ground where he'd sometimes go at night – but his days were mostly centred on the kitchens, where he had another nice mud hole not far from the back door, within easy trotting distance of any food scraps that came his way. Which they did. Constantly.

And not just from the cooks. Like his predecessors, he'd often stand outside the diggers' mess, where Dave Willis recalls the men would throw a bag of chips out the window to the pig. He'd raise his hoof, break open the bag, and gobble the contents. He was partial to grazing among the flowerbeds planted around the buildings, much to the displeasure of the gardeners, some of whom had been known to chase him with a rake. And on a memorable occasion one of the Willys made his way through the scrub where a cross-country run was in progress and consumed the contents of a picnic hamper belonging to some of the spectators cheering on the runners. He ran *wee-wee-wee* all the way home.

Still, these were merely snacks. Breakfast was Willy's first hearty meal of the day, followed not long after by morning tea, which the young Willy from Tully frequently spent with his saviour and mentor, Major Leahy.

'He'd often come to the Headquarters building where my office was as 2IC,' Peter remembers, 'and stand patiently outside. It was usually around eleven o'clock, and the cooks often made us a chocolate cake. Well, I'd give Willy some cake which he'd wolf down, and then he'd lay down on his back. I had an old bass broom – a yard broom with stiff bristles – and would give him a rub on the tummy. He'd grunt with happiness, and then go out to the kitchen door and wait for lunch.'

You may ask, was there ever any risk the pig might try to escape? 'What . . . with chocolate cake for morning tea? What do you reckon? He enjoyed it!'

They were, however, sometimes fearful the 'hygiene wallahs' might come round and that the battalion would find itself in all sorts of trouble. Dave Willis recalls the medical corps made several attempts to remove the mascot pigs, all of which were resisted.

In the meantime Willy became the life and soul of the party. Apart from his informal meals, he'd sometimes attend battalion functions. Dave Willis once took Willy into the sergeants' mess, the pig wearing a bow tie because it was a formal occasion. He'd also go to the officers' mess, but Peter Leahy recalls that Willy generally stood at the door and wouldn't go in until he'd been offered a jug of 'Bundy and coke' for god's sake!

He even took part in those games of skill and daring that military officers sometimes play after a good mess dinner. One evening, visiting officer cadets from New Zealand and Victoria were invited to play indoor football. The room was cleared, a large tarpaulin put on the floor and sealed on two opposite sides by people standing on it. Two teams of five cadets crawled under the tarpaulin and a football was thrown in – the idea being to score a goal by forcing the football out the opposite open side. Trouble was, the officers threw in Willy as well . . . and then stood on all four sides of the canvas.

'There they were! A big black pig, a football and ten cadets sealed under the tarpaulin and they can't get out. It was so funny . . . people screaming and hollering and the pig snorting! We were falling about laughing. Honestly, I was almost physically ill with laughter. It was so good! This huge, powerful animal, and lazy as all get out . . .'

Nor was it just fun and games for Willy. He made his presence felt even at the most serious of regimental events. Peter goes on:

'One day we were having a battalion parade to award the champion company of the year – Delta Company, I think it was. Well, the pig rose out of the creek, marched across the footy ground and over the road to where we were on parade. Everyone was whispering "There's Willy . . ." and the CO trying to ignore the bloody thing. Anyway, he waddled almost in front of OC Delta Company, looked around, and planted the biggest shit you've ever seen. And everybody else thought, "Yep, that's what we reckon, too." '

Which of course is one of the purposes of a mascot like Willy. Not merely to represent the inner life and unity of a regiment, but also to act as a kind of jester in a medieval court: able to offer humorous and even ribald commentary on some of those petty irritations, nonsenses and disciplines of an establishment in a way its human members rarely can.

'The diggers loved Willy,' Peter Leahy recalls with immense satisfaction. 'I mean, his performance on parade is about as irreverent as you can get, isn't it?'

Yes, but not quite. There was better to come – although it's true that the best mascot stories generally revolve around bodily functions and other acts of nature. And this brings us to the incident of Willy's curry dinner. Precisely which one of the several Willys may be a matter for debate, for one legend often gets conflated with another: but the story stands in any event, as a triumph of its kind.

Now, the 3rd Battalion Royal Australian Regiment was quartered just across the road from 5/7 RAR at Holsworthy Barracks. As may have been gathered, whatever delight soldiers may take in their own mascots, they can have a certain contempt for the mascots of other units. It's all part of the identity game. And so it seems that the 3rd were no great admirers of the 7th Battalion's Willis Secundus. In fact, when Willy in his wanderings crossed the road from his own battalion into 3 RAR lines, he would sometimes be captured and subjected to indignities. He came back one day from the 3rd with parachute wings painted on his flanks – as if pigs might fly! The 3rd was then responsible for the army's conventional airborne forces capability and wore the parachute wings badge on their right arm, as they also wore the maroon beret of parachute units worldwide.

Late one afternoon Willy crossed the road into 'enemy lines' once too often, and was discovered eating the roses outside 3rd Battalion HQ. He was not only captured, he was arrested. Placed in the battalion cells. The clink. And warned that he'd be paraded before the CO next morning on a charge. Trespass, no doubt, if not theft.

It was getting towards dinner time and in the close confinement of the cells Willy was beginning to feel hungry. He began to grunt and to forage about. And finding nothing in the clink to eat, made it known to his guards that he was missing the kitchen door.

At length someone at 3 RAR rang 5/7 RAR to advise that they had their pig in prison, that Willy was facing a charge, and would be brought before punishment parade – defaulters – next day.

Then he added, 'By the way, he looks hungry, what should we feed him?'

As it happened, the 5/7 man knew something about pigs. And being not only fond of Willy but anxious, like any soldier, to rescue a mate fallen into enemy hands, replied that there was one thing he liked above anything else.

'What's that?' asked the 3 RAR chap, as if taking an order for a condemned man's last meal.

'Curry,' replied Willy's pal, knowing full well that the dish is a powerful pig enema. 'He loves curry.'

'Right-oh. I'll tell the cooks.'

'Thanks.'

So that night Willy was fed a large bucket of curry and rice. And then nature set to work.

They say the cells were inches deep in pig excrement. Dave Willis, with precise military analogy, says the curry went through Willy 'like Sherman going through Georgia'. It took days to clean the place out. General Leahy said the rumour was that a fire hose was used to do the job. And Dave Willis adds that, 'Any poor bastard who got arrested and placed in the 3 RAR cells had to put up with the stink for months.'

Willy was immediately freed from incarceration and hastily escorted under guard back across the road. Apparently 3 RAR never apprehended him again.

Free at last! Free at last! And the rejoicing from his soldiers at 5/7 RAR was long and loud.

'We all thought: Willy won that round.' Peter Leahy still laughs at the memory. 'It doesn't get any better than that.'

Recent Conflicts

1990–2017

In recent years, Australian forces have been engaged in a number of smaller wars and military peace-keeping operations.

Our servicemen and women took part in the Gulf War (1990–91) following Iraq's invasion of Kuwait. Australian forces returned to the region in 2003 as part of the 'coalition of the willing' to overthrow the regime of Saddam Hussein in Iraq.

The armed services were also involved with the international coalition that overthrew the Taliban government in Afghanistan in 2001 as part of the 'war against terrorism'. Some units were still there in 2016, making it the longest Australian involvement in any war.

Australian peace-keeping forces have also helped deliver humanitarian aid to Rwanda and Somalia (1993), and a larger deployment went to East Timor in 1999, following that country's popular vote for independence from Indonesia. Civil and military forces have also served peace-keeping roles on Bougainville (1997) and in Solomon Islands (2003).

CORPORAL COURAGE

Goes AWOL

Corporal Courage was in trouble. After ten years' exemplary service as a mascot with the 2nd Cavalry Regiment, the wedge-tailed eagle had finally chucked in the army. He'd had enough. Taken wing. And gone Absent Without Leave.

It happened late one November afternoon in 1997 after his regular training session. Six times he'd flown around the parade ground at his Darwin barracks. High in the air one moment – then swoop down to perch on his handler's glove, with a mouse to eat as reward. Talons sharp. Feathers folded. Eagle eyes aglitter. The very essence of strength and invincibility.

They'd just finished, and were heading back to the mascot's cage, when a newspaper photographer arrived.

'You're too late,' said the handlers. 'Corporal Courage has done his work for the day. He's tired. He's on his way to bed.'

'Please. Just one shot of him in the air. My editor expects it.'

So they turned and went back to the parade ground. But the eagle was indeed getting tired. Tired of the army telling him what to do. Tired of other people always making up his mind for him.

Bugger this, he might well have thought to himself. And as he took flight, Corporal Courage resolved that this time he wasn't coming back. Mouse or no mouse. The army could stick it. He would be free. At liberty to do whatever he wanted, for the first time since joining up as a fledgling.

Higher he rose, his great black wings beating. But, rather than make the usual circuit, Courage spied a good stretch of bushland a few kilometres off, and headed for that instead.

On the ground his handlers were shouting, waving their arms and making all kinds of threats if he didn't return at once.

'What's going on?' asked the photographer. 'What's the eagle doing?'

'He's absconding,' cried the chief handler. 'Going AWOL. I'll *bust* him when I find him.'

But Corporal Courage took no notice of that. No more orders and people pulling rank on him. He was going to please no one but himself from now on, and live as the wild eagles do.

Of course he was in trouble with the military. He knew he'd blemished his service record. But who cared? How exciting it would be to hunt his own food. How delightful to build his own nest. Perhaps to raise his own family. To look after himself for once, instead of the army taking care of his every need – bed, board and lodging – and making every decision for him.

Courage spread his wings and rode the wind down to the bush, whistling for sheer joy.

Matters were not so pleasant at the barracks.

His handlers were in a fine temper, their weekend ruined. They'd been planning a fishing trip. Now they'd have to organise a search party to hunt for an eagle who'd done a bunk. Blast Corporal Courage! They'd rip his stripes off him. The bird could be anywhere up to forty kilometres away.

Actually, he was much closer than that. He'd found a tall gum tree in the nearby scrub and roosted on an upper branch to collect his wits after the sudden escape. What fun. What next?

Evening was drawing in quickly, as it does in the tropics. Corporal Courage certainly felt a little peckish; but after the titbits of mice at the parade ground, he wasn't exactly hungry. Perhaps wait until tomorrow to start hunting. Besides, he was in a strange place, and didn't know his way about. Better to stay where he was.

The shadows deepened. Night fell. And there was no moon.

At the barracks, the first search party returned after a fruitless hour looking for the wretched bird. They'd try again tomorrow.

Perched in his gum tree, surrounded by the night noises, Corporal Courage was feeling a little insecure. The sounds were not unfamiliar. Possums moving. Owls calling. The rustle of nocturnal creatures through the bush. He heard them every night. It's just that there was always a wire cage between him and the outside world. In this new environment, Courage felt somewhat exposed.

He needn't have worried. Wedge-tailed eagles have a charisma of their own. Most wild things know enough to leave them alone – although it's true small birds, like rainbow lorikeets, sometimes hopped into his cage, where he'd swoop down for a snack . . .

Corporal Courage spent a fitful night dreaming about them.

When morning came, a posse of thirty soldiers gathered to continue the search further out. They drove straight past the bit of bush near the barracks where they sometimes exercised. Nobody gave it a second thought. The bird would be well away by now.

Courage watched them go. He stretched his wings and thought about breakfast. He was really feeling quite hungry.

Yet catching something to eat wasn't as easy as the wild birds made it appear. For no one had ever taught Courage how to hunt. It was one thing to pounce on the little birds that strayed into his cage. But it was quite another thing to learn how to hover silently in the sky – to spot likely prey – and to know the precise moment at which to swoop and seize it. The exact speed, momentum, angle and direction needed for a successful kill.

Such things require experience, which this eagle didn't have. There'd been no need for it. Courage was only six weeks old when recruited as a trooper, and since then the army had provided his every meal: mice, rats, ox tail and the occasional dead snake found by the roadside. All delivered fresh, every other day, to his cage door. He didn't know how to get them for himself.

Still, instinct is a powerful thing. The bird rose, circling into the morning air, his wings catching the updrafts, and borne aloft by the wind currents. His powerful head moved slowly from side to side, his eyes searching the landscape beneath him.

The world was not as full of edible prey as army rations had led Corporal Courage to imagine. For hours he watched, scarcely seeing a thing to eat: and even when he did, the result was a farce. Breakfast turned into lunchtime. It was heading towards dinner, and still the bird was hungry.

There was something! Some small, furry animal was scuttling through the grassland. The eagle stalled. Turned. Waited a moment. Then began his plunge with talons at the ready. Rabbit for tea.

Unfortunately, he still had the short leather jess straps, with which the handler held him, attached to his legs. They dangled and twirled in the downward rush, making a faint whistling sound. Corporal Courage was going too fast anyway, and the sun was behind him. His shadow passed across the earth. The rabbit sensed the danger and quickly decamped.

Missed again.

This pathetic performance was repeated throughout the afternoon. As the search party returned at dusk, Courage flew back to his gum tree. They were all hungry. No one had anything to show for their day's work.

The eagle cursed his clumsiness. Perhaps there was something to be said for army life after all, where wholesome meals were served on time and without so much fuss and bother.

So Corporal Courage passed his second night of freedom.

He woke early next morning, ravenous. Those dreams of beefsteaks and little birds in his cage at home had been only too vivid. Long before the search party set out again, the eagle was up and looking for breakfast. But once again his hunting was as unsuccessful as the soldiers'. Worse, hunger became overlaid with fears for his own safety.

Banks of monsoon clouds had begun to gather on the horizon. Corporal Courage heard the rumble of distant thunder. The wet season was approaching; and while that carried the promise of plentiful food supplies, it also brought new dangers.

Every year a pair of dominant wild eagles migrated north to breed during the wet, and the barracks were in the middle of their territory. They were well aware that Courage also lived there – and nature allowed for no competition in these matters.

Often they'd land on top of his cage, whistling their warnings and tearing at the green shade cloth with hooked beaks and talons, trying to get at him. Of course they couldn't break through the wire, but the mascot knew the wild eagles would kill him if they had the chance. It was always a stressful time.

Now, in the open, there was no stout cage to protect him. To be sure, Corporal Courage had his freedom – but his enemies were also at liberty to attack him. And military theory holds that two against one are generally assured of success.

The mascot's courage began to fail. At last, he flew back to the gum tree without having had any breakfast, lunch or afternoon tea for a second day. He sat dejected on the branch, feeling as if his throat were already cut. Even those soldiers' woollen berets and canvas gloves he'd chewed over the years would be tasty now.

His head bent low. Wings folded around him. Thinking . . . wondering . . . wishing . . .

Perhaps the army wasn't *such* a bad life. It was all the eagle had known. His handlers provided for him – and the only thing they asked in return was for Courage to behave himself on show. To sit beautifully, in full plumage, on the mascot's stand (known as 'Eagle Rock') during ceremonial occasions. To fly proudly from one side of the ground to the other after parade every Thursday. To be nice to photographers, and not go AWOL during training flights.

It wasn't a lot to ask. For ten years, the bird had done just that: rising swiftly through the ranks from trooper to lance-corporal to corporal – and hoped to become a sergeant, just like his predecessor.

She had been a big girl – twice the size of the male – who had served as a mascot for twenty years. She had even met the Queen. And when the eagle died unexpectedly one weekend in 1987, they popped her in the freezer, then had her mounted and displayed in a warlike attitude for everyone to see outside the regimental sergeant-major's office.

That was something! The unhappy bird, sitting on the gum tree, might even have aspired to it himself, one day. If only he were still there. Plaintively, in the late afternoon, Corporal Courage began to whistle his regrets and wish that his luck might change.

It did.

Some of the search party, almost giving up hope of finding the mascot, decided to have a quick look through that bit of bushland on their return. There wasn't much chance he'd be there, but still . . .

They heard the sad sound of the eagle whistling. Stopped. Looked up. And there he was.

A handler held out something to eat. The fattest, juiciest, sweetest, most succulent mouse Corporal Courage had ever seen.

With a shrill cry of delight he swooped down, gobbled it up, and sat on the handler's glove (his jess straps firmly held), with a look of pure happiness on his face.

Naturally, when they returned to barracks, Corporal Courage was charged with having gone AWOL and faced a court martial. Some thought the punishment severe: his stripes removed; reduced to the ranks; and put in the clink for seven days. He had indeed been busted.

The eagle, however, couldn't thank the army enough. He'd show them in future what a well-behaved mascot could do. He'd soon get his stripes back again.

And as for the clink – well, Courage felt that freedom could be overrated. He was perfectly content to stay in his cage. It was safe. Airy. Sheltered. Had nice views. Enough room to stretch his wings for a bit of a flap. And the food kept on coming.

Trooper Courage didn't care if he never left it again.

IT'S WARRANT OFFICER COURAGE NOW!

Time flies – and so do eagles – and chastened by his demotion to the ranks after absconding, Courage resolved to be a better bird.

Happy to say, he succeeded. He rose through the ranks again . . . and ten years on from the first edition of *Animal Heroes*, Courage is now Warrant Officer Class 2. It's the highest rank to which any mascot may aspire, just one step below WO Class 1, the most senior non-commissioned officer level. And it is surely an appropriate military position for any creature of presence and ability to occupy. After all, everybody knows that warrant officers run the army.

Mind you, Courage has not been faultless during this time – and was even quite insubordinate on occasion.

In 2005, not long before he launched the first edition of this book, the then Chief of Army, Lieutenant-General Peter Leahy, was visiting the 2nd Cavalry Regiment in Darwin, and naturally was introduced to Sergeant Courage (as he had then become). Who proceeded to peck his Chief on the finger with a sharp and predatory beak. It hurt. That bloody bird . . . !

There was every chance he'd be sent back to the ranks again. Courage was indeed formally charged with assaulting a superior officer and appeared before a military tribunal. But counsel pleaded leniency on his behalf, and after careful deliberation it was decided instead to issue him with a severe reprimand and a fine of seven days rats and mice. No beefsteak for a whole week.

Since then Courage has behaved more or less as he ought. Certainly he's not had to face any further disciplinary proceedings – and in November 2010 he was promoted to his present exalted status.

He's also had to get used to a change of habitat. In late 2014 he moved with the 2nd Cavalry Regiment from Darwin to the Lavarack Barracks at Townsville, and a new and much larger cage in the 'Waler' lines. The name is a nice reminder of the regiment's origins with the Australian Light Horse: even today when the cavalry soldiers wear their slouch hats (as opposed to the usual black berets) they're adorned with emu feathers. The sturdy Walers the light horsemen rode, however, have long ago been replaced with vehicles: tanks, Australian Light Armoured Vehicles (ASLAVs) and armoured personnel carriers (APCs).

Yet the original functions of the cavalry remain: its capacity to move quickly across a battlefield, to undertake reconnaissance and surveillance, to engage in rapid attack. It's the reason the regiment chose a powerful eagle mascot. And hence Courage's regular duties, when the regiment is at home, are to spend much of the time supervising his soldiers at work about the base, as any responsible warrant officer should.

As one of his handlers, Lance-Corporal Joseph Blundell, points out, the daily routine of Courage is pretty unchanging, as it usually is with the military. Up at reveille and taken down to the parade ground for a breakfast flight by his two weekly handlers. The area's not really large enough for many full regimental parades, although the eagle's formal parade-ground training is kept up.

At the command 'Fly mascot!' Courage takes off from a gloved hand at one end of the arena and flies to the other end where a handler stands with a piece of meat – mouse, rat or small piece of beefsteak – on his glove. Lands. Consumes it. And flies from there to his stand – another 'Eagle Rock' – at the side of the parade ground. Until 'Fly mascot!' and he's off again. And so on until breakfast is eaten.

Sometimes he'll fly free, sometimes on a long tether rope attached to the leather jesses on his legs. It depends on the handlers and the weather. Lance-Corporal Blundell says Courage hasn't absconded again – except once, when he flew off for a few kilometres. No doubt remembering his earlier experience of going AWOL, however, Courage quickly flew home again.

'After flying, he goes with his handlers to wherever they're working about the base,' Joey says. 'If they're working in the compound with the vehicles, as we mostly are, he'll go and sit with them all day on his portable stand, tethered by a short chain on his leg. Actually, we've had to get a special lock for the chain, because he learned to pick the old one and fly away. Sometimes if we have to go to a regimental meeting, he'll come and stand at the back of the room. And sometimes if we have to go to another unit on the base for a lesson or lecture, Courage will come too. A guy went to a dental appointment one day, and Courage went with him. Don't know how much courage the dentist needed . . . He's even been to the Rugby League. Courage is a strong supporter of the Townsville Cowboys, and is an honorary member.'

Courage certainly has a lot to teach them about flying tackles.

His outings are not just about the workplace and the footy, he also makes an occasional visit to see friends at the Billabong Sanctuary. When the regiment moved from Darwin to Townsville, Courage stayed at the enclosure with Bob Flemming and his staff for a couple of months while his own new quarters were being built. The Sanctuary still helps out with Courage's food supplies, and in return the 2nd Cavalry Regiment bird handlers have been helping to train Billabong's male wedge-tailed eagle, called Thunder, to come to the glove and be rather more amenable around human visitors. Thunder's temperament was fairly stormy to begin with, as his name implies; but he's now much better with people, and indeed Bob Flemming says he's also 'hitting it off' with Courage.

Courage's own disposition can vary from day to day, as with most of us. 'He gets along fine with Thunder,' Joey Blundell observes. 'In fact Courage is pretty good with most other birds. A lot of them try to annoy him – plovers and that, and magpies are the worst for swooping. But Courage is top of the food chain in bird world, and he doesn't much care about other birds. Sometimes a silly wagtail will get into his cage . . . and get out again. Though some mornings we'll go in and there are rainbow lorikeet feathers everywhere . . .

'Still, he can be moody. He doesn't like a *lot* of people, but he likes being *around* people, if that makes sense.' (It does.) 'He's okay to sit on his stand for hours, though sometimes he'll get really angry if people try to tease him . . . to stare him down. He'll spread his wings as if about to jump and attack. At other times anyone can go up and pat him. And sometimes, you know, he's really sooky. He comes up, and you pat him, and he'll snuggle into you . . . And then he can be tired and crazy, and start wanting to do stuff . . . throwing his dog toys around. Like anyone else.'

There's one thing they're having a little trouble with, and that is to engage Courage's amorous emotions. He has been introduced to a female wedge-tailed eagle at the Billabong Sanctuary known as Aurora, after the Roman goddess of the dawn. She apparently seems quite interested in *him* – but to date Courage is not very much interested in *her*. Perhaps he's lived by himself for too long. He celebrated his twenty-ninth birthday in August 2016 at a party with his handlers and a beefsteak birthday cake.

Still, it's to be hoped some wedge-tailed goddess lights up his dawn fairly soon. The species can live to some forty years, and this warrant officer is getting on.

SIMPSON

Afghanistan, 2002

Simpson was feeling hungry. So were his friends – Murphy, Roy and HG. They'd had a hard day of it, out with the Australian special forces in Afghanistan. It's a tough, mountainous country, ravaged by war and poverty. Soldiers operating in the arid hills have to take everything with them, carrying heavy loads.

Now, back in the Australian compound at the Bagram Air Base, the four friends had time to relax off duty: to rest awhile in the shade, and turn their minds to food.

They'd already had a long drink and a few nibbles – slices of apple and carrot, to sharpen the appetite. Simpson was looking forward to his meal. He even became a little impatient and stamped his foot. So did Murphy, Roy and HG. Surely it was dinnertime.

Yes! There was the bell, and there were the men making their way to the mess. Simpson and his mates joined them, and went inside – four grey donkeys, taking their places in the canteen queue.

They were always assured of the soldiers giving them something to eat: fruit, veg, and salad. They'd even help themselves to a bread roll from the plates if men weren't quick enough. The donkeys pretty much had the run of the place. Originally they'd been bought as pack animals, but soon turned into camp pets.

When the Australians joined international forces to overthrow

the Taliban regime in Afghanistan, as part of the war against terrorism, they naturally took the latest military technology with them:
motor transport, armed patrol vehicles, and so on. Yet the troops
also found a use for donkeys: those sturdy, dependable beasts of
burden that people have been using in that part of the world since
time immemorial.

The donkeys helped the special forces to blend into the surrounding landscape, but they also had a more practical purpose.

The mountains around Bagram rise sheer from the valley floor.
At least in the early stages of their deployment, the Australians
had trouble getting heavy supplies into the hills using four-wheel
vehicles. So they bought the four sure-footed donkeys from local
farmers, to help carry their gear up the steep, stony slopes.

The donkeys must have thought all their birthdays had come
at once. Life in Afghanistan is hard and unremitting for man and
beast. Even at the best of times, donkeys labour long in the fields
and on the roadways, often overburdened, overworked, and under-
fed. Where human existence is precarious, and there are more sticks
than carrots, the welfare of animals is not generally a high priority.

Thus, when the four donkeys were led down the road from
Bagram village, through the gates and into the Australian compound known as 'The Ranch', they entered a life of comparative
ease.

Weekly supplies of hay were bought in for them, though they
quickly learned to accept fruit and other titbits from the soldiers.
They came to expect it. Men enjoying a quiet snack often found
themselves nudged by a donkey muzzle. *What about some for me?*

Stables were set up in one of the buildings, but the donkeys wandered more or less where they liked around the air base. Even into
the soldiers' own barracks. More than once was a sleeping soldier,

peacefully dreaming of home and loved ones, woken by the wet kiss of a donkey standing beside his bed.

Such familiarities were not always welcomed and cries of, 'Get out of it, you mongrel!' echoed through the place from time to time.

Yet, on the whole, the donkeys quickly became an accepted part of daily life. And the bond of undemanding affection that so often exists between soldiers and their animals established itself.

The donkeys were given names, which were written on their headbands. Simpson was medium grey and Murphy was one of the two lighter grey animals – called after the celebrated man of Gallipoli and his donkey, who we met earlier in this book.

The other two were named after the well-known Australian comedy duo. Roy was the second light-coloured donkey. HG was quite dark. He was the bossy one – the one who tried to keep the others in order. If another donkey was ahead of him in the canteen queue, HG often kicked him out of the way and took his place.

And the bossy one was often the leader when the donkeys were tethered together by their leading reins and set off in a line to work. They each had a pair of large saddle bags, in military camouflage, loaded with supplies and slung over their backs.

During the early part of the deployment they could be away in the mountains for several days at a stretch. But as time went by, and the forces became better established, there was less demand upon the donkeys as carriers. For really heavy loads, the locals use mules or camels – and the Australians didn't acquire any of those.

So Simpson, Murphy, Roy and HG spent much of their time about The Ranch. They even had their portraits painted.

An Australian artist, Peter Churcher, spent several weeks at Bagram painting scenes around the air base for the Australian War Memorial. He noticed the four donkeys at once: intrigued by the fact that, even in this age of high-tech warfare, the little animals were still part of military life.

One of the soldiers who cared for the donkeys was soon returning to Australia. Home beckoned, but he wasn't looking forward to saying goodbye to Simpson, Murphy, Roy and HG. So he asked Peter if he was going to paint the donkeys.

When the artist replied that he would, the soldier smiled.

'They're my little project,' he said. 'I look after them, feed and water them at the end of each day. I'm attached to them, and would be very pleased to see them in one of your paintings.'

It was quite touching. And Peter went one better than that. He not only painted Simpson, standing with his saddle bags at the hitching rail under the courtyard trees, he also included the soldier who cared for him. It's now in the AWM collection.

In fact, the artist did two paintings of the donkeys. On his final day Peter used the last of his paints, mixed with olive oil from the kitchen, to do a picture of Murphy and Roy kitted up with all their military gear. It's now hanging in the artist's own studio.

Peter Churcher remembers the donkeys as amusing, gentle creatures, with a lot of character, and treated with much affection and respect.

'If you were sitting down, drinking water or eating a piece of fruit, suddenly you'd feel a warm, fuzzy nose prodding you on the arm. This donkey would be just standing there. They weren't skittish – more like big dogs. I kept wondering what was going to happen to them at the end of it all . . .'

As it turned out, when the Australians partially withdrew in 2002, the donkeys were traded for some fine Afghani rugs. The rugs were sold to raise money for the SAS Trust Fund, which helps the families of deceased soldiers. The donkeys were probably sold back to the farmers. No doubt, having been so well cared for by the special forces, Simpson, Murphy, Roy and HG fetched a good price.

They were pretty special themselves. Not all donkeys in Afghanistan get their portraits painted, or have had the chance to line up in a canteen queue when the dinner bell rings.

DOLPHIN PATROL

Iraq, 2003

A bottlenose dolphin called Makai, trained by the US Navy, dived through the murky waters of the port at Umm Qasr, ready to place a marker beside what instinct told him could be a dangerous mine.

His grey body flipped easily through the fast-flowing current, the marker float attached to a special device on his nose. He was going to place it on the seabed next to the target. And although the water was dirty, his in-built sonar echo location guided him surely to the spot.

Click, click, click. His echo bounced off the sea floor, telling Makai what was there.

Click, click, click. Yes, that's a rock. Quite safe. Part of my marine world. Over there was a rusty anchor. Harmless.

Click, click, click. An old car body has been dumped here in the harbour. I think it's okay, though someone will have to check it later.

Click, click, click. That was it! Not just a strange metal object, but the particular sound of the echo suggested it could also contain explosives. That it was a mine.

Deeper Makai dived, with his marker buoy.

It hadn't been easy for any naval mine clearance diver – human or animal – to work at Umm Qasr. The water is thick with silt washed down by the Tigris and Euphrates rivers into the Persian

Gulf. And the harbour has had so much junk tipped into it over the years that the business of inspecting all of it for mines had been extremely time consuming.

It took three days for the joint US, Australian and British diving team to clear a berth for the ship *Sir Galahad*, and another fortnight to completely clear the port of the mines laid by the former regime of Saddam Hussein.

During the search one of Makai's eight dolphin companions, Takoma, became so distracted that he took off for a few days' recreation up the coast. It didn't amuse his human colleagues. There they were in the middle of a tough operation, and he went AWOL.

But Makai and the others stayed on duty, working with their handlers in the sectors being cleared by US divers. While conditions were such that the dolphins perhaps couldn't perform at their peak, Australian and British divers who saw them were still impressed at the way they'd been trained to act as sensors to detect and mark potential underwater mines. Divers examined over one hundred objects at Umm Qasr, of which forty had been marked by the dolphins.

Within the range of their abilities, the highly intelligent marine mammals are very good at what they do. They've been part of the US defence program for more than fifty years, and have given a whole new dimension to the idea of animals in war. Dolphins are used to mark suspected mines. Sea lions are trained to put electronic tags on enemy divers. Pilot whales and belugas help recover dummy torpedoes from the ocean depths.

Of course, marine creatures can't distinguish between friendly humans and enemies. What they do is alert their handlers to the presence of a potential target. It's up to the handlers to decide what to do next.

So it was with Makai at the port of Umm Qasr.

His biological sonar, or echo location, led him to this metal object in the water. And *click, click, click*, the particular sound of the echo suggested it might be a mine.

Makai fixed the spot in his memory and swam back to the surface. He rose near the rubber raft where his handler awaited him, the dolphin's head lifting clear of the water.

Click, click, click. His handler got the picture. Makai was telling him there was a possible target below.

The man took the specially designed marker device and fitted it over the end of Makai's long nose. It was made out of yellow plastic, and looked a bit like a gas mask or one of those chewy things that big dogs like. In fact, the marker was sometimes called a 'dog bone'.

'Off you go.'

Makai dived again. Down, down, down, swimming powerfully through the murky current.

Click, click, click. There it was.

The dolphin quickly manoeuvred himself and dived to the sea floor, where he placed the device in the mud and sand next to the possible mine. Then, with a strong, twisting movement, he withdrew from the section attached to his nose. The buoy broke free and floated to the surface attached to a line.

Later, a human diver would know exactly where to go to determine if the object was a mine and, if so, disarm it. Of the hundred objects inspected in the water at Umm Qasr, four turned out to be live mines. Many other mines were found ashore in storage.

As for Makai, he swam back to the surface and bobbed up beside the raft where his handler was waiting. Mission accomplished.

He received his fish as a reward. As with every animal trained to perform, it's all a game. The reward is everything.

So it went through the long day. One dive after another, as little by little the human and dolphin navy divers cleared their section of the harbour at Umm Qasr.

At the end of his shift, Makai swam casually beside his handler's raft back to the wharf. Sometimes he was so tired he even flipped himself onto the raft to hitch a ride.

Once ashore, Makai was loaded into a sling on the back of a truck, and driven to the dolphins' enclosures not far from the harbour. Tanks of good, clean water, with plenty of fish to eat, and a vet to check his health.

Here he could spend the night socialising with his mates (even Takoma, who'd just come home from his little AWOL sojourn up the coast). And then to sleep, until morning . . .

. . . when Makai returned to duty, as a full-time Mine Hunting Marine Mammal System, on active service with the naval divers in the Persian Gulf.

SNAPPA

Gets promoted

Lance-Corporal Soult-Walter Crock, affectionately known as 'Snappa', was due for another stripe. Promotion to full corporal.

She'd been enlisted into the army as a saltwater crocodile mascot at the age of only four. And no one could say she hadn't performed her duties since then with ferocious determination.

For the first few years of service, Snappa lived with her soldiers – in a compound at the 102 Field Workshop in Townsville, North Queensland. She was still fairly small, as crocodiles go, and of the lowest rank. But her efficiencies soon showed, and Snappa was promoted to lance-corporal. Her first stripe.

Snappa certainly kept people up to the mark when she appeared at the workshop. No slacking then! And on parade, it was a marvel how everyone snapped to attention in her presence.

For Snappa grew in stature. Ever larger, as crocodiles do. She not only kept her soldiers *on* their toes, she started to snap *at* those toes. Hopes of further promotion were delayed when she had a go at the brigade commander. High time that Snappa transferred to quarters better suited to her size and temperament.

So the engineers built her a new and secure pen at Billabong Sanctuary, just down the road from the barracks. Snappa moved in around 1988, and soon found herself attracted to a very large male crocodile called Weipa. She also discovered a new role, as a mother. Between them, the two produced hundreds – if not thousands – of offspring over the years. Crocodiles are very prolific.

Still, Snappa kept her military associations. She was rather too big and undisciplined to go on parade any more (2.5 metres long, weighing one hundred kilograms, and still growing). But whenever a mascot was needed for ceremonial purposes, the crocodile allowed one of her small sons – 'Barry Crocka' – to be her deputy.

They once took him to a mess night, his mouth taped to prevent snapping tendencies, and passed him around. Barry took his mess duties seriously. He became overexcited and messed himself on some of the guests. Which is not nice at a dinner party.

In 2003, after the Field Workshop became part of 3 Combat Services Support Battalion, it was decided to make Lance-Corporal Soult-Walter Crock the official mascot of the whole unit. Not only that, but after so many years of dedicated service, Snappa deserved a promotion to corporal. Her second stripe.

Now, there's a correct military procedure for doing these things. Before any promotion went through, her OC, Major Nick Faughey, had to fill out a Soldier Performance Appraisal Report. Snappa passed with flying colours.

Major Faughey found her persuasive and convincing in oral communications. An inspiration to any young soldier in the determination and aggression needed at times of conflict. Her job knowledge and skills were of a high standard. Fit. An excellent swimmer, Snappa could hold her breath underwater for extended periods. The OC thought she'd be an ideal candidate for a clearance diver course (and she'd certainly clear any divers from the water in double quick time).

Of course, no one is perfect. Major Faughey had to admit that

Lance-Corporal Crock needed to work on her interpersonal rela-
tionships. Things were rather strained and tense in her workplace,
for she tended to be overly aggressive and snap at anyone who got
into her personal space. At least with humankind.

As for her own kind, well Snappa had already been counselled
on her 'promiscuous' behaviour, having hatched so many babies
with Weipa, but it seemed to have no effect on her at all.

'Her saving grace in this regard,' the OC reported, 'is that she
has been in a stable monogamous relationship for many years.'

Still, that's a private matter. Militarily, Snappa was a role model
in her regard for army traditions. Focused and single minded, she'd
done picket duty in her compound for fourteen years without a single day off (and without a single day's pay).

Major Faughey recommended that Snappa get her promotion. The unit commander, Lieutenant-Colonel Daniel, agreed.
The paperwork went down the line to the Defence Department in
Canberra and back again. Approved. Soult-Walter Crock could
receive her second stripe.

On the day of the ceremony, a select party went up to the
Billabong Sanctuary. Lieutenant-Colonel Daniel and Snappa's
handler stepped into her enclosure. Proceedings were formal but
necessarily brief. They were conducted under the watching eyes
of Snappa's mate Weipa, who was becoming increasingly assertive
at the intrusion. If you thought Snappa was big, consider *him* –
600 kilograms (six times her weight) and over twice as long.

Snappa lazed in the pool, once again allowing her son Barry to
deputise for her. The young croc was held with his mouth bound and
draped with the regimental insignia. In the corner of the pen, the big
male was getting more agitated, and Snappa was starting to rouse
herself too. The difficulties crocodiles have in workplace relations

with their human colleagues were becoming only too apparent.

Lieutenant-Colonel Daniel didn't waste a lot of time on speeches. He pinned the corporal's second stripe onto Snappa's insignia – and got out of there quick smart.

In any event, there was no need to stay for congratulations. Actions speak louder than words. The people had no sooner left the pen than Weipa launched himself into the pool with Snappa. The two crocodiles rolled around in the water, tails thrashing, jaws snapping, expressing their delight in the most obvious way.

Afterwards, Corporal Soult-Walter Crock lay in the sun with a smile of satisfaction on her face. Another nest to build. Another clutch of eggs. Another little Barry Crocka to raise.

Imagine what she'll do when they promote her to sergeant.

SNAPPA'S PROMOTED AGAIN . . . AND AGAIN

Well, since the first edition of this book, Snappa not only made it to sergeant in 2008 . . . she's been promoted again to Warrant Officer Class 2 Soult-Walter Crock. It's the same superior rank as her acquaintance, the high-flying WO2 Courage, who sometimes sees her in the enclosure at Townsville's Billabong Sanctuary when he comes with his handlers to visit the eagles.

In fact soldiers from 3 Combat Services Support Battalion recently built a new and vastly improved enclosure for Snappa – one that meets the finest modern biosecurity standards. Which is only proper for a mascot that has spent the last thirty years or so on constant patrol – guarding her patch with fierce warrior spirit and keeping any unwelcome intruders well away.

Snappa's latest promotion came on the fiftieth anniversary of the formation of 102 Field Workshop (now part of 3CSSB) in May

2016. A splendid dinner was hosted at the Lavarack Barracks by the present CO, Lieutenant-Colonel Gabrielle Follett, attended by some 180 serving and former members of the battalion.

It was a grand evening and it had been hoped that Snappa would grace the meal with her toothsome presence as well. But alas, she just keeps growing, and in the end her size and the logistics told against her. Better for everyone they didn't risk Snappa having one of the guests for dinner.

Still, a Certificate of Promotion approved by the Chief of Army was on display, and the owner of Billabong Sanctuary, Mr Bob Flemming, was there with another of the little Barry Crockas as a substitute for Snappa. He brought along a few more reptiles as well . . . several pythons to drape around willing necks. Much more suitable than a saltwater crocodile for close human inspection on a social occasion.

As for Snappa, it cannot be said she enjoyed her promotion in the same happy manner as she had with her mate Weipa. Sad to report, the big male crocodile with which she shared the enclosure has died – himself promoted to Glory, as they say. But the good news is that Snappa won't be a widow for long.

In early 2016 a very large saltwater crocodile was captured swimming off Townsville's Strand beach – a popular tourist resort and, as always, safety must come first. The croc measures some 4.3 metres long and has been described as 'a fifty-year-old bruiser', for he's missing an eye and quite a few teeth, having seen a fair bit of action in his life.

He was successfully caged and taken to the Billabong Sanctuary . . . where they've called him 'Jupiter'. He's certainly a king in croc heaven. Apart from the missing bits and battle scars, Bob Flemming says he's otherwise in good health. He will soon be introduced to Snappa, and it's hoped she'll find her 'bruiser' attractive enough to mate up. Yet more nests for her to build. More clutches of eggs to lay. More little Barry Crockas to hatch, in hopes of further promotion.

But it won't do Snappa any good. She may not know it, but Warrant Officer Class 2 is the furthest a mascot can ascend in the chain of command. Heaven indeed.

BORIS

The 'devil dog'

East Timor, 1999. A large black sniffer dog called Boris stood in his cage on the back of a patrol truck, his military nose twitching with excitement. Such exotic smells. Such different people. Such new sights.

Boris and his handler, Sapper Lee Doyle, had just flown into Dili from Darwin with an explosive detection dog (EDD) team. It was only a fortnight since Australian troops had first entered East Timor with the international peace-keeping force (known as INTERFET). The town's streets were still devastated after a violent campaign by militia rebels, following the popular vote for independence from Indonesia.

Dili was largely deserted. People had fled in terror, or been dragged off by the militia. Buildings lay in ruins, looted and burned. The stench of death, decay and desolation hung heavy in the tropical air. There was much for Boris to smell.

The patrol truck drove through the rubble until it stopped outside the walled compound of a deserted coffee factory, where the troops had their temporary base. As they waited to pass through the gate, Lee Doyle saw a rusting sheet of tin on the footpath, propped up with a stick. It was a 44-gallon drum, squashed flat. And beneath it he saw the ragged figure of a girl.

She crawled from under her shelter, and stood looking at them. Her clothes were torn and her hair filthy. A little girl, no more than six, silently staring at these strange soldiers.

'Hello,' smiled Sapper Doyle. 'What's your name?'

She moved shyly towards them, as if she might speak. Then she noticed Boris – this big black Labrador-kelpie-cross – standing in his cage and eyeing her. She cried out in fear. A devil dog! And the girl disappeared beneath her tin humpy.

Over the coming weeks, however, the dog, the young soldier and the child would come to know each other much better.

Whenever Sapper Doyle was on picket duty at the compound, he'd see the girl huddled under her lean-to, or playing with other children in the street. The first time he and Boris went on a job, Lee stopped the truck and held a packet of sweets out the window. Without once looking at Boris, she edged across and took the lollies.

'Mister . . .' And she ran off again.

Next day, Lee had more sweets and a tin of baked beans for her. The girl was very hungry, and the soldier had enough to spare from his ration pack.

This time she was less nervous of him, though still frightened of the devil dog. There are few dogs in Timor, and none as large and black as this one. What dogs they have are often small and destined to be eaten. Perhaps the girl thought Boris intended to eat her. So she avoided him, even though the dog had done nothing except sit placidly in his cage and take in the scene.

Yet as the days passed, the child's confidence grew. Each morning she came to wait for her handout as the dog truck left.

The dog teams spent much of their time searching nearby villages, and down at the wharves. Using a tennis ball reward, the dogs are trained to detect about a dozen specific odours, one or more of which are present in almost all known explosives and weapons. As the INTERFET troops gradually made Dili more secure, streams of refugees began to return, many of them by sea.

Boris and his mates had to check their belongings for hidden arms or ammunition. Often thousands of people arrived each day, and the work was long and tiring. But Lee usually found time to stop and give something to the girl who had nothing.

One day, Sapper Doyle and the Timorese interpreter approached the child. Boris wasn't with them, and she spoke without fear.

'Mister . . .' It was her only English word.

Her name was Sandra, the interpreter said, and she was all by herself. Her father had been murdered by the militia in front of the whole family. Sandra, her mother and older sister were taken over the border into West Timor. Somehow, Sandra managed to escape, and had journeyed alone back to Dili, over rough, mountainous country.

Lee Doyle was very moved by her story.

'You can't sleep in the street, Sandra, waiting for your mother and sister to come home. Is there no one to look after you?'

'I don't know any other family.'

'Then I'll see what we can do.'

Near the compound was a partly damaged house, where an elderly couple lived. Lee spoke to them through the interpreter, and they agreed to take Sandra in. By way of return, he promised to provide them with whatever food the soldiers could spare.

At that early stage of the East Timor operation the troops still relied on their ration packs. Yet the men were generous and donated tins of food – meatballs and spaghetti – biscuits, fruit and bread rolls to the collection. As such things were in short supply in Dili, Sandra and the old couple became the envy of the neighbourhood.

When Lee wrote home about Sandra and the story was printed in the newspaper, toys, clothes, books and piles of other goodies started arriving in the military mailbags. Far more than Sandra could ever use. They had to call a stop. The surplus was distributed to other children in Dili and the nearby countryside.

Talk about popular. Whenever the vehicle with the dog cages on the back appeared, it was immediately surrounded by boys and girls chanting, 'Mister! Mister!'

And if Sandra wasn't there, they'd rush to find her.

Even Boris was accepted after a time. The children often barked at the big black devil dog in his cage. But as his response was generally just a wag of the tail, there came the day when Sandra plucked up enough courage to touch him through the wire.

Boris licked her hand. A few days later, she climbed onto the back of the truck and gave Boris a pat. And not long after that, Lee found a whole mob of kids sitting on top of his cage – and laughing.

HOME

'Stay, Boris!' Lee Doyle gives his dog a command, and Boris sits in the Queensland sun, eyes alight and tail thumping, as his master hides a tennis ball.

'Seek on, Boris! Seek on!' At once the dog is up and hunting along the garden bed for the telltale scent. Still playing his games.

In fact, it's all games now. It's 2004 and Boris has retired from the army. At ten years old, there are touches of grey around his muzzle. And although he is willing as ever when it comes to tennis balls, he's slowing down. He's given in his papers and gone home with Lee and his wife, Deanne, as their full-time family pet.

For the really good news is that Australia's military working dogs are coming back. Unlike the ten trackers left in Vietnam, today the dogs return from overseas with the troops. Strict health protocols have to be followed while the dogs are away, and quarantine requirements may vary over the years. One dog that contracted brucellosis in East Timor didn't make it through quarantine. But the rest, once cleared, could go straight back to military duties.

The first military working dogs to return to Australia were from the United Nations peace-keeping task force to Somalia, known as Operation Solace, in 1993. Three German shepherd explosive detection dogs – Duke, Mick and Tia – went with the 3rd Combat Engineer Regiment.

According to Seamus Doherty, who handled Mick, the team was told before they left that the dogs would not be coming back. But the brass encountered so much opposition – not just from the soldiers but from their families as well – that they eventually relented.

Arrangements were made for the dogs to go into quarantine when the tour ended, but it wasn't straightforward. Simon French, who had Duke, tells how the dogs escaped when the plane landed at Nairobi. Duke and Mick started scrapping, and Tia took off down the runway. They were caught at last, and departed for nine months' quarantine in Britain and Australia.

A few years later, Tia and Mick both served with Australian peace-keeping troops in Bougainville – just as some of the six East Timor dogs went on to work with the twelve explosive detection dogs that accompanied our forces under the Regional Assistance Mission to Solomon Islands (RAMSI) from 2003. In the case of Boris and Lee Doyle, their first job when they returned to Australia was to work with the sniffer dog teams checking the stadiums and athletes' luggage for the Sydney 2000 Olympic Games.

Indeed, in forty minutes Boris and Lee could make secure a grandstand that would have taken humans many days to search: and you'd be fairly sure there were no hidden bombs. In Iraq, British soldiers swept five buildings for arms and found nothing. They called in their springer spaniel sniffer dog, Buster. In five minutes Buster found a cache of guns, grenades, explosives and drugs hidden in a wall cavity, for which he was awarded the Dickin Medal.

CANINE AND WAR DOG SERVICE MEDALS

For many years Australian veterans involved with military working dogs and government service dogs – such as those working with police and customs – have fought to have their four-legged comrades recognised by some kind of presentation medal.

From the Boer War onwards the argument has always been that the animals face the same dangers, and in their own ways show the same courage as humans. Certainly they can also ultimately sacrifice their lives. But the answer from the authorities has always been, 'No! Animals cannot be equated with people.' Some of the handlers who worked with Australian war dogs in Malaya apparently got around the prohibition and managed to arrange for *British* service medals to be awarded to their canine companions instead. They applied by forwarding the military registration numbers tattooed inside their dogs' ears to the British authorities.

Officially the Australian authorities still do not award service medals to animals – in particular, these days, dogs working with our armed forces and civilian services. Yet in more good news the long-standing efforts by the Australian Defence Force Trackers and War Dogs Association to gain some recognition for their companions-in-arms have at last borne fruit.

Around 2007 the association's former president, Lieutenant-Colonel George Hulse of the Royal Australian Engineers (Ret.), convinced the authorities that the association was really making the argument on behalf of the human end of the dog and handler team. After all, a dog doesn't know what it's getting a medal for, but the handler certainly does.

On this basis George was given the green light to have designs prepared for two medals. One was a Canine Service Medal awarded for five years accumulated service with government military or civil authorities. The other was a War Dog Operational Medal awarded to a dog with at least twenty-eight days on deployment in a combat zone. There were two stipulations for the design. The medals couldn't look like a human medal, hence they're square not round. And, again unlike human medals, they couldn't have an obverse and reverse side: all the information had to be on the front of the silver medal.

The finished design for the medals depicts a Vietnam dog handler and his tracker dog, together with the dog's name, number and service branch. The Canine Service Medal has a ribbon with three coloured stripes representing the navy, army and air force. On either side of the central red army stripe are two narrow white bands, representing the police, customs and other government non-military working dogs. They also are entitled to the medal. As George Hulse says, 'The military working dogs keep the bad guys out of Australia. The police and customs dogs keep the bad guys off the streets at home.'

The War Dog Operational Medal is given only to military working dogs. The ribbon also has three stripes representing the navy, army and air force (the army colour being green on this ribbon). Down the centre of each stripe is a narrow red band, representing the blood spilt on a battlefield. Again, as George points out, 'It's

inevitable in a war zone that blood will be shed. That's the significance of the three thin red lines.' The ribbon also comes with a
metal clasp stating in which theatre of war the dog served.

Well, the designs were submitted and in 2007 word came back
from the civil and defence awards authorities in Canberra. They
wouldn't officially condone the service medals being given to the
dog handlers or their units: but equally they didn't want to stand
in the way. Provided the medals remained unofficial, and were
awarded by the association at its own expense and in its own time,
they could go ahead.

Which is what happened. The canine medals went into pro-
duction in 2008 and the first ones were sent out to those units and
individuals who applied for them. They're produced by the same
firm that makes the medals for servicemen and women, and they
come in much the same presentation boxes. Due diligence is done,
of course, on each application received; but once approved the
association sends the first medal to the individual or unit free of
charge. If a duplicate is required, the cost is around $60.

Which seems a small enough price to pay, heaven knows, for
the enormous service the dogs render our community in terms of
human lives saved and the reduced cost to society from criminal or
enemy activity. Not to mention the acknowledgement, long denied,
of the special nature of that bond between mankind and our most
faithful friends. A bond that makes the work of those protecting
our safety and national security – in the words of bureaucratic
jargon – so much more effective and efficient.

'Come, Boris!' Lee Doyle calls to his dog, still lazing in the backyard
sun. 'Come, old feller!' And he shows him the tennis ball about to be

planted in the garden bed. 'Seek on, Boris. Seek on!'

It's 2009 now, ten years since East Timor and Sandra, but at the familiar words the old dog slowly gets to his feet. His hips are going, but he's still ready for work. Lee didn't apply for the Canine Service and War Dog Operational Medals for Boris when they were introduced. The dog would certainly have been entitled to them. But he was retired by then and well . . .

Yet the light still glimmers in his eyes as the grey muzzle sniffs along the borders for the scent. At around sixteen years old, Boris's life is drawing to its close; but right to the end he is still trying to play his games. Hide and seek.

It's been a good life – his years in the army and the time at home afterwards with the growing family. When the first edition of *Animal Heroes* was launched at the Australian War Memorial in Canberra by the then Chief of Army, Lieutenant-General Peter Leahy, Boris was there, together with Lee in uniform, and the dog pretty much stole the show. And although Lee has since left the service and gone into business, the old ways between them have never ceased.

'Good boy . . . seek on!'

It's true that these last couple of years Boris has become more Deanne's pet and the two girls'. . . the muscles weaker, the aged bones more stiff. Sleep is more to his liking than a day at the office: though whenever Lee produces the ball, Boris is always willing to please him, even if the games are fewer and not as quick as they once were.

There it is!

His nose at least is unfailing. And Boris picks up the worn tennis ball, shuffles back to Lee with it, and sits by his feet.

The man looks down with that look of compassion and tenderness that only those who have truly known a dog can understand.

Boris has started having fits lately. They're getting worse, and the dog sometimes can't use his legs for a while afterwards. The family's not quite sure what it is, but Lee knows that it won't be long before he and Boris take their last ride together.

'One more time . . . ?'

One more time.

Boris died on 2 February 2009.

VERY SMALL CREATURES

Here's a chapter about the countless very small creatures that are so much part of a soldier's life . . . the ants, flies, lice, spiders, reptiles, scorpions and a multitude of other creepy-crawlies that abound on the battlefields of the world.

Most of them don't have names, except ones that would be unprintable in a book for family reading. Nor are they exactly 'animal heroes' in the accepted sense. But they share some of the most intimate aspects of service people's existence in the field – their very bodies, clothes and bedding. Indeed, soldiers sometimes regard them with as much hostility and even fear as their human enemies. As a headline in the Sydney *Sun* newspaper put it during the Second World War, for those fighting in New Guinea the bite of a malarial mosquito 'can be as dangerous as a tommy-gun'.

It wasn't that much of an exaggeration.

FLIES

Of all the insect pests that have campaigned with Australian fighting forces over the past century, none have been more vilified than the flies of Gallipoli. Men swore that every fly in the world went to Anzac – attracted by the summer heat, open latrine pits and so many unburied bodies. They had much to feast upon . . . and blew from there into the mouths of the living to bring disgust, disease and death.

Among their victims was fourteen-year-old James Martin, dead of enteric (typhoid) fever in October 1915 after only seven weeks on Gallipoli – so far as we know the youngest of the Anzacs, and almost certainly the youngest Australian soldier to die in war. The medical historian of Gallipoli, Dr A G Butler, observed that the history of disease at Anzac was in no small measure the history of the flies there. There were no fly-proof latrines until it was already too late, when the cold weather came and the flies had gone. Mess tins became infected. 'Black swarms of flies carried infection from the very bowel to the food as it passed the lips,' he wrote. In September and October alone, after the worst of the fighting was over, of the 50 000 Allied soldiers evacuated from the peninsula through Mudros, nine out of every ten were sick.

The men responded to this disgraceful predicament in many ways, but mostly with that kind of laconic black humour typical of the Anzac temperament. Thomas White in *The Fighting Thirteenth* cried that no Australian ever had such nightmare flies as those of Gallipoli. Tins of jam couldn't be opened – except in the dark – without immediately becoming 'a dense mobile black', and a biscuit with marmalade had to be held by one hand 'and guarded by the other until the teeth closed on it'.

In *The Anzac Book* an ambulanceman called Carruthers sang what he called 'A Hymn of Hate' to the flies. Flies getting into his eyes, ears, nose and mouth every time he went into the trenches to do his country's duty. Nothing drove them away. He'd retire to his dugout, and the flies followed him. Smoke till he almost asphyxiated himself, and the flies were active as ever. And whatever terrors the food held for men, the flies were fearless. 'Stepping boldly on the edge of a syrup-covered biscuit, they immediately get their feet entangled; but they will not retreat . . . Instead they will struggle to the centre, where they gladly give up the contest and die.'

As, of course, did a sufficient number of men who ate such a contaminated biscuit.

It all got too much for Trooper Ion Idriess of the 5th Light Horse. He was in his trench on the Anzac ridges, trying to eat a biscuit and jam and finding the flies beating inside his very mouth. His response was to hurl the jam tin away and to scribble the words subsequently made famous in his 1932 book *The Desert Column*: 'Of all the bastards of places this is the greatest bastard in the world.'

We sense that Dr Butler, who analysed what he called 'the disease debacle of Gallipoli', would only agree.

The flies that so plagued the Anzacs were just as infuriating to the men of the Second AIF during 1939–45, though for the most part without such lethal consequences. And unlike their fathers on Gallipoli they sometimes had quite novel fly-catchers – which leads us to a couple of true animal heroes.

A NSW soldier fighting in the south-west Pacific told of a duck called Flannel, looked after by a corporal signalman, who taught her to come running for a meal of delicious swatted flies by tapping his morse code finger on the floor. Visitors to the signals office, including senior officers, would join in the game. And one day, when nine NCOs were in sigs tapping away on the floor, Flannel feasted on 115 flies in the one sitting. Alas, fattened up on so many insects, she mysteriously disappeared – presumably to become a feast for somebody else.

The 1943 army volume *Khaki and Green* tells the uplifting story of Robbie the Chameleon, who became the bosom companion of a soldier called 'Smithy'. In his shady tent under the desert sun of El Alamein, unable to sleep one afternoon because of an annoying fly, he was surprised suddenly to find the pest disappear in a flash of green and yellow. Looking around he found the six-inch chameleon on his shoulder – and from then on the two formed a partnership of mutual advantage. They went everywhere together, Robbie camouflaged on the soldier's khaki, and any fly that came within twelve inches of Smithy would be caught by his mate's rapid-fire tongue.

The creature's duties soon extended from Smithy's shoulder to looking after the mess tins in the canteen. It took the chameleon a little time to adjust his colour to the silvery metal, but once disguised no fly ever got past him.

Robbie travelled with the unit to Palestine, bravely facing the perils of a military life. He once fell with Smithy into a slit trench as they were meandering home from a happy night in the canteen; but he no sooner recovered from that shock than somebody dumped a tomato-sauce bottle on his tail, and thereafter the tip always stayed an ashy grey.

Robbie's end, alas, was tragic. One day he fell into a mess tin of very hot tea. Smithy fished him out – though even as Robbie lay expiring on the man's hand, he made every valiant effort to turn the same brown nicotine colour as the stain on his master's fingers. Faithful unto death.

FLEAS

The fleas of Gallipoli were just as reviled by the diggers as the blow-flies. No sooner had the sun set and the flies retired for the night than operations would be handed over to the fleas; ambulanceman Carruthers acknowledged the flies could have found no worthier allies.

It wasn't guerrilla warfare but a full frontal assault the moment he lay down to sleep, as battalions of fleas in open or close formation attacked. They bore down on every flank – and if driven off they only returned in greater numbers, having apparently unlimited reinforcements.

'Counter-attacks in the dark are all in favour of the enemy,' the serviceman lamented, 'and morning finds they have withdrawn their forces to advantageous cover in the blankets from which it is impossible to dislodge them.'

Corporal George Smith of the 24th Sanitary Section, poured out his feelings in verse:

The fleas they wander nightly, as soon as I've undressed,
And after many weary hunts I've had to give them best.
As the ants have also found it, there is very little rest
In my cosy little dug-out on the hill.

LICE

Just as vexatious are lice that infest the clothes, blankets, hair and bodies of soldiers exposed for any length of time to rough conditions in the field.

When the mounted troops of the Australian Light Horse and Camel Corps were fighting through Egypt and Palestine in 1917–18, mobile disinfectors and barrel delousers were used to kill lice in uniforms and bedding – though neither method was very effective. High pressure steam was needed to do the job properly, and that was in short supply – as was water of any kind – in the desert campaign.

The most reliable method of removing lice, or 'chats' as they were sometimes called, was to do it yourself . . . picking them from your clothes by hand each morning and night. It became a habit, especially at Gallipoli, when uniforms (or what passed for them) were taken off and deloused almost every time a soldier came out of the trenches. Unless, of course, he was fortunate like the soldier mentioned by Thomas White of the *Thirteenth*, who somehow acquired a tame monkey. Whenever this soldier's shirt became too 'chatty' he'd toss it across to the monkey who spent many a happy hour picking out the lice. And eating them.

Another soldier, whose sweetheart enquired what 'chats' were, sent one home imprisoned on a letter under a piece of gummed stamp paper.

'No wonder there was so much illness,' White exclaimed.

Others also turned to verse on the subject. A soldier named Park in *The Anzac Book*, for example, saw a gunner scanning his sunburnt knees:

> *I asked him why he was searching*
> *And what he was looking for,*
> *But his only reply was a long-drawn sigh*
> *As he quietly killed one more.*

The times and locations may change, but these soldierly rituals can stay very much the same over the years. As do their artistic representations. Murray Griffin painted an evocative picture of the prisoners of war at Changi, in Singapore during the Second World War, debugging their bed frames by washing them with hot water.

Manual debugging of clothes and bedding was also necessary of course – although for other POWs incarcerated in far worse conditions elsewhere, such luxuries as bedding were almost unknown, even if the torments of lice and other low forms of insect life remained as bad as ever.

SCABIES

Prisoners incarcerated at the infamous Outram Road Jail in Singapore were forced to sit cross-legged all day in narrow cells that were infested with lice and scabies. The female scabies mites, as is their wont, burrowed into living flesh to lay their eggs that, as the larvae hatched and ate their way to the surface skin, caused the most terrible rash. The only relief was by incessant scratching, which made it far worse.

The Japanese guards at Outram Road eventually responded by making the prisoners sit for several minutes every so often in a revolting 'scabby bath' diluted with a bit of disinfectant – and to dunk their heads in it. As a method of eradicating scabies it was quite ineffective. Not until one of the senior guards ordered the cells themselves to be disinfected was the disease brought under some control.

MOSQUITOES

Perhaps the most insidious insect enemies confronting soldiers fighting in tropical theatres – and elsewhere – are anopheles mosquitoes, over forty species of which are known to cause malaria in humans. One bite can bring on the shivering, aching disease that may put servicemen and women out of action from a few days to several weeks – and, in the worst cases of cerebral malaria, even kill them. It's been estimated that over 400 000 people die from malaria every year.

As the Sydney *Sun* observed in its article of January 1943, a mosquito bite could be 'as dangerous as a tommy-gun' for Private Alf Jones, fighting in New Guinea: 'The Jap sniper "pinged" from his tree top; but the sting that laid Alf low was delivered silently, viciously.'

Defensive precautions have always been essential, and indeed part of the daily (and nightly) routine. Rubbing insect repellent on the skin and along the seams of clothing. Spraying stagnant water around camp sites with kerosene. Regularly taking quinine tablets and other anti-malarial drugs . . . though you need to be careful. Certain drugs cause serious side effects in some people, ranging from physical illness to depression and hallucinations – there are even claims of them inducing suicidal thoughts – to the extent that several court cases have been brought by former soldiers.

The humble mosquito net is another important line of defence when sleeping. Soldiers carried lightweight nets during the Second World War, and we've seen how the Darwin dog, Gunner, slept under the net with his master. The nets were also used in Vietnam. Corporal Bob Bettany, who was a dog tracker team commander, says the net was mandatory when you laid your bed out, as they were for the INTERFET force in East Timor. Sapper Lee Doyle, who was with his dog Boris, says the Australian nets had to be hitched to a stay with hoochie cord and weren't all that effective. The troops started buying much better imported nets at the local market. They opened up on frames like an umbrella – and sunshade versions of them can still be seen every summer at Australian beaches.

The military dogs in Timor and Vietnam didn't have mosquito

nets, but they were sprayed every day with insect repellent and given a daily drug. 'We had to worry about ticks,' Lee says, 'because they can affect the dogs especially. We groomed them consistently – twice a day – inspecting them for ticks and lice. Every morning when they went for a walk, the first thing we did back at base was to check them all over, and again in the afternoon. The thing we most worried about was the dogs getting injured.'

TICKS . . .

Of course ticks attack both animals and humankind, hooking themselves into the flesh with backward pointing teeth to feast on blood. Their anticoagulant saliva can be toxic to animals and in people may cause rashes, fever and even partial paralysis. Hence the need for regular inspections and to remove them quickly.

People have their own systems, but General Peter Leahy, former Chief of Army, was taught this method as a young soldier: 'You get a couple of ten cent pieces, catch the arse end of the tick between the coins, and turn them anti-clockwise to pull them out. If you just try to scrape them off, the barb will stay in your flesh. I went home after a bush exercise, had a swim, and my mother said "What's that on your back?" There was a big infection from a tick still partly caught in my skin.'

. . . AND OTHER CREATURES OF FOREST, JUNGLE AND DESERT

In late 1943 the Melbourne *Sun News-Pictorial* published several photos of some of the insect life – magnified many times to increase their ferocious appearance – with which our soldiers were contending in New Guinea. There was the malarial mosquito . . . a tiger beetle . . . a huge centipede of the kind mentioned by Keith Eddison, writing home to his mother from Port Moresby in 1943. He'd found one in his tent 'nine inches long and as thick as your finger. I swear he'd pull your leg off in one go.' He went on to tell her of one poor fellow at the outdoor picture show who was bitten by a centipede that got into his trousers!

The need to constantly check bedding for snakes that may have slithered in during the day . . . to shake out your clothes . . . to look inside your boots before putting them on – all are a constant in every military routine across the years. Lee Doyle says the instructions in Timor were always to put your socks over your boots at night to stop nasties, such as a venomous black scorpion, from getting inside. Peter Leahy stuffed his socks *into* his boots.

The Anzac soldiers' magazine *Kia Ora Coo-ee* from the desert campaign of 1918 called the scorpion the worst of all the insect pests of Palestine, and quoted the bible, 'My father has chastised you with whips, but I will chastise you with scorpions.' Charles Barrett added, 'Many of us have been chastised with scorpions and are not much the worse for it.' Though try telling that to a soldier in Vietnam, lying in jungle ambush, finding the leaves moving as a scorpion approaches with stinging tail erect . . . and having to flick it discreetly away without revealing his position to the enemy.

Spiders were next on the list of pests to be feared in Palestine . . . especially quite large ones, like the tarantula. 'It is a hideous creature,' said the *Kia Ora Coo-ee*, 'with four talon-shaped jaws that work fiercely when the spider is angry – it is rarely in a gentle mood.'

A lifetime and half a world away in Singapore, Lee Doyle was getting into formation for a night ambush exercise when he noticed some small holes, the size of a fifty cent coin, in the hill where they were lying. He thought they were birds' nests – but as soon as the sun went down dozens of large hairy legs started coming out of the ground. Tarantulas! The soldiers immediately began ramming sticks and stones into the holes to block them. Not good for an ambush, trying to keep quiet and not get into trouble.

For soldiers serving in Iraq, the so-called camel spiders were just as detested. They're actually part-spider and part-scorpion, combining the two nasties, and are very large – up to fifteen centimetres long. A number of myths have grown up around them – that they can be half man-size, or that they eat both men and camel's stomachs. They don't. Nevertheless their pincers are very strong, able to cut through the skin and bones of small birds . . . and while their bite is not life-threatening to humans, it can still cause an ugly rash.

In any event, Australian spiders can often be just as intimidating to soldiers on manoeuvre at home. Lee Doyle still has unpleasant memories of walking on night exercise into the webs of the large golden orb spiders strung from the trees in the scrub around the combat training centre at Tully in North Queensland. And Peter Leahy tells of making an evening bivouac while on an exercise in a forest south of Sydney . . . and finding in the morning that they'd scraped their sleeping pozzies in ground infested with funnel web spiders. Nobody, fortunately, was bitten.

To Charles Barrett, in *Kia Ora Coo-ee,* ants could scarcely be classified as an insect pest, 'indeed they are rather welcome guests in a bivvy'. But to soldiers settling down for the night in a Vietnamese jungle, the sounds of what they called 'chopper ants', on the move and eating everything in their path, were not so benign. And for Bob Bettany, Vietnam's green ants could positively be a danger to life and limb.

Once, travelling with a section of about eight men in an APC, the hatch open to give some relief from the jungle heat, the vehicle's long antennae dislodged a green ants' nest woven from leaves in the overhanging trees . . . and it dropped right into the crowded vehicle. Men and ants everywhere. 'It was pandemonium,' Bob says. 'You just wanted to get away from the mongrel things. They've got a painful bite like the North Queensland green ants. Of course you're shut in, so you have to scramble through the hatch and jump off the top of the APC. Honestly, it would be a movie cameraman's dream.'

Another scene worth filming would be a certain foot patrol Bob Bettany was with, on his first tour of duty, along a fairly straight creek not far from Nui Dat. He was 'arse end Charlie', bringing up the rear and able to see the leading man.

'All of a sudden it was like a silent contact drill in motion,' he says. 'I couldn't believe what was happening in front of me. There were no shots fired or anything like that, but blokes were weaving left and right and dropping down into the water.

'Then somebody yelled out "Bees!" and I did what everyone else was doing, and hit the water to escape. I was okay, but some blokes got stung and had allergic reactions. The patrol was cancelled and we had to make our way to the nearest medevac and get choppered out.

'Small creatures! Mate, you've opened up a can of worms . . .'

SCARAB BEETLES

And finally, let's end this review of very small creatures with one that proved truly heroic and useful to a First World War soldier called 'Booligal Bob'. He was not exactly in the field at the time – in fact he was penned up in an army clink in Palestine for having told a certain sergeant that he had no father.

As Bob related the story to *Kia Ora Coo-ee,* when he ran out of cigarettes in the clink his cobber got the necessary together, yarded up half a dozen scarab beetles (the very ones regarded as sacred creatures in the Egypt of the Pharaohs), and squatted down on the other side of the compound's wire fence from Bob, pretending to read a book.

'After a while he digs a straight line under the wire, fastens a smoke to one of the beetles, and puts him in the furrow. The insect marches straight ahead, and I got the cigarette. Others followed, and when one of the scarabs showed signs of going on strike, another one was detailed to do the job.'

Initiative. Ingenuity. Mateship. The diggers have always been famous for it.

SARBI

Among the many animal heroes that have served with Australian forces in recent times, by far the most celebrated has been the explosive detection dog (EDD) Sarbi.

The black Labrador-Newfoundland-cross was taken by a Taliban warlord after a fierce firefight in Afghanistan in 2008, during which her handler, Corporal David Simpson, and a number of other soldiers were wounded, and one American dog handler died. Sarbi was kept captive, as a trophy canine prisoner of war, for some fourteen months . . . before being found and rescued by American forces following an assault on the warlord's compound.

Reunited with her soldiers, and getting the all clear from quarantine, the dog returned home to a real hero's welcome. Public and media interest in her was intense, for here was a 'good news story' from the long war in Afghanistan. Such was Sarbi's fame that she retired not long after her return to live the rest of her days with David Simpson.

Sarbi was only this country's second military animal – after Murphy, the Gallipoli donkey – to be awarded a Purple Cross by the RSPCA for the work done by her and all the sixty-two explosive detection dogs that served in Afghanistan: finding hidden bombs, weapons, ammunition and communications equipment, and thereby saving many lives. Even so, forty-one Australian soldiers have been killed there and ten military working dogs died. They also paid the ultimate price.

A book was written about Sarbi. Her portrait was painted. She has her own Facebook page. The dog attended an open day for animals in war at the Australian War Memorial, where I had the pleasure of meeting her. A park was named after Sarbi in the northern Brisbane suburb of Warner. Sarbi attended the opening with David's family in early 2015. It was one of her last public functions. Not long afterwards Sarbi began suffering seizures due to the onset of brain cancer, and sadly had to be humanely put down.

But even in death Sarbi is still with us. At their own initiative David and his wife Kira decided to have her body taken to a taxidermist. It's not a very usual thing for people to do these days. But with the assistance of the Australian War Memorial, Sarbi has been mounted and can be seen by anyone visiting the Afghanistan exhibition at the AWM in Canberra.

She now has her own special place there – joining those other animal heroes at the AWM from earlier conflicts, like the dogs Roff and Driver, and the pigeons with their Dickin Medals. *Requiescat In Pace.*

Sarbi was raised with her brother Rafi by a family living at Bowral, in the southern highlands of New South Wales. The two were bought from a nearby pet shop and grew to be strong, alert and clever young dogs. Both were black in colour, Sarbi with a distinctive white zigzag blaze on her chest, and both loved chasing tennis balls.

Shortly before the dogs turned three, in 2005, the family moved to Sydney. As often happens, there wasn't enough room for two very active dogs, and with regret an advertisement was placed in the local newspaper. *Brother and sister need a new home.* It was spotted by Corporal Murray Young of the Explosive Detection Dog section at the School of Military Engineering at Holsworthy Barracks. They sounded just the kinds of dogs suitable for training in what is now a very highly regarded service of the army. They showed their potential when he went to see them . . . and in fact Murray took the two dog recruits back to the barracks with him that same day.

Corporal Young took on Rafi's training himself. Sarbi became the responsibility of Corporal David Simpson. David had wanted to become a military dog handler since his youth. He'd joined the army for that very purpose, although it took him a few years to get into the EDD section, even spending some time with an artillery unit working with missile systems. David managed a transfer to the engineers eventually, serving in East Timor for several months. But at last in early 2000 David was accepted by the EDD section where, after completing the training course over several months, he became one of the Doggies (as they call themselves). Soon afterwards he helped to secure the Sydney Olympic Games sites with the explosive detection dogs, in the same way that Lee Doyle did with Boris.

Until Sarbi's arrival in 2005, other people had trained all the dogs David worked with. Sarbi was the first EDD he trained up himself. And the dog soon showed she had qualities that made her particularly suitable for the demanding work. Sarbi was over the puppy stage and not easily distracted. She was responsive to his commands; had a good nose; quickly established a bond between herself and her new master; and was 'fanatical' about chasing tennis balls.

Indeed, if Sarbi had any faults, one was that if she couldn't find a ball (or if, in the course of her training, none were present) she'd pick up a stone and bring that back to her handler instead. David quickly had to correct that. She could break her teeth or swallow the stone!

Another problem was that, as the bond between the two developed, Sarbi became almost too protective of her handler. As anyone who's had a dog knows, there is nothing like going to sleep with your animal to strengthen that bond. It establishes an absolute sense of trust and affection, for in sleep we are all at our most vulnerable. So it was when David and Sarbi went to sleep side by side, on exercises in Australia with the swag out in the open and even more so on the battlefields of Afghanistan.

'If I was sleeping, Sarbi wouldn't let anyone else come near me,' David says. 'She'd growl and keep them away. That could be seen as a good trait in her for me . . . though no doubt a bad one for others. There were a couple of times when I didn't have to do picket duty at night, because no one could get close enough to wake me up.'

Other EDD handlers report the same thing. And a growling dog can also alert you to the presence of other people or animals near the camp at night. It's one more layer of protection, which impressed our SAS and commando troops in Afghanistan so much that they now have their own dog programs. They use mainly German shepherds and Belgian Malinois, trained in consultation with the RAAF Security and Fire School military working dog program at Amberley in Queensland. Many now have patrol and some EDD capability, and are often known as combat assault dogs – an evocative name, although officially they're all military working dogs.

As for Sarbi, she passed her course well and, as EDD 436, she first went on active duty with David and the other Doggies at the 2006 Commonwealth Games in Melbourne: searching for hidden devices in public venues, spectator stands and securing the athletes' village. It demonstrates, at these times of heightened terror threats, the great service these dogs render our community. They don't just have a military role, important as that is. They have incalculable value in helping to make safe visits by heads of state, international trade and economic conferences, major sporting events and other large-scale civilian gatherings at home.

In March 2007, Sarbi went on the first of her two overseas deployments with David to Afghanistan, as part of Operation Slipper. The dogs were used there from late 2005 to 2014, working out of Camp Russell at Tarin Kowt ('TK') in Uruzgan province with the engineers and infantry to search routes and compounds for the reconstruction task force. The dogs also went with the SAS and commando forces on many of their special operations – and, as mentioned earlier, became greatly respected for their capabilities.

It was difficult work in the mountainous, rugged country, and very dangerous. In TK the dogs ran their noses over vehicles coming onto the base at the checkpoint, on the lookout for hidden explosives and weapons. They were also adept at detecting unexploded grenades and mortars on the practice range that might otherwise have been used by the Taliban.

Outside, the place was no less hazardous for the dogs as they searched for improvised explosive devices (IEDs) and unexploded mortars, checked vehicles and helped clear village compounds (with all their interesting new animal and human smells) of hidden weapons and ammunition. Indeed, the majority of casualties suffered by coalition forces in Afghanistan were from IEDs detonated either by direct contact on the roads or by remote control, for the Taliban occupied large parts of the province.

The dogs sometimes wore protective goggles (known as 'doggles') in the field – not against the glare so much as to prevent the fine dust from the roads and helicopter lift-offs getting into their eyes. In fact when travelling in a helicopter they very often had earmuffs, held in place with elastic stocking, against the noise. Pre-deployment training was mostly done at Woomera – a fair Australian equivalent to Afghanistan's environment – but for the early stages of deployment, until they got used to the terrain, the dogs generally wore padded canvas and rubber booties to save their paws on the hot, sharp-stoned ground. Some dogs even wore little socks with their booties, for the powdery dust in their paws could coagulate with sweat and form hard lumps that made them limp, and would have to be removed.

There were three dogs with the 2nd Combat Engineer Regiment on Sarbi's tour, and one of them was killed: Merlin, accidentally run over by an Australian Light Armoured Vehicle (ASLAV). Another dog, Razz, with the Special Operations Task Group supporting the SAS, was blown to pieces when a massive IED was detonated on the road out of a forward operating base known as Anaconda.

Fortunately Sarbi and David were both fine when they returned to Sydney at the end of their first tour in October. But they were home for only eight months before Sarbi and Sergeant Simpson – he'd been promoted – were deployed back to Afghanistan for their second rotation in June 2008.

Uruzgan province had become noticeably more dangerous. There'd been many more attacks by the Taliban on coalition forces, many more casualties, and the force's role expanded to actively search and destroy enemy compounds and strongholds. And it was during such an operation in July that Sarbi made one of her most significant finds: a cache of communications equipment, including mobile phones still with their SIM cards, hidden in the mudbrick wall of a compound. It had been missed during an earlier search and was to prove of value to the intelligence sections.

A couple of months later, however, came the ambush and fire-fight by the end of which Sarbi had disappeared.

It was 2 September. A convoy of five American humvees carrying a combined force of about three dozen Australian, US and Afghan soldiers was returning across country to Anaconda base. They'd been on an operation in which some seven Taliban fighters had been killed. The vehicle drivers were avoiding the roads, believing they'd been planted with explosives. Indeed, the Afghan interpreter ('terps') had picked up a lot of chatter on the insurgents' radio channels, including threats to 'kill them all'.

David and Sarbi were in the convoy, together with US Sergeant Greg Rodriguez and his golden Labrador, Jacko. Nearing home, about five kilometres from Anaconda, the convoy came under attack in a narrow valley by an enemy force estimated at perhaps 200 men. Fire was coming from both sides of the valley, some in front, and some from a compound in a cultivated green strip on the valley floor (until an American F/A-18 fighter dropped a 500-pound bomb on it).

The convoy quickly grouped closer together, soldiers returning fire from the ground and from the machine guns mounted on their vehicles. But the attack was severe and the coalition patrol began to suffer injuries. One American soldier was hit, and as Sergeant Rodriguez ran to his aid he was shot in the head and killed. His body was brought back to the humvees, which began moving slowly off toward the base, the soldiers on the ground keeping up a running fight beside them.

The attack turned into a 'rolling ambush', the fighters on the hillsides keeping pace with the convoy – setting up their guns and rocket-propelled grenades, firing, and leapfrogging the next man to set up again further along the valley. It became very slow going for the patrol, injuries were mounting, and the fighting extended over several hours.

It was during this time that David was wounded three times and Sarbi became separated from him. David was fighting from the ground, the dog attached to his body armour by her lead and clip, when a rocket-propelled grenade exploded close by. David was hit behind the knee by shrapnel – and another piece severed Sarbi's lead. With the noise of the humvee's heavy weapons, Sarbi moved a little out of the firing zone: she didn't run off, but rather kept at a distance of about fifty metres and moved in parallel with the convoy as it crept forward. David couldn't see her at all times, but he did sight her occasionally during the contact to determine she was there. It's quite possible that Sarbi copped a bit of 'frag' from a stone or shrapnel chip as the initial grenade exploded, although David says he examined her thoroughly when she returned, over a year later, and couldn't find any wounds.

Still the rolling ambush went on. At one point David found himself together with an SAS trooper, moving to the left and right of the vehicle for cover and to return fire, depending on where the fewest enemy bullets were coming from. There was a burst of machine-gun or automatic fire from a hole in the mountainside to the right. The SAS man took a round in the calf and buttocks, and his weapon was shot out of his hands. David was hit in the hip by a ricochet, which knocked him to the ground. Luckily a lot of speed had come off the bullet, though it left a large bruise. He returned fire into the cave and crawled to the back of the humvee, continuing to provide covering fire. David even grabbed the SAS soldier's weapon and passed it to the wounded trooper taking shelter under the vehicle – not realising it had been rendered totally useless.

He was conscious of seeing Sarbi a couple of times in the distance, reassuring himself that she wasn't going to 'leg it' and take off. But suddenly his immediate concerns were with his injured companion. The humvee began to move off . . . and the SAS trooper sheltering underneath only saved himself by grabbing the axle and being dragged along a short distance until David attracted the driver's attention and stopped the vehicle.

Three hours or so into the contact, David was beginning to tire with the injuries to his legs and hip. The machine gun on the back of a nearby humvee was being manned by the interpreter. To give him a spell David decided to jump on the back of the vehicle and take over the gun. But just as he was stepping up to it, two rocket-propelled grenades exploded – one above the humvee, the other beneath it.

'The guys in the vehicle behind thought we'd actually hit an IED,' David recalls. The force of the explosions knocked him off the vehicle, onto the ground – and a few moments later the interpreter rolled off, suffering serious head wounds. It was then that SAS Trooper Mark Donaldson (who later became a dog handler and whose German shepherd, Devil, was killed in Afghanistan) ran from the humvee behind, through fire, to pick up the injured interpreter and carry him back to the vehicle and some safety. It was an act of such singular gallantry that Trooper Donaldson was awarded the Victoria Cross: one of four won by Australian soldiers in Afghanistan.

As for Sergeant David Simpson, he lay on the ground for a few seconds gathering himself. Shrapnel had inflicted further wounds to his arms and shoulders, though fortunately his body armour had protected more vital parts.

'By that time the vehicle I'd been on had gone too far ahead to catch up, and it was too far to go to the one behind. About thirty metres off there was a ditch near the road, and I took cover there for a while. That's where I saw Sarbi again in the distance a little bit. I called her towards me . . . and she got about five metres away when one of the vehicles fired over the top of her again. She took fright and moved away once more. And that was actually the last time I saw her during the fight.'

The firing didn't stop until the convoy was a kilometre or less from the base camp gates. David scrambled into the back of a vehicle for the ride home.

'At that point one of the guys cried out that he could see Sarbi. I called to her, but we couldn't stop because of the number of wounded . . . Nine of the twelve Australians had been hit, including myself, there was the dead American soldier and the seriously injured interpreter. It didn't cross my mind to ask them to stop. Sarbi could see where we were going and I was happy she'd be able to come back in herself. Apparently – I don't know if it's true – but apparently she got close to the base, although the Afghan security forces shooed her away. They didn't realise it was our dog, or else we may have recovered her.'

As it was, the next thing David heard about Sarbi was that his dog had disappeared – officially listed as Missing in Action.

He and the other wounded soldiers were evacuated to a military hospital at Tarin Kowt where, over the next week or more, David began to hear reports that Sarbi had been seen a couple of times with village people in the district around Anaconda. As soon as the medics discharged him, David flew back to the operating base to see if he could find her.

'I was there for another ten days or so, helping the intelligence guys . . . putting out radio blasts to the locals to let them know our dog was missing and that we'd provide a reward if they gave information that led to the dog's return. Unfortunately no one took up the offer and she stayed out there. I wasn't allowed out of the base myself because of the injuries. But I'd go and look out the walls to see if I could sight her. Yet by that time . . .'

It was with a heavy heart and a foreboding he might not see Sarbi again that David returned to Sydney at the end of his rotation in November 2008. He went back to the EDD section, being posted to Townsville with a new dog, Tana. But always in his mind was the question of what had happened to Sarbi.

'We maintained contact with some of the intel guys. I'd get reports that she'd been seen somewhere . . . or was thought to be dead now . . . and then another report would come in that she'd been seen. It was fairly up and down during that period . . .'

And then in October 2009, nearly a year later, when David was back at Holsworthy for a course, he got a phone call from his colleague Corporal Murray Young, then in Tarin Kowt, to say it seemed that Sarbi had been recovered and was safely back at Anaconda base.

'He hadn't yet seen her . . . couldn't definitely say it was Sarbi until she'd been returned to TK and had her microchip scanned. But he seemed fairly certain it was her . . . And I was pretty confident too,' David says. 'I was very happy. I rang my girlfriend Kira, now my wife, to tell her the news with a big smile on my face.'

Once the dog was back with the Australian forces at Tarin Kowt, Murray Young had no doubt it was Sarbi. After all, he was the one who'd collected her and brother Rafi from their original owners at Bowral. Now back with her soldiers, Sarbi was given her first bath for a year, feted and welcomed by everyone, and returned to life with her canine friends in the dog kennels. Where she was placed on a strict diet – this lithe military working dog had put on at least five kilos during her time away. Whatever else she may have been doing, Sarbi had not been starving and having to forage for herself in a barren country.

The puzzle of exactly what happened to Sarbi during the fourteen months she was missing is still unsolved. It seems likely that, having been unable to get back into camp on the day of the ambush, Sarbi had been taken by local villagers. Eventually she'd been handed over to the local Taliban warlord, Mullah Hamdullah, who kept Sarbi partly as a kind of 'war trophy', and partly because his wives liked her and had the dog accompany them as they moved about the district. Hence Sarbi's very comfortable existence. No wonder she put on weight.

Certainly Hamdullah appears to have refused an early offer of a reward for the return of the dog, or to exchange Sarbi for his father who was being held by the authorities (knowing, apparently, that his father was soon due for release). Thereafter things are a bit unclear. The early stories suggested that Hamdullah at length grew tired of the dog and so began negotiations with the forces at Anaconda base to hand her over for the reward (which was nowhere near as substantial as the amount Hamdullah had been demanding).

Now, however, David believes it was rather different. To be sure it is likely Hamdullah kept her as a war trophy – as a kind of canine prisoner of war. 'If the Taliban got an anti-aircraft weapon, rather than fire it and shoot an aircraft down, they'd often hold it as a trophy weapon. It would be held for esteem and the prestige, and I think Sarbi would have been part of that.

'One of the things I heard is that Hamdullah tried to retain the dog for the reward, but apparently that wasn't true. The intelligence I got was that the American green berets – the US Special

Forces – had done a hit on a target . . . a compound . . . and when they finished with that they found Sarbi there. They didn't know she was in the compound. It was only afterwards that they saw her and worked out she was possibly an Australian military working dog. Somebody gave her a few commands in English. *Sit! Stay! Seek On!* . . . and watched her chase a tennis ball. Yep, she was responding, so they took her back to the base.'

The news that Sarbi had been recovered broke on 11 November 2009 – Armistice Day – when Prime Minister Kevin Rudd was visiting the Australian base at Tarin Kowt. It went around the world. Media attention on the dog and her story was huge. Sarbi's photo was everywhere amid the plans to start bringing her home. Here was a positive story from a war that had already gone on for eight long years and had claimed a lot of lives. Her return was a huge boost for public morale as well as that of her soldiers . . . playing into that sense of hope and renewal we all need. That which was lost had been found, and we all felt better for it.

David saw Sarbi for the first time since her return when he arrived at Tarin Kowt in early April 2010 for his third rotation. It was naturally an emotional reunion, though like every handler his affection was balanced with discipline. He gave the dog a thorough examination, finding no wounds or other damage: if anything, excess pampering had been her problem, and he ordered her to lose a lot more weight. 'Sarbi was pretty chunky,' he remembers.

Seven weeks later he saw Sarbi off as the dog boarded an aircraft bound for Dubai, where she would spend six months in quarantine – and received a great many distinguished visitors. At length, in December, she landed back home in Sydney, though even then she underwent another month in quarantine. Not until early January 2011 was EDD 436 returned to David Simpson at the School of

Military Engineering dog kennels at Holsworthy Barracks.

'When Sarbi arrived I could see straight away she was fine to go back to work,' David says. 'So I did an assessment, took her out on searches, wrote a bunch of reports saying *Yep she's fine . . . there are no adverse reactions from her time overseas and she's fine to work.*'

But it had to go higher, and in the end the senior military brass decided that Sarbi wasn't to go overseas again as a working dog – she was to retire. The dog had become so celebrated in the media, the view was probably correctly taken that if anything further happened to Sarbi on deployment, it would be The End. For them, that is. In terms of Sarbi's public fame it was just The Beginning.

She retired from service and went to live with David and Kira and their golden Labrador, Vegas, who had been the soldier's first EDD. Sarbi had already been presented with her War Dog Operational Medal, with Afghanistan clasp, and the five-year Canine Service Medal. When she was presented with the RSPCA Purple Cross, in April 2011 at the Australian War Memorial, she wore both square medals proudly over the left shoulder, on the green silk jacket of the Incident Response Regiment, with the motto *To Protect*.

The Purple Cross was given in recognition for the resilience and strength Sarbi had shown during her captivity. But David prefers to believe it honours the work that she, and all the dogs, had done on deployment. The explosives and equipment they'd found, and the number of lives they had saved. Sarbi was only one of over sixty military working dogs that went to Afghanistan, of whom six explosive detection dogs and four SAS dogs died. It's undoubtedly true, however, that Sarbi's celebrity ensured that all of them received their share of public acknowledgement with the Purple Cross.

———

Sarbi lived for about four years with David, Kira and Vegas after her retirement. A substantial book, *Saving Private Sarbi*, was written about her by Sandra Lee. The park in northern Brisbane was named after her in late February 2015, adorned with a bronze statue by sculptor Kathy McLay of the dog sitting with her paw raised as if about to shake hands . . . a typical Sarbi gesture, as it is with many dogs. David and Sarbi went to the opening, and a photo was taken of her sitting next to her bronze representation.

Shortly before the family moved from Sydney to Brisbane in 2015, EDD Vegas died. The golden Labrador was around sixteen, a good age for a dog, and she'd had a happy life. In her working days she'd even got to meet the Queen during a royal visit. Then, less than a month after the park opening, Sarbi began to have seizures. They became more frequent . . . the treatment was getting invasive . . . and it was discovered the dog had a brain tumour. With great sadness, David and Kira decided to have her put down in late March. 'It was hard,' he says, 'but you have to do the right thing for the dog.'

At the same time the two decided that it might be nice if Sarbi were mounted.

'We contacted the Australian War Memorial before she passed away, to see if they'd be able to assist with the mounting and that she'd be donated to them afterwards. They said, "Yep, we'll do that." When she did die, Sarbi was kept in the fridge at the vet until she was transferred to the taxidermist in Melbourne.'

And how do they feel about it?

'Good, I think, from the effect Sarbi had when she did come back. There were so many people who loved to hear the story of how she returned, we thought it would be a good idea to let everyone else who visits the War Memorial in Canberra have the same experience . . . to recognise what the dogs did and the lives they saved . . . and of course to hear how she was found. I hadn't quite realised it at the time, but many people saw Sarbi as not just a good news story from Afghanistan – although it is certainly that. But people also liken it to their own life experiences . . . of not giving up, of maintaining hope.'

Which of course is David Simpson's own story as well.

Now, having left the army and the Explosive Detection Dog section with the rank of Warrant Officer, David Simpson looks back on Sarbi as the best all-round dog he worked with. The other dogs he took on his five deployments to Afghanistan were good, but each had faults. PJ was fine at detecting, but didn't work well around the noise of gunfire and battlefield explosions. Sonic had another great nose . . . but he'd bark and jump around in cars and helicopters, which again is something you don't want in military emergencies. Tana was easily distracted and would chase creatures like chickens. It's not the best thing during a village search, although in retirement he is doing very valuable work helping as an assistance dog with veterans suffering post-traumatic stress disorder and other difficulties.

ASSISTANCE DOGS

In recent years a number of state-based organisations have begun programs to provide properly trained and accredited canine (sometimes called K9) helpers specifically for returned servicemen and women suffering from nightmares and flashbacks, anxiety attacks and withdrawal symptoms in public, usually as the result of combat stress. The number of available dogs is still relatively small and demand is high, but some contact points can be found in the Sarbi chapter notes for those who may be interested.

It's quite remarkable what the dogs can do: wake someone from a nightmare; give practical support about the house, and a feeling of security and confidence in public; seek help; retrieve medicines; fetch a telephone; interrupt an anxiety attack, and perform a good many other tasks tailored to the needs of their owner. Above all, the dogs give comfort, independence, companionship and even a sense of responsibility for another life. There have been a number of reports where the presence of an assistance dog is said to have helped prevent a suicide. And thus it may be thought they are still saving lives.

Which is surely the best tribute that can be given to all of them. They are all animal heroes . . . all serving human beings and meeting their needs at times of crisis, both on the battlefield and away from it.

In death, as in life, *We Will Remember Them*.

WAR DOG SCHOOL

We're in a search house at the Explosive Detection Dog training section at the School of Military Engineering, Holsworthy, where a young tan and black kelpie-cross called Ace is being assessed as to whether he has the makings of an EDD. He's come from an animal shelter not far away; and although he's been at the school for a couple of weeks, being tested for temperament and what the Doggies call 'prey drive', this is Ace's first day in the search house.

There's not much doubt about the dog's obsession with tennis balls.

He's already had one session today with the trainers and they're just getting ready for the next one.

'Good boy Ace!' cries Sergeant Ben Bartolo, one of the four men from the Training Development Cell in the house. He bounces a tennis ball. Ace scampers around after it. Picks it up and runs back. Ben takes the ball from his mouth and throws it to Corporal Murray Young – the same Murray Young who collected Sarbi. Another bounce.

'Good dog!' The simple words of praise and encouragement for a dog are the same the world over, as is the affectionate petting of the ears and neck. 'Clever boy!' It's all part of the business of 'razzing' the dog. Revving him up. Building the excitement in Ace for when they're ready to get serious. Not that he needs much more of it!

The room in the training house is a fair size – as large as an average suburban lounge. There's a short passageway with doors off it, and at the end a two-way mirror with a couple of holes beneath it, one above the other. A few more bounces of the ball and they're ready to start.

'Come, Ace!' Ben Bartolo squats down and holds Ace by the khaki webbing harness all military dogs wear at work. Murray Young runs forward and places a milk crate beneath the lower of the two holes in the wall under the mirror. He runs back, radiating excitement and a sense of play to the dog, and stands behind Ace with Sergeant Bartolo.

'Hang on!'

Just before the game (or, from the human point of view, the training session) begins, Sergeant John Cannon, trade manager for the EDD section and a handler with a lot of experience, notices something wrong.

Two mirrors high on the passage wall need adjusting so that Lance-Corporal Shaun Ward, who is standing out of sight behind the two-way mirror, can see what is happening at the two holes beneath it. They're both about the size of a tennis ball. The lower one, with a grille in front, has a piece of plastic explosive (PE4) in it. The one above is a chute that goes through to Shaun on the other side.

The mirrors are set.

'Right-oh!' And Murray comes from behind Ace with the tennis ball in his hand. He shows it to the dog.

'Look Ace! See the ball.' And as the dog starts to squirm with excitement, eager to escape Ben's grip on the harness, Murray runs to the end of the hall and places the tennis ball on the milk crate, just below the hole with the explosive in it. He runs back and opens his hands in front of Ace, showing him the ball's not there now.

'Where is it?' The physical actions and voices of the men are all ramping up the level of excitement in the room. It's a good game!

'Seek on, Ace.' The same words that every military working dog has heard these last sixty years or more. 'Seek on!' Ben releases his hold on the harness and Ace is off like a shot down the hall.

He's seen exactly where Murray put his ball on the milk crate. And as he picks it up in his mouth, his remarkable nose – thousands of times more powerful than a human's – catches a whiff of the plastic explosive. To the trainers this is what they call the 'odour pool' – though to the dog it's just another smell at first. Ace runs back to Ben with the ball. It's passed up to Murray standing behind him.

'Good boy!'

They play this game a few more times. The dog resolutely stares at Murray each time he places the ball on the milk crate, every repetition helping to imprint just a little more on Ace's mind the association of the smell of the explosive with the tennis ball reward.

Then comes a variation. Murray only *pretends* to put the ball on the crate. He makes the gesture, but in fact the tennis ball goes into his pocket.

He runs back and shows his hands to the dog. Nothing there again.

'Seek on!' Ace rushes up to the milk crate, but this time the ball isn't there.

He does catch the odour of the plastic explosive however. And as he does so Shaun, watching from behind the mirror, drops a tennis ball down the chute. For Ace, the tennis ball reward appears as if by magic.

They play this a few more times before a further variation is added. Murray takes the milk crate away and stands at the back of the room. Now Ben is the one who has the ball, showing it to Ace.

As the handler, he's holding the dog by the harness . . . and, when he's ready, *pretends* to throw the ball down the passage towards the hole.

'Seek on!'

Ace is released, and at once rushes down the passage – but there's no ball to be seen.

It should be here, but it isn't!

He casts around for a bit.

Where is it? And of course his nose catches a whiff of the explosive's odour. And immediately the tennis ball appears down the chute like a conjuring trick.

That's clever! The dog picks up the ball, runs back to Ben who takes it from his mouth. *Let's play that game again!*

So it goes on for another three or four times until, even to a casual observer like myself, Ace quite clearly pauses in his search at the hole with the explosive in it. And when he does, immediately the tennis ball appears. Each time the dog's attraction to the odour pool (and the associated tennis ball reward) is becoming just that little bit more noticeable.

At last, after about ten minutes, the session comes to an end. This time, still holding Ace by the harness, Ben *really* throws the ball down to the end of the hall. It hits the wall, bounces a couple of times, then dribbles along the skirting board around the corner and out of sight.

But instead of letting Ace run after it, as the dog is expecting with much delighted anticipation, Ben takes him away. Back to the kennels. Full of praise.

'Good boy, Ace!'

The dog knows exactly where the ball is. Down the passage in that room, just sitting there for him next time he comes in. Ace can't wait to get back!

'It's like any stage show,' says Sergeant Cannon. 'You always need to stop when the audience is cheering and wanting more. Don't leave it until they start to get bored.'

Not that there seems much likelihood of young Ace losing interest in this game any time soon. Although this is perhaps one of the simpler training routines, it's an effective one. And even on this first day in the search house, John Cannon thinks Ace has further shown he has real potential as an EDD . . .

At the back of the room is a stack of cement construction blocks, like a row of shelves, in which are placed sealed tins with holes punched in them. They contain a variety of substances: tea, coffee and so on. But during a training session one of them will have a piece of explosive in it – and the tennis ball reward will be thrown when the dog pauses at the right one. The handler throws it from *behind* the dog, hitting the block near the correct tin, so that to the animal it seems that the ball is appearing – again by magic – from the source of the odour.

Another method is to use a little wire cage, about twelve centimetres square by two deep. A small piece of explosive is in the cage, which is hidden somewhere in a room – behind a couch, say – or outdoors. Again, when the dog pauses at the scent, the reward ball is thrown to the couch from behind, so that for the dog it seems to be coming from the odour pool.

The wire is there to prevent the dog's nose coming into contact with the explosive, as is the grille in front of the hole in the wall. Not only can explosive substances be poisonous, but the trainers don't want the dog to think that the explosive is the reward. The last thing you'd want on a real search is for a dog to start scratching away at a potential bomb. It's the association between the odour and the tennis ball that matters.

Hence, the whole emphasis when EDD training starts in earnest is for the dog to adopt what is known as a passive response – that is, to 'stand off' and sit when it detects a particular odour it associates with the tennis ball reward. The same is true for the drug detection dogs used by customs officers with Border Force. Sitting is the ideal, though EDD section will accept a drop. For some dogs the drop is a natural response. The aim is for the dog to adopt the passive response of its own volition, without a human command.

As David Simpson observed of his training with Sarbi: 'If the dog makes the decision itself to sit, and you reinforce it with the command, it will learn a lot better, because it doesn't have the distraction of you talking to it or physically manipulating it. The dog's actually had something in its head saying, *Nothing's happening here, I might just sit down*. Then it gets a reward for that and it thinks, *Gee that went well* . . . Actually thinking about it, and making that decision for itself, will make work and training much better.'

The games with the tennis ball never stop, as we saw with old Boris. He was playing them with Lee Doyle right to the last. Even on deployment the tennis ball is used when exercising and going through the daily training routines back at base. In the field, of course, there is no tennis ball. No games around potential bombs! Once a dog indicates a likely source of explosives or weapons, there is rarely time even for a quick sit.

'Come!' The dog is called back immediately and the 'techs' are advised there's something for them to investigate. Again, you don't want your highly trained animal – and very good mate – sitting beside what is possibly an unexploded device.

As we saw with the Vietnam tracker dogs, each animal has its own distinctive point or indication, and some are so subtle that only the handler can tell. Even then it may be missed – with potentially

disastrous results in the field, as Denis Ferguson found with a dead
enemy's rifle pointing at him in Vietnam, or Bob Bettany who kept
following his enemy into a dangerous creek. In Sarbi's case, her
point was very obvious. When she got a whiff of something nearby
she'd slow down, stiffen up a little, and stalk it until she was close
enough and confident about the scent. Then she'd do a slow-motion
sit. Or try to, until she was called back. Indeed, one of her paws
would often come up in the classic 'handshake' gesture.

But you wonder how the dogs respond when during a real
search, having found an odour they associate with the reward,
no tennis ball is forthcoming. Do they stop working? Not at all,
John Cannon says. 'A good detection dog will work very well when
it's given a consistent reward. It will work even harder when that
reward is *in*consistent. The dog's had thousands of tennis balls . . .
a few times without won't matter.'

Sergeant Cannon explains that the school trains the dogs to
detect a number of distinct odours, one or more of which are used in
almost all known explosives. They begin with one, as we saw when
Ace started out on his first day. Once that becomes imprinted on the
dog they move to another explosive, and so on, each stage becoming
a little easier as the dog begins to learn what's required – or rather,
what this game is all about.

If Ace is accepted by the school his training will take about four
months, at which point he graduates as a properly accredited EDD
and is assigned to a handler with a military unit. Not all dogs are
suitable, of course, and drop out of training, just as many of those in
the initial assessments turn out to be unsuitable.

There's no specific type of dog they look for. John Cannon
says they come in all shapes and sizes, although in broad terms
Australian working dogs or crosses of them – Labradors, kelpies,

collies, springers and heelers – seem to produce the best dogs for this sort of work. The one common denominator is a powerful prey and retrieving drive.

And they come from many different sources as well: some from private homes, like Sarbi and Rafi, where the family moves location; or there may be not enough space; or the manic ball drive can prove too much for a distracted private owner. And they all keep their existing names (unless, say, it's Goldilocks or Cutie, which aren't really appropriate in a military environment). Some, like Ace, come from animal shelters, approached by the EDD section asking if they have any dogs with the characteristic obsession they're looking for.

'Some even have been saved at the last moment,' John says. 'We've sometimes rung a pound or animal shelter and asked if they have anything suitable. "Hang on five minutes!" It turns out they've been able quickly to rescue a dog already on the vet's operating table about to be euthanised. And it's gone on to lead a valuable life.'

It's true, of course, that even a dog with the most obsessive ball drive may not turn out to be suitable for the work of an explosive detection dog. In that case, if the dog came to the team from the public, it's rehomed from the barracks. But if it came from a shelter, it's returned to that shelter to find another home.

Back at EDD section with Sergeant Cannon at the School of Military Engineering, the young kelpie Ace, like every other candidate, is put through a whole series of tests during his two-week assessment, of which the prey drive is one. He's done well so far, but even that could fade once he settles in to his new surroundings – sufficient to get him out of the pound, but quickly dropped once he's achieved that. Then there are other requirements. Is he afraid of loud noises? Does he mind working on slippery surfaces or in confined spaces? Is he aggressive with other dogs? Okay around people and vehicles? Does he cling to his handler or stride out in front, inquisitive for the ball and the world around him? All those positives that suggest he'll make a good EDD. And even some of the negatives, such as aggression, can be the sort of thing that's desirable in a police or special operations assault dog.

Readers will be pleased to know that Ace passed his assessment. He's no longer a Candidate Dog (CD). He's now a Training Dog (TD). That's ace, Ace!

Once accepted by the EDD section, the dogs begin an intensive course with the specialists in the training cell or with soldiers learning to become dog handlers. Not infrequently the dog, like Sarbi, will become the trainees' own EDD – and indeed retire to their family home when its working days are over.

At Holsworthy, the dogs each have their own night kennel, although some may share a day run. There's an agility course within the kennels compound, for the dogs need to be able to work in all kinds of situations. The daily routine is pretty unvarying. As soon as the trainer comes in they take each dog for a walk, then let it run about for a bit while they clean the kennels.

The dogs' quarters are know as the Sabre Kennels, after a beautiful (if somewhat temperamental around officers) white German shepherd called Sabre, who was one of eleven dogs trained at the School of Military Engineering (SME) as a landmine detection dog in the early 1970s. The plan was to take them to Vietnam, but Australian troops withdrew before they were deployed. Sabre's mounted body can still be seen at the SME museum, wearing a red uniform jacket with a sergeant's three stripes on the shoulder.

'Today, though, we don't give our military working dogs a

rank,' John Cannon laughs. 'Otherwise they might outrank the handler – and who would give the orders then . . . ?'

With the kennels cleaned, the sappers go for their daily PT exercise – usually a run, accompanied by their dog, but not if they go to the gym for a workout. In the field, however, they always like the dog to do some outdoor exercise with them. Then back, a quick shower for the handlers and a clean up for the dogs, breakfast, and then begins the day's training. It's nice if the dog has had some basic obedience training. *Sit! Stay! Come! Drop!* But in any event they very much pick that up in the course of their schooling.

As with Ace, training usually begins in one of the two search houses. Once the passive response to the first scent is mastered, they move on to the other odours, using the same techniques – the hole in the wall, cement blocks or the little cage. The dog also has to learn how to search a house methodically: scenting all around the skirting boards and walls up to just above head height. There's no point in the dog rushing into a room and searching randomly. It might miss something. If there's a table or similar, the dog can jump onto it – or the handler can lift it onto another object to sniff higher up the wall. Of course it also has to search roof cavities, cellars, under the house and inside furniture. In fact, the trainers say that if a good dog detects a substance inside a cupboard, for example, sometimes it will sit if the odour's on a higher shelf and drop if it's lower down.

From indoors, training moves outside: learning to search building exteriors, of course, then the other four main types of search: route, area, vehicle and people.

The route searches along roads and tracks were particularly important in Afghanistan, where improvised explosive devices caused such death and injury for the coalition forces. Handler Sapper Darren Smith, his companion Sapper Jacob Moerland and

EDD Herbie were all killed in a single IED blast. It was the first death in action of an Australian military dog handler, although a number of British and American handlers have been killed in the line of duty.

Darren Smith was an active member of the Australian Defence Force Trackers and War Dogs Association committee until his death on 7 June 2010; and he is the focal point of the national memorial at Wacol in Brisbane. The association's former president and current historian, George Hulse, says that Darren's death really brought home to their own people the risk handler and dog are constantly asked to take. Now 7 June is celebrated as a national day to honour not just the military working dogs but all service dogs and their handlers.

Vehicle searches were also very important in Afghanistan. At one stage the dogs used to conduct vehicle searches on the leash; but when John Cannon went to Afghanistan with his dog Sam, and Sapper Phil Grazier with Jasmine, Cannon decided to change it. In late 2005 they were the first EDD deployment to that theatre (man and dog actually travelling together first class in the airliner because of temperature problems in the cargo hold). The place was replete with explosives and John realised that searching with the dog on leash at vehicle checkpoints was far too dangerous. He had a blast wall erected to protect the handler and had the dogs search off leash: a practice they've continued to the present. It should be added that Sergeant Cannon also introduced the dark glasses – the 'doggles' – for Sam and his companions to wear as eye protection against the clouds of fine dust in the country, and that practice continued throughout the deployment as well.

Another problem for the dogs can be the sound of gunfire on their sensitive ears. You can't have a dog that is 'gun shy' when you're in action. At EDD training they're introduced to the noise in gradual steps. For a dog like Ace, when still on assessment they look for his reactions to thunder and other loud noises about the place. What's he like in a revving vehicle and, later on, in a helicopter? But once accepted for training, they start taking the dogs to the range when firing practice is underway. They stand well back at first . . . but little by little they move closer to the guns and the noise of the explosions . . . watching for the dog's response . . . letting their ears adjust to it, so they won't take fright and flee when faced with the real thing.

Some dogs just don't get used to it and have to be rejected as EDD, though they might still have other roles to play, as assistance dogs, for example. And even a well-trained dog can take sudden fright, as we saw with Sarbi when the rocket-propelled grenades were exploding around her and she stood off, following her soldiers from a distance (which, for an unprotected animal, could very well be seen as a sensible precaution).

Once a dog has completed its basic training, it is important to constantly maintain discipline both at the School of Military Engineering and after the dog has been assigned to its handler. The handlers only have one dog at a time, with which they bond and are fully responsible for.

At Holsworthy the regimen is for a dog to do at least one of the five basic searches every day – a building, route, area, vehicle or person search – using the tennis ball reward. And to reinforce the imprinting, a different explosive is used each time. Full records are kept on each EDD, and on the monthly sheet they like to see each odour having been used at least twice, giving the team a few spare days to focus on problem areas – difficulty with a particular odour, say, or searching vehicles.

Upon completion of their training, the dogs are assigned to handlers in a range of units, including the Combat Engineer Regiments and Special Operations Engineer Regiment. The Royal Australian Air Force is by far the largest user of military working dogs in Australia, training their own patrol dogs at Amberley as a key element of protecting air force bases around the country. The RAAF Fire and Security School also trains military police dog handlers and consults with army engineer and special forces dog handlers and trainers.

It's clear that over the past decade and a half there's been a very substantial acceptance in the armed services of the great value of the military working dog – and numbers have grown considerably. Of course the figure waxes and wanes a bit according to the level of engagement. When the first explosive detection dogs were sent to Afghanistan at the end of 2005 there weren't enough of them trained at full operational level, and some had to work back-to-back rotations (with different handlers). Many of the handlers also served two or three deployments or more. Still, the fact that sixty-two explosive detection dogs went to Afghanistan (compared to twelve to Solomon Islands and six to East Timor) plus the military working dogs with the SAS and commandos, speaks eloquently of the level of their military appreciation. Outside the EDD section a memorial to the dogs that have died has the following ode:

> My eyes are your eyes
> To watch and protect yours.
> My ears are your ears,
> To hear and detect evil minds in the dark.
> My nose is your nose,
> To scent the danger of your domain,
> And so you may live, my life is also yours.

The national monument at Wacol unveiled in 2012 is perhaps the first in the world to recognise the service rendered by both military and civil law enforcement service dogs. George Hulse says it's still to be decided whether all dogs that have served since the 1950s will be named (that would run into some thousands) or just those that have died. In any event, he cannot speak too highly of the help given to the ADF Trackers and War Dogs Association by the Queensland RSPCA. 'They bent over backwards for us,' he says, 'making land at the Wacol campus available for the memorial, and Society members helping gratis with the architectural design and project management of the monument.'

Even so, the memorial cost the association about $250 000, and it was hard work raising that sum from public donations. It was made somewhat easier by the fact that the design also includes a memorial to Sapper Darren Smith, his dog Herbie, and Sapper Jacob Moerland – reinforcing the notion that the dogs and their handlers offer their lives in the service of all of us.

George Hulse, who served with the engineers in Vietnam, puts it this way: 'I had some of my soldiers killed in Vietnam and badly wounded, and my heart went out to every one of them. If I could use a dog to save a soldier I would, but I wouldn't put a dog there deliberately to be killed saving our lives. They're there to help us, and they are no good to us dead. The death of every military working dog affects me of course, but I'm not going to shed a tear in the same way I would for soldiers when I hear they've been killed in action.'

There are memorials to the military working dogs in almost every state and territory of Australia. At the Australian War Memorial in Canberra there is not only a beautiful memorial to all animals in war, designed by Steven Holland using the damaged bronze head modelled on Sandy from the original Light Horse memorial destroyed at Suez. In 2015 a bronze sculpture of a sapper and his dog, *Elevation of the senses*, by Ewen Coates, was unveiled to honour all the explosive detection dogs and their handlers. It's a splendid work, full of emotion; the bronze tennis ball sitting on top of the soldier's kitbag brought tears to my eyes. The ball is almost unnoticed and unremarked upon by visitors – but of course it is *everything* in the bond between human beings and their working service dogs. So with the teams that went to Somalia and East Timor. So with young Ace, starting out on his first day of training in war dog school at Holsworthy.

Ewen Coates's sculpture stands near Poppy's restaurant, not far from the Australian War Memorial front steps, looking down Anzac Parade towards Parliament House. It is flanked on the other side of the entrance by Peter Corlett's statue of Simpson and his donkey, one bronze boot worn smooth by the countless numbers of visitors who have touched it. No doubt trying, as only we can, to make some connection with all the legend has come to represent. Those same visitors have draped both of them with garlands of red poppies, for honour, and for remembrance.

When *Animal Heroes* was first published in 2005, the cost of producing a fully-trained military working dog was estimated to be around $30 000, the value increasing by about $5000 a year during the animal's service life. Today the cost is put at several times that figure: a sum of $100 000 is sometimes mentioned, but it's very general. An accountant could certainly work out the annual salaries of the trainers, handlers, vet fees, kennelling costs, equipment amortisation, transport and so on. But how do you calculate in monetary terms a value for the human lives that have been saved, or the replacement cost of buildings, property and infrastructure that were not destroyed, thanks to the services provided by an explosive detection dog, a patrol, sniffer, police or combat assault dog? It's extremely difficult, indeed, to know just what to include when estimating the savings of something that *didn't* happen.

Ultimately, of course, the worth of any animal with which we live and work, in peace as in war, cannot truly be measured in terms of economic inputs and outputs.

How do we put a monetary value on a small slate-grey carrier pigeon, following its instinct and flying through storm and shellfire, to deliver a message of help for a patrol trapped in New Guinea?

Can we estimate in dollars and cents the hope, the solace, the joy, the will to live, that Judy gave Freddy Bloom, Sheila Allan, and the women and children interned with them in the squalor of Changi Prison?

> *. . . all the tears that I didn't shed . . . have now rushed out.*

And what cost the bond, the fellowship, the depth of those feelings so painfully denied when the men of Vietnam and Malaya were forced to leave their dogs behind as unwanted engineers' equipment?

> *Have you ever seen a dog cry?*

In the end, these things can only be measured by human values. Things like love, loyalty, devotion, laughter, tears, mateship and sacrifice. Things that belong to animal heroes, and which are beyond price. Often they are beyond the power of words to adequately convey, though many soldiers have tried.

Brave Soul that sprung in the colt of you . . .

wrote an Australian light horseman in 1918, of his pal who had shared all their hardships, and now was left behind in Palestine . . .

O! If then there be for the likes o' me
A Heav'n – it must hold you, too.

Seventy years later, a young RAAF police dog handler, Grant Teeboon, discovered that his German shepherd, called Swede, had developed osteoarthritis, and suffered increasing pain as he worked.

It was up to Grant to decide when the time had come to put Swede to sleep. His first military working dog. As he thought about this, Grant wrote down a few lines which turned into a poem of twelve verses. The emotions we feel for our dogs – and the words with which we try to express them – are pretty much the same the world over. Let this verse stand as a tribute not only to Grant's dog, but to all those animal heroes who have served with Australia's fighting forces at home and abroad over the past century and more of our nationhood.

So why, you may ask when you quiz,
Is the friendship between us so fine?
Because the life he lays down will be his,
And the life that he saves will be mine.

CHAPTER NOTES

ABBREVIATIONS

AWM – Australian War Memorial

AWM224 etc. – AWM file number (spacing will vary)

NAA – National Archives of Australia

RELAWM – AWM relic or heraldry items (note spacing); ART – AWM art collection.

Readers are urged to view the many photographs of animals in war on the 'Collection' database at the Australian War Memorial website www.awm.gov.au. Search for dogs, horses, mascots etc., as well as individual names.

INTRODUCTION

Thanks to Dr Brendan Nelson, Director of the Australian War Memorial, for his moving foreword. For more on Horrie, Cassius, Sandy, Pigeon VC, Murphy and mascots, see their respective notes below. The 2009 travelling exhibition A is for Animals, was the first mounted by the AWM specifically for children.

The **RSPCA** policies opposing the training or use of animals 'where injury, pain, suffering or distress is likely to be caused' are Policies C01 and C03, available on the RSPCA website www.rspca. org.au. Thanks to Jane Speechley for her help.

COLONIAL WARS

Chris Coulthard-Clark in his *Encyclopaedia of Australia's Battles* pp 1–55 gives a good overview of the principal clashes during the 'Black Wars'.

THE SUDAN DONKEY

A photograph of the Sudan donkey at Duntroon can be seen online at the Canberra & District Historical Society, www.canberrahistory. org.au. ID 15475, search 'Soudan Donkey'. Also search the Australian War Memorial collection for 'Sudan'.

Also spelled 'Soudan'. The Sudan campaign was, as Ken Inglis observes, in many ways 'a rehearsal' for Australian involvement in the Boer War, the First and, to some extent, the Second World War.

An article by Tom Gunning, a member of the NSW Contingent, recalling the donkey's 'capture', in *As You Were 1947* pp 99–100, suggests the donkey went to a property at Narellan, NSW. **Return** of the contingent and the humour provided by 'the very uncomfortable-looking donkey' in the rain at Circular Quay, *SMH* 24 June; *Sydney Mail* 27 June 1885. 'Flower of the British army', *Sydney Mail* 27 June 1885. **Hop cartoons** ridiculing the donkey, see *The Bulletin* 27 June, 4 July, 18 July, 24 October 1885; 13 June 1896; 9 July 1898 (reporting the donkey's death); and news that he was then still alive at Duntroon on 10 March 1910.

Historical accounts of the contingent and the return of the donkey are in Stanley, *But Little Glory*, especially the article by Coulthard-Clark p 26 and accompanying photo; Inglis pp 131–57, who says the donkey at Duntroon was 'a ring-in'. However, an article by Coulthard-Clark, 'The Soudan donkey at Duntroon', in the *Canberra Historical Journal* March 1982, and *Duntroon* p 32, suggests the Duntroon connection is correct. The Royal Zoological

Society of NSW minutes of 2 July 1898 note that a 'list of deaths was read' at the meeting, but there is no mention of the donkey.

'Enobesra' was concocted at RMC in 1923. The story of Samson and the jawbone of an ass will be found in Judges Ch 15, v 15–17. Sir Frederick Scherger became Air Chief Marshal in 1965, and Lieut-Gen Sir Reginald Pollard became Chief of the General Staff. For many years the trophy was in the officer cadets' mess, but around 2002 it went missing. See Coulthard-Clark *Duntroon* p 103 and Moore pp 69–71. **Enobesra replacement,** sincere thanks to Lieut-Col John Bullen (Ret), Major David Evered, Captain Jack Westhorpe and WO2 Steve Medforth, curator Army Museum of Officer Training RMC Duntroon, for their kind assistance.

Thanks also to Dr Coulthard-Clark, former RMC archivist Ross Howarth, Nola Sharp of the Mitchell Library and Allan Helman, who all helped with this story. For general articles on the Sudan campaign see *Wartime* Issue 21; the AWM website 'Encyclopaedia' entry and collection photographs; Dennis.

BUSHIE

Bushie's portrait, by Wollaston J Thomas, on an AWM postcard is in the Australian War Memorial collection, RC01119. Also search the AWM collection for 'Boer War' for more photos, records and memorabilia.

Photo of Bushie with Lieut Battye *Sydney Mail*, 3 March 1900 with background and Darley's speech. **Airey,** ADB online. **Parade,** Sydney *Telegraph* 1 March 1900. **Bushmen's Contingent movements,** Smith pp iv–vi, 55–9; Wallace. **Horse statistics, horse killer,** Yarwood p 172. **Scorched earth, concentration camps,** see articles in AWM online encyclopaedia. South African History Online puts the number of deaths at 26000 people, 80 per cent of them children: www.sahistory.org.za, search 'concentration camps'. **Rustenburg,** Smith p vi. **Elands River,** Coulthard-Clark *Encyclopaedia* pp 84–5. **Bushie photo,** *Sydney Mail* 30 June 1900. **Daspoort,** *SMH* 12 Oct 1900. **Bushie given to Roberts,** *SMH* 21 November, *Evening News* 27 November. **Roberts at Cowes,** *The Times* 3 January 1901, inc *Court Circular* 3, 15 January 1901.

A letter to the author from the Royal Archives states they can find no reference to Bushie in their records. However, as Andrew Slater was the Land Steward for the Osborne Estate the letter acknowledges there may be some truth to the story. Lieut Battye didn't end up taking Bushie to meet the Queen as he'd hoped. He came down with enteric fever and was invalided home with his father in November 1900.

Bushie 2, A second Bushmen's collie dog called Bushie turned up in an article published in the *Ballarat Star* 10 June 1901 from the *Argus*. It apparently belonged to a Victorian policeman, Constable Horn, who gave it to a friend going to South Africa with a Bushmen's Contingent. Its adventures as described were hair-raising: stabbed aboard ship by a sailor; infected by ticks and losing the use of his back legs for a time during the march from Marandellas (now Marondera) to Mafeking; lost during later fighting and found by a Scottish regiment; shot in the breast and recovered; captured by the Boers and escaped (twice); and eventually reunited with his soldiers and returned home to Constable Horn in Melbourne. The story might be true – but occurring at much the same time and locations as the NSW Bushie, it seems almost too much of a good thing. See also photo and caption AWM P11043.002.

DRIVER

Photographs of Driver and Minnie can be seen online in the Australian War Memorial collection, A02639 and C04359. Also search the AWM collection for 'First World War dogs'.

AWM93 7/4/225, letters and reports from Driver L E Ross, curatorial notes; Chatto pp 8, 145; Long (manuscript kindly made available by Elizabeth Burness).

MURPHY

Photographs of Simpson and his donkeys can be seen online in the Australian War Memorial collection, A03114 and P03088.013. Also search the AWM collection for 'Gallipoli donkey'.

AWM27 172/3 *The story of 'The Man with the Donkey'*, *compiled from AWM records*; AWM27 397/9 *Request to Australian and NZ Forces for information on the location of 'Murphy' after evacuation from Anzac*, March 1916, unavailable online. Bean, *The Anzac Book*, p 53, 'Jenny'; Bean, *Official History*, vol i, pp 552–5; Carlyon pp 266–71; Cochrane esp Ch 6; Curran esp Ch 12; Dennis p 548.

ZEP

Zep's passport is in the Private Records held at the Australian War Memorial collection, PR86/342. A photo of Frank and nurses with the ambulance can also be seen, P02686.026. Also search the AWM collection for 'Zeppelin'.

AWM PR86/342 *Papers of C.F. and E.H. Fryer*; author interview with Mrs Barbara (Judy) Holt, who donated the Fryer material to the AWM on behalf of her family; remembrance booklet for Charles Francis Fryer, kindly loaned by Judy Holt.

LAST RACE

A rare photograph of the races held at Tripoli, Syria, in February 1919 can be seen online in the Australian War Memorial collection,

Jo6619. A probable re-enactment of the charge at Beersheba can be seen at P03723.001. Also search the AWM collection for 'light horse' for many photos.

Billjim is invented, but the name was often used by the light horsemen of themselves (possibly a combination of common Australian and New Zealand names). See also AWM database encyclopaedia entries for 'Kangaroo Feathers and the Australian Light Horse' and 'Waler'. **Last race at Tripoli,** 22 February 1919, Darley pp 170–2, Olden pp 298–300.

Horse disposals, Nutting p 64 states 667 horses of the 4th Regiment were destroyed at Tripoli, the remainder handed over to the 11th and 12th Regiments and the 5th Cavalry Division. See document in AWM25 29/62 for GHQ orders on destruction of horses. For overall numbers see notes for Sandy, below. **Saluting, lamp, donkey,** Gammage pp 140–1; **Turkish POWs** p 144. **Bill the Bastard,** Jones p 21; the gallant animal later became an officer's packhorse. **Beersheba,** Gammage pp 133–4; Jones pp 96–106. Some thirty-one light horsemen were killed and thirty-six wounded in the charge of 31 October 1917. At least seventy horses died.

Sir Harry Chauvel commanded the Desert Mounted Corps. In 1950 Lady Chauvel unveiled a memorial in Sydney to the horses. It says in part: *They suffered wounds, thirst, hunger and weariness almost beyond endurance but never failed. They did not come home. We will never forget them.*

BULLET, TRICK AND NELL

Apart from Bullet, Trick and Nell, E02318, the Australian War Memorial collection also has a fascinating photo of two German messenger dogs in action during a gas attack, H12391. Also search the AWM collection for 'messenger dog'.

AIF War Diaries, 2nd and 4th Aust Div Signal Coys, May–August 1918 (AWM4 rolls 408 and 410). Bullet's 19 hour run, with 16th Bn, 18 June 1918. **Messenger dogs,** Bean, *Official History*, vol vi, p 39. Officially, Nell was War Dog 103, Trick WD 102 and Bullet WD 101.

BILLY BANTAM

A photo of Billy Bantam with Driver Tom Igoe can be seen online in the Australian War Memorial collection, E02722. Jackie's photo with Walter Farrell is P01835.014, Robert sitting on his drum is EN0104.

AWM265 21/5/26 *Mascot bantam of the 13th Bn*, inc letters from Mrs Igoe; White p 62; *Smith's Weekly* 30 October 1926, 'Fighting Chook'. **Jackie**, also see P01836.003, Jackie perched on a stack of rifles.

ROFF

Roff's mounted body can be viewed online in the Australian War Memorial collection, RELAWM04369. A photograph of him with Lieutenant-Colonel Marks at Villers-Bretonneux is E02225 and with the dogcart E02723. Also search the AWM collection for 'messenger dog' for more photos and memorabilia.

AWM93 7/1/55 *German Messenger Dog* inc letters to AWM from Capt McKillop, George Starke and others 1926; letters from Lieut-Col Marks 1918; McKillop, vets, AIF staff and others 1919. Background notes kindly made available by Elizabeth Burness. Names in caption to RELAWM04369. Monash p 241; White p 136; also see Chris Goddard, 'Roff's War', in *Wartime* issue 20. Roff was placed at the Bitterne Manor Farm Quarantine Kennels. The AWM file documents the last sad year of his life.

SANDY

You can see Sandy's head in its glass case online in the Australian War Memorial collection, J02105. A photo of one of General Bridges' chargers and rider in Egypt is J02136, and search the AWM collection for 'First World War horses'.

Chris Coulthard-Clark, 'One came home' in *Wartime* issue 19. **Voyage,** Jones p 23. **Horses at Gallipoli,** Bean, *Official History*, vol ii, pp 78, 169. **Bridges,** Dennis p 120. **Sandy's return,** AWM13 7026/2/31 and AWM27 397/10. **Camels,** *The Kia Ora Coo-ee* pp 13, 19; Gullett *Australia in Palestine,* esp p 125, 'The Camel Brigade' by Trooper Bluegum (Oliver Hogue), also p 78, 'The Horses Stay Behind'. **Numbers,** Yarwood pp 180–1: of the 135 000 horses who left Australia in WWI, 43 000 were used by the AIF, the rest by British and Indian units.

Fate of horses, AWM25 245/112, *Disposal of Animals on Demobilisation*, shows that when the war ended, the AIF had about 15 000 horses and 6000 mules in Europe. Almost all were sold to farmers or for horsemeat. The fate of the horses left in Egypt and Palestine is more contentious, some historians suggesting they were either all shot or 'sold into slavery' (e.g. Cooper p 47, Gammage p 138). Yet the majority appear to have been transferred to Imperial (mainly Indian) army units, and continued their military lives.

A document in AWM25 29/1, *Disposal of AIF Animals in Egypt June–August 1919,* by Col Kendall of Veterinary Services, states that 6126 AIF horses were transferred to Imperial units for War Department purposes, seventy-two were sold, and 111 destroyed. Before the transfer, 2583 horses and mules had been destroyed (which Kendall assumes are those classified as aged over twelve or unfit, and destroyed by AIF units themselves, as at Tripoli). A cable (AWM25 245/112) of 15 January 1919 from Australian

Administrative HQ states that few surplus riding mounts were left 'after refitting Indian Cavalry Division and other Imperial formations, thus assuring quick satisfactory disposal majority AIF animals'. No doubt some Australian horses were among those sold in Egypt after the war, whose mistreatment led to the establishment of the Brooke Hospital at Cairo in the 1930s, see Cooper p 48.

RSPCA Memorial, RSPCA brochure; Bird; 2004 author interviews with Dr Hugh Wirth and Steven Holland. The memorial was unveiled in 2009. The Desert Mounted Corps memorial, unveiled at Port Said in 1932, was designed by C Web Gilbert and completed by Sir Bertram Mackennal. Destroyed during the Suez crisis of 1956. Replicas are at Albany, WA, and in Canberra. The second horse is said to have been modelled on a NZ mare, Bess (Bird).

COCKY

Cocky can still be seen online in the Australian War Memorial collection, RELAWM08024, together with photos of Mrs Bon. Also search the AWM collection for 'cockatoo bird'.

AWM93 7/4/86 (donation of exhibits by Mrs A F Bon 1922–1930): includes letters from Mrs Bon and former nurses of the No 1 Rest Home to John Treloar, then director of the AWM. See esp letters from Nurse Bertha Bennett and Nurse R N O'Connor. The file includes notes about Cocky by Treloar, based on conversations at the Windsor Hotel with Mrs Bon; and a note by Treloar to the director of the National Museum in Melbourne, with directions about Cocky after the bird died in early July 1925. A letter by Mrs Bon states he was then forty-seven years and six months old. See also caption to RELAWM08024.

Casualty rates, Of the 330 000 Australian servicemen who went to the First World War, there were 226 000 casualties, of whom 60 000 were killed: a casualty rate of 68.5 per cent, the highest among all the countries of the British Empire, *The Australian Encyclopaedia*, vol 6, p 387.

HORRIE

The photo from which Horrie's statue was modelled can be seen online in the Australian War Memorial collection, 076877. The AWM also has his soldier's jacket with two corporal's stripes, RELAWM32386, and the smuggling pack, RELAWM32387. Also search the AWM collection for 'Imshie'.

Author interviews with Norma Allen, Betty and Brian Featherstone, Ian and Leonie Moody, who are two of Jim's children, and the late Joan Moody, Jim's second wife. All generously gave access to their material. Idriess *Horrie the Wog Dog* pp 78 war dog, 124 messenger dog, 163 Imshie and bulletin, 222 Hobo, epitaph by kind permission of ETT Imprint and Idriess Enterprises. Moody pp 78 pack, 83 smuggling, 85 Imshie and Horrie home, letters, poems, articles etc. Letters to Jim from his father, Henry, March 1945, kindly loaned by Leonie Moody. NAA: files A432 1945/480 *Destruction of dog, Horrie*; A11984 V213 *Legislation – Commonwealth – Breaches 'Horrie the Wog Dog'*, esp letters from Moody, Wardle and the Director-General of Health, Dr J H Cumpston; WWII Defence Service Records VX13091 J B Moody and NX11568 D M Gill. *Daily Telegraph* 13 February 1945; *Truth* 18, 24, 25 March, 22 April 1945; *Daily Mirror* 25 April, 28 June 1945; Melbourne *Herald* 15 March 1945. Verse by 'Charlie'.

Horrie in retirement, thanks for their help and advice to Ted Bennetts, Betty Featherstone, Tom Griffiths, Richard and Sandra Hubbard, Ian and Leonie Moody, Greg Nankervis, Garry Power, Andrew Rule, Pam and Bill Simpson. Horrie's statue can be seen at the small remembrance park in the main street of Corryong. Andrew's article on Horrie appeared in the Melbourne *Herald Sun* 19 April 2013. For the Bennetts' connection to Horrie see also Perry p 230 ff.

Cautionary note, There is some doubt about the Bennetts' version as another district man, Dick Griffiths, joined up at the same time as his friend Eddie Bennetts and had the consecutive service number. He also went into the 2/1 Machine Gun Battalion and 2/1 Anti-Tank Regiment, and knew Moody. Horrie may have gone to him – but Dick's son, Tom Griffiths, has no recollection of his father ever talking of a smuggled dog or of Moody. His family then lived at Upper Towong on the other side of Corryong to Cudgewa. As another piece of circumstantial evidence, Bill Simpson, who has lived on part of Selsey Station at Cudgewa since 1977, says his father knew the Bennetts family from boyhood – and he sometimes spoke of a dog that had saved lives during the war being smuggled back to Australia. **Benji,** There's a suggestion the dog's name might be a contraction of *Bennetts* and *Jim*, but it's impossible now to verify.

I should say that not everyone accepts the Horrie substitution story. It's thought that, on balance, Horrie was probably destroyed by the authorities and that Jim Moody invented the story afterwards, possibly as cover for his remorse at handing over the dog. The main evidence for this view is Henry Moody's letter of 16 March 1945 – only four days after the dog was put down – in reply to correspondence from Jim that apparently confirmed the dog was Horrie.

It's good evidence on the face of it, but is it conclusive? I doubt it. If the substitution story is correct, it seems most unlikely Jim would tell his father of it in writing so soon after the event. Henry was in Melbourne dealing with the press and public, and the risk the secret might leak out would be acute – putting in jeopardy the dog and everyone involved, including Henry himself. On the other hand, if Henry spoke publicly believing Horrie was dead, it would add a further dimension to the deception.

In the absence of firm contemporary evidence we're unlikely to know for certain. But the oral evidence of three people that Jim told the substitution story to, under pledge of secrecy, after the heat died down; the fact that Moody had already smuggled Horrie into Australia; his opportunity to make a switch in the week's grace before handing over the dog; and the currency Horrie's story (if not the coda) had in the Cudgewa district, suggest to me it is more likely than not to be correct.

Mascot smuggling, Australian soldiers tried to smuggle many mascots home. A letter from Wardle in NAA files states that in March and April 1942 (when Horrie got ashore) quarantine officers seized twenty-one dogs, seventeen monkeys, three squirrels and a cat, rabbit, parrot and other birds found aboard returning troopships. See also *Salt*.

One other verse, by Tom Evans, sent to Jim Moody about Horrie demands a place in this book:

> *But Red Tape said 'We'll strangle him,*
> *At each end hard we'll pull it.'*
> *But then they thought it might give way,*
> *SO THEY GAVE THE DOG A BULLET.*

PIGEON VC

Pigeon 879 DD 43 Q, from the Manus Island contact, can be seen with his Dickin Medal in the Australian War Memorial collection, 134260. Also search the AWM collection for 'pigeons'.

Author interview with Keith Wrightson, a lieutenant with the

Australian Corps of Signals' Pigeon Service in New Guinea during WWII; Wrightson interview with Andrea Close, ABC Radio 2666, Canberra, 11 October 2002. The ABC kindly made the tape available. AWM database encyclopaedia, 'Short history of the Australian Corps of Signals' Pigeon Service from 1942', and also 'Dickin Medal'; Kilgore Ch 2, 'Pigeons at War'. At the time of writing in 2016 Keith is still with us, though at ninety-four he has just closed his pigeon loft at home after seventy-nine years' continuous pigeon racing.

Fate of pigeons, Keith Wrightson estimated up to 10 000 pigeons were left behind in New Guinea when the war ended. There are no natural food grains suitable for them in the country, and cost and quarantine regulations prevented their entry to Australia. It was felt humane to gas the birds, and only very few bodies were returned for display, although these did include the two Dickin Medal winners.

GUNNER

A lovely photo of Gunner with Percy Westcott can be seen online in the Australian War Memorial collection, 044608. Also search the AWM collection for 'Second World War dogs'.

Author interview with Percy Westcott. *The Canberra Times*, 15 August 1981, p 2 article by Frank Cranston on Gunner. In 2016 Percy is happily still with us and retains the fondest memories of Gunner.

REDLEAD

There's no photo that we know of Redlead, but a splendid shot of a mascot kitten peering from the barrel of a ship's gun is online in the Australian War Memorial collection, 304910, and HMAS *Perth*, 301162. Also search the AWM collection for 'Second World War pets'.

Author interview with Mrs Norma Collins, widow of Bob Collins who died in 2000. The kitten's name was spelt as one word. Cassell pp 123–5 is based on interviews with Bob. AWM database encyclopaedia entries for HMAS *Perth*: 'The cat who knew'; Dr Peter Stanley transcript, 'The loss of HMAS *Perth*, 1 March 1942'; items from the collection including Christmas card, map, news clipping; entry for HMAS *Perth* on RAN history site (www.navy.gov.au). See also Whiting p 86; and Parkin *Sunda Strait* Ch 9 for *Perth's* last battles.

JUDY

For photos, search the Australian War Memorial collection of 'Changi', 'Selarang Barracks' and 'Second World War Singapore'.

Author interview with Sheila Bruhn (née Allan); correspondence with Virginia Kanka, the late Freddy Bloom's daughter; correspondence with Hilary Kinghorn, the late Iris Parfitt's niece and co-executor of her estate. Extracts from *Weekly POW-WOW* at the Imperial War Museum, London, kindly researched by Edward Mann and Barbara Large.

March, Allan p 36, Bloom pp 24–5, Parfitt p 2. **Cells,** Parfitt p 10, also Bloom and Allan. **Sparrow,** Allan p 61, Bloom p 76. **Votes,** Bloom p 81. **Nipper,** *Weekly POW-WOW* 27/1/43, plus various references to the dogs, cats, sparrows, goat and hen. **Window,** Bloom p 42. **Quilts,** Allan p 174 ff. **Secret police,** Bloom p 115 ff. **Judy leaping,** Bloom p 139. **Judy's death,** Bloom p 147, Allan p 178. John Allan died in June 1945, two months before the war ended. Sheila came to Australia and has lived here ever since. Her diary was published in 1994. Freddy Bloom's letters were published in 1980.

THE DAWN DOG

A picture of Eros and some of these other dogs are in the photo pages of this book. Also search the Australian War Memorial collection for 'dogs Korea', 'dogs training'.

Author interviews with the late Lance Abbott, George Gray and Allyn McCulloch. **Prince** served in Malaya 1955–7 with George Gray and other Australian dogs including Jewel, Pedro, Tex and the mascot Wild Dog. Four Labrador-crosses from Australia – Rank, Toddy, Gunnar and Simba – served in Malaya and Sarawak during the period of Confrontation 1964–6. They were trained in South Australia by Mason Clark.

Dogs' scenting, Grant Teeboon, formerly of the RAAF Military Working Dog Training Flight, says if the human olfactory membrane were flattened out, it would be the size of a postage stamp compared to a large handkerchief size for a dog. We can smell a stew. A dog could tell you the history of every ingredient in it.

PEDRO

I've been unable to find a picture of Pedro, but there's a splendid photo of Prince in Malaya online in the Australian War Memorial collection, HOB/56/0710/MC, and a number of the other war dogs including Wild Dog, P05001.035. Also search the AWM collection for 'dogs Malaya Emergency'.

I am grateful to the late George Gray for sharing this story and his recollections of early days with Eros, Prince, Tiger and the military working dogs in Australia. He read this story and suggested corrections before his passing.

STAN'S BAD HABIT

There's a picture of Stan in the photo pages of this book. There are many other photographs of mascots in the Australian War Memorial collection, search for 'mascots'.

My thanks to Ted Chitham, secretary of 8/9 RAR Association, for sharing his recollections, and also for permission to draw on information about the mascot, published on the association's website: www.89rar.asn.au. There were four successor Stan the Rams before 8/9 RAR was disbanded in 1997. I acknowledge WO2 Mark Gattenhof and staff of the Infantry Museum, Singleton, NSW, and the president and members of the Royal Australian Infantry Corps' Sergeants Mess, who kindly made photos of Stan available, and the Department of Defence for permission to publish them.

CASSIUS

There are a number of photos of the eleven Vietnam dogs to be seen online in the Australian War Memorial collection, search for 'dogs Vietnam', and also by their names: Caesar, Cassius, Janus, Julian, Juno, Justin, Marcian, Marcus, Milo, Tiber, Trajan.

Author interview with Norm Cameron; Cassius' autopsy report in AWM98 R72/1/3, which shows he collapsed at 10 a.m. and was presented to the vet at 3 p.m. on 12 May 1967. **Tiber,** author interviews with Norm Cameron, Mal Collison (who was at 'Coral'), Ros Leonard (formerly Selleck); Melbourne *Herald* 10 May 1969; Melbourne *Sun News-Pictorial* 18 June 1970 and 13 October 1975, where Tiber was still alive after the fall of Saigon, and promoted to acting Warrant Officer.

Marcus, author interviews with Ian Atkinson, Bob Bettany, Denis Ferguson, Peter Haran; *Wartime* issue 18, 'Dogs of War' by Elizabeth Stewart; Haran, *Trackers*, p 196. Peter Haran kindly gave permission to reproduce the photo from *Trackers*. See also 'Black Dogs' by Trudi Tate in *Quadrant* September 2001. Bob Bettany was secretary of the Australian Army Trackers & War Dogs Association. Memorials to Australia's military working dogs are at Alexandra Headland in Queensland, and at Goolwa in South Australia among other places – see also notes to last chapter 'War Dog School'.

Fate of dogs, Simon Whitehead has done much research into the Vietnam dogs, but there are still gaps in the record. Marcus apparently was handed to a New Zealand military family in Saigon in 1971, when his eyesight was failing. Caesar was given to the British air attaché in September 1970 (letter in AWM98 R72/1/3); and Justin was photographed in Saigon with the manager of the Chartered Bank, who took him in December 1969. Milo also went to a Chartered Bank family, and David Cree, who handled him in 1971, received two Christmas cards from him. The files suggest that Trajan went to a banking family, Janus and Juno to US families, Julian and certainly Tiber to Australian and Marcian to British diplomats. Trajan's Regimental Record of Service (his AAB-83 form) is at AWM98 466, the only one of the Vietnam dogs' known to still exist. It incorrectly calls him 'Trojan'. See also AWM98 72/1/1 and /2.

WILLY'S CURRY DINNER

Pictures of Willy and the tiger are in the photo pages of this book. There are quite a few photos of mascot pigs in the Australian War Memorial collection including the 'tiger pig', COL/67/0316/VN, and others at various stages of the food chain. Search the AWM collection for 'mascots pigs', 'pigs'.

Thanks to General Peter Leahy, now Professor Leahy, Director of the National Security Institute at the University of Canberra for Willy's story. Thanks also to Sergeant Dave Willis, now retired but still living at Holsworthy with his memorabilia, for his embellishments and photographs. One of the Willys apparently remained with the battalion until 1998 when he died of ill health (perhaps not unconnected to overindulgence). He was carried in his funeral procession on the lowered ramp of an APC, and his ashes were divided between the officers' mess and sergeants' mess. In December 2006 the two battalions of 5/7 RAR were unlinked and they were re-raised as separate units once more. Now one urn with Willy's ashes is with 5 RAR and the other with 7 RAR. RIP Willy. Thanks to Chris Shannon, 5/7 Association secretary, for this later information. See www.57rar.com. The battalion still has a pig mascot, currently cared for by Urrbrae Agricultural High School students in Adelaide, which appears on festal days (no more wallowing outside the kitchen door). Cartoons also feature in the Adelaide *Advertiser*. Thanks to the CO, Lieut-Col David McCammon for this advice.

CORPORAL COURAGE

The Australian War Memorial collection has many photos of different mascots. Search for 'mascot birds'.

Author interview with Cpl Kyle Stewart, a member of the search party, and the mascot's chief handler (2004). Biographical notes on Courage I and II kindly supplied by 2nd Cavalry Regiment. Trooper Courage rose through the ranks again, becoming Sergeant Courage in 2002. In the first edition of this book I inadvertently called him 'Sergeant Courage' throughout. He was a sergeant at the time it was written, but the AWOL offence took place when he was still a corporal. Apologies. **WO2 Courage,** Thanks for this update to 2nd Cavalry Regiment, now based in Townsville – in particular WO Anthony Lynch and Lance-Corporal Joseph Blundell, who is one of Courage's team of handlers; and also to Bob Flemming of Billabong Sanctuary. Two handlers are rostered to be in charge of the bird each week. Courage turned 29 on 14 August 2016. He weighs approximately 2.4 kilos. **Courage I** is now in the foyer of regimental HQ.

SIMPSON

Peter Churcher's painting of the Afghanistan donkey Simpson can be seen online in the Australian War Memorial collection, ART91913. Also search the AWM collection for 'Afghanistan donkeys'.

Author interviews with Peter Churcher and WO2 Neil Dailey, Army History Unit, who visited Bagram in August 2002; Lieut-Col Stephen Delaney, Capt Jason Logue, Don Barnby and Mick Malone. AWM captions to Churcher's paintings. *Rendezvous*, Journal of the SAS Association, December 2003, p 15. I acknowledge the kind assistance of the CO and men of SASR. The Department of Defence kindly gave permission to publish the photograph of the donkeys being led up the mountain in Afghanistan.

DOLPHIN PATROL

There's a picture of the Mine Hunting Marine Mammals in the photo section of this book. Also search online for 'marine mammal program'.

Author interviews with Leut-Cmdr Scott Craig RAN, who was with the joint mine clearance team in the Gulf and observed the dolphins at work; Capt Matt Grant. Article by Leut-Cmdr Michael Maley RAN, Deputy Underwater Mine Countermeasures Commander for Operation Iraqi Freedom, in *Navy News* 22 May 2003; articles in *The Times* 29 March and *The Australian* 31 March 2003.

Information and photographs of the dolphins, sea lions and other Marine Mammal Systems may be found on the US Navy website www.public.navy.mil/spawar/Pacific/71500/. In 2004 it stated that the survival rate of the Navy's marine mammals has been around 95 per cent, equal to their survival in the wild. Also search 'Marine Mammal Program', and see an article in *Business Insider* 13 March 2015, available online.

SNAPPA

There's a splendid photo of Snappa in the photo section of this book. Also try the Australian War Memorial collection. Search for 'crocodiles', etc.

Author interview with Maj Nick Faughey, formerly OC 102 Field Workshop, who kindly made available Snappa's Soldier Performance Appraisal Report. Further material from Capt Matt Grant, and staff of Billabong Sanctuary. See also *Army News* 27 March 2003 and *Northern Services Courier* November 2003 for Snappa's promotion. The crocodile was hatched in 1981, and enlisted as a mascot in 1985. **Promoted again,** Thanks to Bob Flemming of Billabong Sanctuary for his photos and helpful information on Snappa and Jupiter in 2016. Thanks also to Capt Adrian Cherry and WO Ken Brown of 3CSSB for the updates and Snappa's promotion. See the Townsville *Bulletin* and ABC News 4 February 2016 for the capture of the '50-year-old bruiser' now known as Jupiter.

BORIS

Pictures of Boris and some of the other dogs mentioned in this chapter are in the photo section. You can also find more photos of the dogs that went to Somalia, Timor and the Solomon Islands deployment in the Australian War Memorial collection. Search for 'dogs Somalia', etc.

Author interviews with Lee and Deanne Doyle. It is not known what became of Sandra and her sister after Lee left Dili. **Military working dogs,** author interviews 2004 with WO2 Michael Pimm of 44 Military Police Platoon, Oakey, Qld; WO Paul Andersen, Flt-Sgt John Baguley and Sgt Grant Teeboon then of MWD Training Flight, RAAF Security and Fire School, Amberley, Qld; Dr Michael

Hibbert and Robin Martin of the Australian Quarantine Inspection.

Somalia, author interviews with Seamus Doherty and Simon French, formerly with 3rd Combat Engineer Regiment (3 CER). Since leaving the service Simon has used a retired military dog to hunt truffles in Tasmania, with considerable success. **Buster,** *International Express* 16 December 2003 (see the story 'Pigeon VC' for Dickin Medal). **Malaya medals,** author interview with George Gray, see the story 'The Dawn Dog'.

Working Dog Service Medals, Special thanks to Lieut-Col George Hulse RAE (Ret), former president and now historian of the Australian Defence Force Trackers & War Dogs Association, who laboured for many years to have the medals introduced for military and civil service working dogs.

VERY SMALL CREATURES

There are many photographs involving these small insect pests in the Australian War Memorial collection. Search for 'flies', 'lice', 'scorpions', 'centipedes', 'fleas' and so on. They include some of the enlargements from New Guinea published in 1943.

Thanks to Bob Bettany, Lee Doyle, Peter Leahy, John Quane and David Simpson for sharing their recollections of creepy-crawlies. I have been unable to locate most of the contributors to the WW1 and 2 volumes listed below. Sydney *Sun* 24 January 1943. **Gallipoli flies,** Hill *Soldier Boy* pp 138–9; Butler Chs XVI and XVII; White pp 43–4; A Carruthers, 3rd Field Ambulance *The Anzac Book* p 44; Idriess *The Desert Column* p 42 by kind permission of ETT Imprint and Idriess Enterprises; Flannel by NX126751 (Sgt W J Crowther), *Jungle Warfare* p 38; Robbie by VX15174 (Capt ED O'Rourke) *Khaki and Green* pp 62–3. **Fleas,** Carruthers op cit; Smith, 'My Anzac Home', *The Anzac Book* p 107. **Lice,**

AWM photos C01453, A02718, A03189, H00799 etc; White op cit; Am Park, 'The Never-Ending Chase', *The Anzac Book* p 30; Murray Griffin painting 'Troops de-bugging their beds, Changi, 1942–3', AWM ART24486. **Scabies,** Hill *Billy Young* pp 50–3. **Mosquitoes, ticks and others,** Sydney *Sun* op cit; interviews with Bob Bettany, Lee Doyle, Peter Leahy, Ian McPhedran; Melbourne *Sun News-Pictorial* 31 December 1943; Keith Eddison in Hill *For Love of Country* p 339; Charles Barrett, *The Kia Ora Coo-ee* August 1918 p 12. **Scarab,** 'Booligal Bob', *The Kia Ora Coo-ee* April 1918 p 5.

SARBI

Sarbi's portrait, by Lyndell Brown and Charles Green, can be seen in the Australian War Memorial collection, ART94166. Photos of more Afghanistan dogs can also been found in the AWM collection, search for 'dogs Afghanistan', etc. George Hulse's site www.aussiewardogs.org also has many photos.

Sincere thanks to David Simpson and his wife Kira for making the time to talk to me, and for the generous use of their photographs of Sarbi. Thanks also to Lee and Deanne Doyle for their friendship and advice; John Quane, secretary of the ADF Trackers & War Dogs Association, for all his help with this project; and Cpl Murray Young and his colleagues in the Training Development Cell at the EDD section, School of Military Engineering, Holsworthy. I acknowledge them more fully in the last chapter 'War Dog School'. Sarbi's story is comprehensively told in Lee *Saving Private Sarbi*.

Assistance Dogs, Thanks to General Peter Leahy and Ben Johnson for information on the Soldier On K9 Support Program, launched in Canberra in early 2017, www.soldieron.org.au. While not a complete list, these are some of the other organisations involved as of late 2016 with assistance dog programs for veterans:

South Australia, www.rslsa.org.au/operation-k9-releases-5th-assistance-dog. The South Australian RSL has been running a successful program with the Royal Society for the Blind for the past three years supporting veterans living with PTSD.

Victoria, www.guidedogsvictoria.com.au/resources/about-our-dogs. Guide Dogs Victoria has placed and re-homed a limited number of dogs as support dogs to assist veterans managing PTSD.

Queensland, www.whiskeyswish.org.au. Whiskey's Wish operates in Queensland and has been successfully training and placing red heelers with veterans managing PTSD in partnership with Service Dog Training Victoria, www.servicedogtraining.com.au.

New South Wales, www.youngdiggers.com.au/dogs. Young Diggers has been training a range of re-homed and rescue dogs to work with veterans as support dogs.

WAR DOG SCHOOL

Sincere thanks to Maj Andrew White, Sgt John Cannon, Sgt Ben Bartolo, Cpl Murray Young, Cpl Kane Tiller and Lance-Cpl Shaun Ward of the EDD section at the School of Military Engineering, Holsworthy Barracks, for allowing me to spend a grand afternoon with them and Ace at the Sabre Kennels. I also acknowledge the assistance given by Sebastian Spencer, curator of the SME museum; Yuri Shukost, Department of Defence media; and particularly the generous advice on military working dogs given by Lieut-Col George Hulse (Ret), ADFT&WD Assn, www.aussietrackers.org. See also George's site, www.aussiewardogs.org. For official military websites see for example the army, www.army.gov.au (search 'military working dog'), and the RAAF, www.facebook.com/RAAF.MWD.

Afghanistan MWD deaths, ten military working dogs died in

Afghanistan (2005–14) either in action or as a result of an accident. The six explosive detection dogs: Razz, Merlin and Andy died in 2007; Nova 2009; Herbie (killed with Sappers Darren Smith and Jacob Moerland) 2010; and Lucky (Ben Bartolo's dog) 2011. The four SAS dogs: Kuga, Quake and Devil died in 2012; and Fax 2013.

Memorials, Apart from those mentioned at Canberra and Wacol, there are memorials to the military working dogs in almost every state and territory. At Alexandra Headland, on Queensland's Sunshine Coast overlooking the Pacific, there is a national war dog memorial, originally erected to commemorate the eleven tracker dogs that went to Vietnam. Plaques have since been added to remember those dogs that also served in other war zones including Malaya, Somalia, East Timor, the Solomons and Afghanistan. Among other places, there are memorials to the dogs at Goolwa, Moonta and Salisbury RSL in South Australia; at Berriedale in Tasmania; Baldivis in Western Australia; at the Ballina RSL and of course at Holsworthy Barracks in New South Wales; and at the Vietnam Museum on Phillip Island in Victoria.

Costs, 2005 author interviews with Grant Teeboon and Michael Pimm; 2016 various former dog handlers. **Finale,** Ode EDD memorial at SME Holsworthy; 'Old Horse o' Mine' by TVB, in Gullett *Australia in Palestine* p 149; Freddy Bloom in 'Judy' and Denis Ferguson in 'Cassius' this book; 'Why' by Grant Teeboon 1987 at www.thepawman.com.au by kind permission.

ACKNOWLEDGEMENTS

A great many people and institutions helped me research this book. In particular, I acknowledge the assistance of a grant from artsACT and the ACT Cultural Council, the always generous advice of the staff at the Australian War Memorial, and the individual men and women who agreed to share their sometimes painful recollections. I mention many of them in the chapter notes. But let me here reiterate my thanks and appreciation to all who have helped me and these animal heroes with their knowledge and expertise.

Australian Defence Force & Department of Defence: WO Paul Andersen RAAF, Flt-Sgt John Baguley RAAF, Sgt Ben Bartolo, Lance-Cpl Joseph Blundell, Cpl Stephen Bowes, WO Ken Brown, Lieut-Col John Bullen (Ret), Sgt John Cannon, the CO and men of the Special Air Service Regiment, Capt Adrian Cherry, Maj Allan Croft, Leut-Cmdr Scott Craig RAN, WO2 Neil Dailey, Lieut-Col Fred Dangar, Lieut-Col Stephen Delaney, Lieut Steven Dickie, RAdm Ken Doolan RAN (Ret), Maj David Evered, Maj Nick Faughey, Cpl Simon French, WO2 Mark Gattenhof, Capt Matt Grant, Cpl Nick Hall, Brian Hickey (who kindly helped to open many doors for me), Lieut-Col George Hulse (Ret), Josh Hutton, Cpl Scott Ihle, David Kirkpatrick, Lieut-Gen Peter Leahy (former Chief of Army), Capt Jason Logue, WO Anthony Lynch, Lieut-Col David McCammon,

WO2 Steve Medforth, Lieut-Col Jim Messini (Ret), Leut-Cmdr Stephen Mullins RANR, WO2 Michael Pimm, Damian Shovell, Yuri Shukost, David Sibley, Sebastian Spencer, Cpl Kyle Stewart, Sgt Grant Teeboon RAAF, Cpl Kane Tiller, Cpl Don Vogelsang, Lance-Cpl Shaun Ward, Lieut-Col Rod Webster, John Wellfare, Capt Jack Westhorpe, Maj Andrew White, Cpl Murray Young.

Australian War Memorial: Ian Affleck, Elizabeth Burness (formerly of the AWM, who generously made much of her collected material available), Neil Burton, Carol Cartwright and staff of Education and Visitor Services, Madeleine Chaleyer, Dr Chris Coulthard-Clark, Ashley Ekins, Chris Goddard, Andrew Grey, Ian Kelly, Dr Brendan Nelson, Robert Nichols, Jane Peek, Dianne Rutherford, Joanne Smedley, Elizabeth Stewart, Douglas Thwaites, Lexie Whitehead, staff of the Research Centre and esales.

National Archives of Australia: Dr Jay Arthur (curator of It's a Dog's Life exhibition), staff of the Reading Room and Access and Information Services.

Royal Society for the Prevention of Cruelty to Animals: Rachel Baker, Jilea Carney, Jenny Hodges, Steven Holland, Jane Speechley, Dr Hugh Wirth.

I thank the following for their kind assistance and advice: Lance Abbott, Norma Allen, Bernice Archer, Ian Atkinson, Don Barnby, Ted Bennetts, Bob and Julie Bettany, Billabong Sanctuary staff, Sheila Bruhn, Colin Burge, Norm Cameron, Vic Cassells, Ted Chitham, Peter Churcher, Pamela Clark (Registrar, The Royal Archives, Windsor), Norma Collins, Mal Collison, Dr Alan Cowan, David Cree, Tim Daniel, Christopher Dawkins (ADFA Library), Margaret Dean, Capt Tony DeFrias, Seamus Doherty, Deanne and Lee Doyle, Betty and Brian Featherstone, Denis Ferguson, Bob Flemming, George Gray, Tom Griffiths, David Hall, Peter Haran,

Sally Hayes, Allan Helman, Dr Michael Hibbert (AQIS), Alan Hilleary, Judy Holt, Ross Howarth, Richard and Sandra Hubbard, Idriess Enterprises, Reg and Laureen Jerome, Ben Johnson, Virginia Kanka, Hilary Kinghorn, Barbara Large, Ros and Ken Leonard, Ellen Linke, Allyn McCulloch, Nicholas McClellan, Dr Michael McKernan, Ian McPhedran, Mick Malone, Edward Mann, Robin Martin (AQIS), Ian and Cynthia Moody, Joan Moody, Leonie Moody, Greg Nankervis, Dr Graeme Pearce BVSc, Sheryl Polglase-Boyce, Garry Power, Graham Price, John Quane, Andrew Rule, Roger Rye, Chris Shannon, Nola Sharp, Neil Smail, David and Kira Simpson, Pam and Bill Simpson, Dr Peter Stanley, Rod Suddaby (Department of Documents, Imperial War Museum, London), Tom Thompson (ETT Imprint), Percy Westcott, Simon Whitehead, Dave Willis, Jennifer Wood (IWM), Keith Wrightson.

Finally, I acknowledge the help and support I received from Ali Watts and Johannes Jakob of Penguin Random House with this new edition of *Animal Heroes* and – as always – the wonderful support of my dear wife, Gillian.

REFERENCES &
FURTHER READING

Adam-Smith, Patsy, *the ANZACS* (Penguin, Melbourne, 1978, 1991).

Allan, Sheila, *Diary of a Girl in Changi 1941–45* (Kangaroo Press, Sydney, 1994, 2nd ed. inc. Changi quilts 1999, 3rd ed. 2004).

Army News, Published by Defence News. For dates see chapter notes.

Australian War Memorial, *As You Were: A cavalcade of events with the Australian Services from 1788 to 1947* (AWM, Canberra, 1947).

Bean, C.E.W. (ed.), *The Anzac Book: Written and Illustrated in Gallipoli by The Men of Anzac* (Cassell and Co, London, 1916).

Bean, C.E.W., *Official History of Australia in the War of 1914–18* (Angus & Robertson, Sydney), vols i, ii, vi.

Bevege, Margaret, *Behind Barbed Wire: Internment in Australia during World War II* (University of Queensland Press, 1993).

Bird, David, *Apex Avenue of Honour & Desert Mounted Corps Memorial* (The Apex Club of Albany brochure, 1998).

Bloom, Freddy, *Dear Philip: A Diary of Captivity, Changi 1942–45* (The Bodley Head, London, 1980).

Butler, A.G., *The Gallipoli Campaign,* Part I of *Official History of the Australian Army Medical Services 1914–18* (Angus & Robertson, Sydney, 1938).

Carlyon, Les, *Gallipoli* (Pan Macmillan Australia, Sydney, 2001).

Cassells, Vic, *Shipmates: Illustrated Tales of the Mascots carried in R.A.N. Ships and Establishments,* (self published, Queensland, 1998).

Chatto, R.H., *The Seventh Company (Field Engineers) AIF 1915–1918* (Smith's Newspapers Ltd, Sydney, 1936).

Cochrane, Peter, *Simpson and the Donkey: The Making of a Legend* (Melbourne University Publishing, Melbourne, 1992).

Cooper, Jilly, *Animals in War* (William Heinemann Ltd, London, 1983).

Coulthard-Clark, Chris, *Duntroon: the Royal Military College of Australia 1911–1986* (Allen & Unwin, Sydney, 1986).

Coulthard-Clark, Chris, *The Encyclopaedia of Australia's Battles* (Allen & Unwin, Sydney, 1998, 2001).

Curran, Tom, *Across the Bar: The Story of 'Simpson', The Man with the Donkey: Australia and Tyneside's Great Military Hero* (Ogmios Publications, Brisbane, 1994).

Darley, Major T.H., *With the Ninth Light Horse in the Great War* (The Hassell Press, Adelaide, 1924).

Dennis, Peter, et al., *The Oxford Companion to Australian Military History* (Oxford University Press, Melbourne, 1995, 1999).

Fischer, Gerhard, *Enemy Aliens: Internment and the Homefront experience in Australia 1914–1920* (UQP, 1989).

Gammage, Bill, *The Broken Years: Australian Soldiers in the Great War* (Penguin, Melbourne, 1974).

Gullett, Henry and Charles Barrett (eds), *Australia in Palestine* (Angus & Robertson, Sydney, 1919). Gullett also wrote vol. vii of the *Official History,* 'The AIF in Sinai and Palestine 1914–1918' (Angus & Robertson, 1924).

Haran, Peter, *Trackers: The Untold Story of the Australian Dogs of War* (New Holland, Sydney, 2000).

Hill, Anthony, *For Love of Country* (Penguin/Viking, Melbourne, 2016).

Hill, Anthony, *Soldier Boy* (Penguin, Melbourne, 2001).

Hill, Anthony, *The Story of Billy Young* (Penguin/Viking, Melbourne 2012).

Idriess, Ion, *Horrie The Wog Dog: With the AIF in Egypt, Greece, Crete and Palestine, Written from the Diary of Private VX13091 J.B. Moody, AIF* (Angus & Robertson, Sydney, 1945; ETT Imprint).

Idriess, Ion, *The Desert Column* (Angus & Robertson, Sydney, 1932; ETT Imprint 2017).

Inglis, K.S., *The Rehearsal: Australians at War in the Sudan 1885* (Rigby, Adelaide, 1985).

Jones, Ian, *The Australian Light Horse* (Time-Life Books, Australia, Sydney, 1987).

Jungle Warfare: With the Australian Army in the South-West Pacific (AMF and AWM, 1944). With *Khaki and Green*, one of the army Christmas Books published 1941–45. The others were *Active Service, Soldiering On* and *Stand Easy.*

Kilgower, Ian and Robert, *Australian Racing Pigeons* (Rigby, Adelaide, 1982).

Lee, Sandra, *Saving Private Sarbi* (Allen & Unwin, Sydney, 2011, 2013).

Long, Valmai, *Mascot of the 7th Field Company 1st AIF*, paper based on interview with Leslie Ross, undated, AWM Education Section.

Monash, Sir John in F.M. Cutlack (ed.), *War Letters of General Monash* (Angus & Robertson, Sydney, 1934).

Moody, Leonie, *Cpl Horrie EX1 (The Wog Dog)*. Produced with the assistance of an Australia Remembers grant 1995, the 2/1 Australian Machine Gun Association and the State Library of Queensland. Three private copies, one lodged at the Library. Contains Jim Moody's diary typescript, official correspondence, private letters, poems, newspaper articles, and photographs.

Moore, Darren, *Duntroon: A History of the Royal Military College of Australia 1911–2001* (RMC, Canberra, 2001).

Navy News, Published by Defence News. For dates see chapter notes.

Nutting, Lieut G.W., *History of the Fourth Light Horse Brigade, AIF* (W.R. Smith & Paterson, Brisbane, 1953).

Olden, Lieut-Col, *Westralian Cavalry in the War: The Story of the Tenth Light Horse Regiment, AIF, in the Great War, 1914–1918* (Alexander McCubbin, Melbourne, 1921).

Parfitt, Iris, *Jail-Bird Jottings: The Impressions of a Singapore Internee* (The Economy Printers, Kuala Lumpur, 1947).

Parkin, Ray, *Out of the Smoke: The Story of a Sail* (The Hogarth Press, London, 1960).

Perry, Roland, *Horrie, the War Dog: The Story of Australia's Most Famous Dog* (Allen & Unwin, Sydney, 2013).

Quadrant magazine, Sydney.

Remembrance booklet for Charles Francis Fryer, 1875–1942 (South Australian Religious Society of Friends, The Hassall Press, c. 1942).

RSPCA, *A Memorial to Animals that Served Australia in War* (RSPCA and AWM brochure, 2003).

Salt, (WWII Army Education Journal) 10 September 1945, p 9 article on mascots.

Smith, Neil, *The Bushies: A Biographical History of the New South Wales Citizen's Bushmen Contingent to the Boer War 1899–1902* (Mostly Unsung Military History, Melbourne, 2002).

Smith's Weekly, (Sydney, for dates see Chapter Notes).

Soldiering On: The Australian Army At Home and Overseas, Prepared by Some of the Boys (Australian War Memorial, Canberra, 1942).

Stanley, Peter (ed.) *But Little Glory: The NSW Contingent to the Sudan, 1885* (Military Historical Society of Australia, Canberra, 1985).

The Advertiser, Adelaide.

The Argus.

The Australian Encyclopaedia (The Grolier Society, Sydney, 1981 ed.).

The Australian.

The Ballarat Star.

The Bulletin.

The Canberra Historical Journal.

The Canberra Times.

The Daily Mirror.

The Daily Telegraph, Sydney.

The Herald, Melbourne.

The Herald Sun, Melbourne (formerly *The Sun News-Pictorial*).

The Kia Ora Coo-ee: The Magazine for the Anzacs in the Middle East, 1918 (Reprint, introduction by David Kent, Cornstalk, 1981).

The Sydney Morning Herald.

The Sydney Mail.

The Times, London.

The Truth, Sydney.

Wallace, R.L., *The Australians at the Boer War* (AWM and AGPS, Canberra, 1976).

Wartime, Official Magazine of the Australian War Memorial (AWM, Canberra, for issues see chapter notes).

Weekly POW-WOW (Changi news sheet, ed. Freddy Bloom. Typewritten copies lodged by Mrs Bloom at Imperial War Museum, London).

White, Thomas, *The Fighting Thirteenth: History of the Thirteenth Battalion AIF* (Tyrrells Ltd, Sydney, 1924).

Whiting, Brendan, *Ship of Courage: The Epic Story of* HMAS *Perth and Her Crew* (Allen & Unwin, Sydney, 1994).

Yarwood, A.T., *Walers: Australian Horses Abroad* (Melbourne University Press [Miegunyah Press], Melbourne, 1989).

Also by Anthony Hill

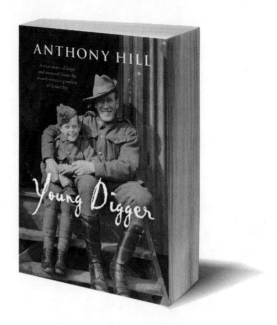

The dark clouds returned and gathered about the boy. His eyes grew distant, and he began to tremble. He heard not only shells exploding, but the cries of dying men . . . He was stumbling over churned earth, looking into the face of an officer, bloodied red as the poppies, ripped apart in the Flanders mud . . .

A small boy, an orphan of the First World War, wanders into the Australian airmen's mess in Germany, on Christmas Day in 1918. A strange boy, with an uncertain past and an extraordinary future, he became a mascot for the air squadron and was affectionately named 'Young Digger'. And in one of the most unusual incidents ever to emerge from the battlefields of Europe after the Great War, this solitary boy was smuggled back to Australia by air mechanic Tim Tovell, a man who cared for the boy so much that he was determined, however risky, to provide Young Digger with a new family and a new life in a new country, far from home.

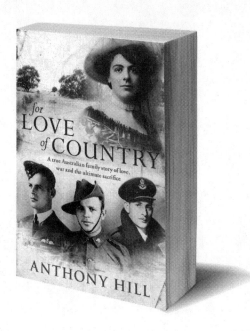

At the close of the First World War, and after surviving a gas attack on the Western Front, Captain Walter Eddison moved his family from war-ravaged Britain to start a new life in Australia. The Eddisons were offered 'land fit for heroes' under the Australian government's soldier-settlement scheme, but the grim realities of life in the remote bush were not easy for a family used to the green pastures of England.

Walter and Marion made the best of their limited prospects, but as they raised their young family on the outskirts of the nation's newly established capital, tensions were again simmering in Europe. When the Second World War broke out, they were forced to confront their worst fears as their three sons headed back to the battlefields they'd tried so hard to leave behind.

Anthony Hill expertly weaves military history and gripping accounts of frontline fighting into this intimate portrait of a family who sacrificed everything for their country, showing how the global conflicts of the twentieth century came home to Australia, with tragic consequences.

Billy Young was a boy of 15 when he joined the AIF in 1941. He was an orphan – hungry, broke, with nowhere to sleep – and the army offered him a feed, a blanket and five shillings a day in his pocket.

The trouble was, the army sent him off to Malaya where he became a POW when Singapore fell to the Japanese. From Changi, 'Billy the Kid' went on to spend the rest of his teenage years in some of the most barbaric Japanese prisons: the notorious labour camp at Sandakan (from which he escaped), and solitary confinement in the horrific Outram Road prison.

Billy survived by a combination of luck, larrikin humour and native cunning, learned as a market boy growing up in Sydney during the Depression. He has lasted into old age by virtue of his extraordinary spirit.

This powerful account of one of the youngest-ever prisoners of war takes us into the hearts and minds of the POWs, who refused to ever wholly submit to their captors.